BULLETS, BOMBS, *and* BAYONETS

A tribute to L/Cpl S.E. Shortliffe and the 43rd Canadian Infantry Battalion (Cameron Highlanders of Canada) CEF, who fought at Passchendaele, 1917.

by Edward N. Ross

 FriesenPress

Suite 300 - 990 Fort St
Victoria, BC, V8V 3K2
Canada

www.friesenpress.com

Copyright © 2016 by Edward N. Ross
First Edition — 2016

Photographs pertaining to Vimy Ridge and Passchendaele have been reproduced from those in the possession of Library and Archives Canada. In addition, a number of images pertaining to the Battle of Vimy Ridge are part of the author's collection.

The cover photo for Bullets, Bombs and Bayonets was photographed by the author in Gallery 2: the South African and First World Wars at the Canadian War Museum, Ottawa, Canada. The author gratefully acknowledges permission for its use. Cover design by Paul Kelly. Author photo by Joanne Ranger.

Efforts have been made to locate the original copyright owners of other photographs that may have been used in this book. If the reader has any information concerning the original copyright owner, an acknowledgement could be included in any revised edition.

All rights reserved. No part of this publication may be reproduced in any form, or by any means, electronic or mechanical, including photocopying, recording, or any information browsing, storage, or retrieval system, without permission in writing from FriesenPress.

ISBN
978-1-4602-9087-3 (Hardcover)
978-1-4602-9088-0 (Paperback)
978-1-4602-9089-7 (eBook)

1. HISTORY, MILITARY, WORLD WAR I

Distributed to the trade by The Ingram Book Company

Bullets, Bombs, and Bayonets is dedicated to Mary Elizabeth (Tibert) Hopkins, my aunt, and the last surviving, immediate-family member of Lance Corporal Stephen Ernest Shortliffe.

With my aunt, Mary Elizabeth Tibert, c. 1944

Table of Contents

Foreword vii

Introduction 1

Chapter One 14

Chapter Two 19

Chapter Three 30

Chapter Four 40

Chapter Five 52

Chapter Six 58

Chapter Seven 73

Chapter Eight 78

Chapter Nine: January 1917 87

Chapter Ten: February 1917 93

Chapter Eleven: March 1917 99

Chapter Twelve: April 1917 . . . . 122 → 125

Chapter Thirteen: May/June 1917 155

Chapter Fourteen: July 1917 160

Chapter Fifteen: August 1917 165

Chapter Sixteen: September 1917 175

Chapter Seventeen: October 1917 189

Chapter Eighteen: October 14, 1917 191

Chapter Nineteen: October 15, 1917 201

Chapter Twenty: October 18, 1917 203

Chapter Twenty-One: October 19, 1917 207

Chapter Twenty-Two: October 20, 1917 211
Chapter Twenty-Three: October 21, 1917 216
Chapter Twenty-Four: October 22, 1917 229
Chapter Twenty-Five: October 23, 1917 244
Chapter Twenty-Six: October 24, 1917 250
Chapter Twenty-Seven: October 25, 1917 259
Chapter Twenty- Eight 268
Chapter Twenty-Nine: Battle Of Passchendaele 272
Chapter Thirty: October 26, 1917 284
Chapter Thirty-One: "Their Names Liveth Forever" 320
Acknowledgements 337
Bibliography 338

Foreword

By Fernand Verstraete Volunteer Research Assistant
and WWI Battlefield Guide, The Memorial Museum
Passchendaele 1917, Zonnebeke, Belgium

Thousands and thousands of people from all over the world have been and still are looking for information about a relative who was listed as missing and declared killed-in-action during the First World War 1914-1918.

And so was the author of this book, Edward Ross.

Doing genealogical research about his family's history, he came across Stephen Ernest Shortliffe, the brother of his grandmother. The photograph of this great-uncle hanging on the wall in his grandmother's house enormously intrigued him. His question to his grandmother asking who the man was, seemed somewhat too much, as her answer was short and filled with sadness.

Edward became more and more captivated by that soldier, who obviously had something to do with the First World War. He learned that the soldier, who joined the 43rd Battalion, Cameron Highlanders of Canada (the Manitoba Regiment) died on 26th October 1917, somewhere in Belgium with no known grave. Edward's interest in the Shortliffe family history led him to start intense research about the life and military career of S.E. Shortliffe; first of all in his own country, examining family documents, then researching military information including battalion and divisional diaries. The final step was to try to find more information abroad in France and Belgium.

He was fortunate to find local (Belgian) websites and discover a lot of information about the First World War, in Belgium, and still more interesting, about the region where his great-uncle was killed: Ieper (Ypres), Zonnebeke, Passendale. He also learned that there was a war museum in Zonnebeke, called "Memorial Museum Passchendaele 1917." What was even more interesting for Edward was that the museum promoted a project; "The Passchendaele Archives," about the British Expeditionary Force soldiers who died between 15th July 1917 and 15th November 1917, during the Third Battle of Ypres, in other words, The Battle of Passchendaele 1917.

Edward didn't wait long before making an inquiry to the museum. It's really fortuitous that his inquiry fell into my hands and that I was asked to look for information about S.E. Shortliffe. I was lucky and happy at the same time, to be able to send written material, battlefield maps, and photographs. Edward's reaction was that he became even more curious and wanted to visit all the places where his great-uncle had passed by, stayed, and fought during his campaign in France and Belgium. In 2012, Edward and I met in Brussels airport, after which I took him to his hotel in Ieper, and the following days we made a thorough battlefield tour, starting near Le Havre (France), where S.E. Shortliffe landed in November 1916 and gradually going northwards till we reached the region of Ieper- Passendale in Belgium.

I will never forget the moving image of Edward standing more or less where his great-uncle died and went missing during the Canadian assault on Bellevue Ridge near Passendale, on 26th October 1917. His salute was simple and sublime at the same moment. On Wednesday, 23rd May 2012, he proudly honoured S.E. Shortliffe by laying a poppy wreath, at the Memorial to the Missing (Menin Gate) in Ieper, during the daily Last Post ceremony.

This battlefield tour allowed Edward to take lots of pictures and obtain other material in addition to what he already possessed while learning about that horrible war, on the Western Front and more precisely in the Ypres Salient, in Belgium. He now has written down all his knowledge about the war, and combined it together with the detailed personal and military life of S.E. Shortliffe in this book. His sense for a smooth style of writing, his well-considered and abundant vocabulary choices, and the systematic structure make this account a literary work everybody will read with much pleasure and interest.

Every Canadian and all others who have a desire to learn something about the First World War will want to acquire a copy of *Bullets, Bombs, and Bayonets,* a magnificent reference work concerning the so called "Great War" in France and Belgium. It's a book that will especially be appreciated by the numerous families in Canada who lost a relative between 1914 and 1918.

Introduction

Take up our quarrel with the foe:
To you from failing hands we throw
The torch; be yours to hold it high.
If ye break faith with us who die
We shall not sleep, though poppies grow In Flanders fields.

From "In Flanders Fields" by John McCrae, May 1915

I have always admired authors who demonstrate a creative ability to entertain, provoke, inform, captivate, and educate through the power of the written word. As English author, Edward Bulwer-Lytton wrote in 1839, "The pen is mightier than the sword."

In my book, *Bullets, Bombs, and Bayonets* I have attempted to capture the essence of war. This book commemorates the memory of all those who fought and died for freedom and honour, including a soldier whose young life was tragically cut short, denying him an opportunity to create a lifetime of dreams and live to see them fulfilled. *Bullets, Bombs, and Bayonets* remembers the sacrifice of my great-uncle Stephen Ernest Shortliffe, and the 43rd Canadian Infantry Battalion (Cameron Highlanders of Canada) who laid down their lives for king and country.

Twenty-five years after my uncle's death in 1917, I was born in a small fishing village in Little River, Nova Scotia to Connie Rae (Tibert) Ross and Edward Vernon Ross on Sunday March 22, 1942, in the midst of the Second World War.

In my youth there were a number of favourite items that I enjoyed seeing whenever I visited my maternal grandparents' home in Little River. Some of these included a huge, Victorian reed organ, which my grandmother occasionally played, another was an RCA Victrola (ca.1915-1928) with a sizeable collection of 78-rpm records to entertain me on rainy days, and last but not least was a photograph. Of the many photographs displayed on my grandparents' parlour wall, this one particular photo interested me the most. It was that of a serious young man wearing an army tunic and a Glengarry cap with a swagger stick tucked under his left arm.

My curiosity prompted me to ask my grandmother: "Who is the soldier in that picture?"

With a touch of sadness in her voice, she quietly but proudly replied, "He was my brother Ernie. He died in the war after being hit in the stomach by an artillery shell."

Although I did not comprehend the significance of my grandmother's explanation at the time, her words, years later, would become my motivation, and her brother, Lance Corporal Stephen Ernest Shortliffe my inspiration to write *Bullets, Bombs, and Bayonets*. My great-uncle was not among the seventy-one Canadian soldiers who received a Victoria Cross in the First World War, or one of the nine to be awarded a VC for the Battle of Passchendaele. He was not mentioned in Despatches nor was he the recipient of a military medal despite his eleven months of combat duty in France and Belgium. Nevertheless, as a wide-eyed, six-year-old boy, Ernie Shortliffe was my war hero, and he continues to be, sixty-seven years later.

The image of my great-uncle and my grandmother's whispered answer were stamped on my brain, ingrained for future recall. Fifty-five years later the name Ernest Shortliffe reappeared while I was searching family files in the genealogy section of the Admiral Digby Museum in Digby, Nova Scotia. The Shortliffe file contained little information, except for a particular handwritten page with the words: "Velma's Parents." Velma was my grandmother's given name. It was at that very moment that I discovered for the first time, the names of my great-grandparents and their ten (two females died not long after birth) children. One of the names on the list was: "Ernest (Lance-Corporal) killed in action 26 Oct 1917." The name automatically triggered a recall of that photo portrait and my grandmother's explanation of his death. Little did I realize at the time I would eventually embark on a journey that would take me to, not only Ernie's place of birth, but also to the battlefields of the Western Front where he went to war.

Stephen Ernest Shortliffe, son of Isaac and Sophia Shortliffe, was born on December 25, 1892 in Freeport, Nova Scotia. He attended school, graduated, and was employed locally before leaving home for Stonewall, Manitoba in 1912. It was in Stonewall where he sought and obtained employment with the Bank of Hamilton. On May 9, 1916 he enlisted with the Canadian Expeditionary Force in Winnipeg, joining the 179th Infantry Battalion (Cameron Highlanders of Canada). Prior to his enlistment, my great-uncle served with the 79th Cameron Highlanders of Canada Militia Regiment in Stonewall as a weekend warrior.

How was I to create a persona where there was no existing evidence suggesting what that individual may have been like? Letters, diaries, personal items, and photographs if they once existed had now disappeared; lost in time. The only person who could have assisted me in my quest was Ernie's sister Velma, my grandmother, who had never mentioned her brother Ernie again following my first inquiry. She died in 1983. What evidence remained was limited information gleaned from military sources, genealogy records, the Commonwealth War Graves Commission, and an obituary notice. Documents provided by Library and Archives Canada included an array of papers, among them my great uncle's Attestation papers, medical records, payroll, field reports, sick parade, and casualty details. Another important source of information was the 43rd Canadian Infantry Battalion (Cameron Highlanders of Canada) War Diaries.

Bullets, Bombs, and Bayonets is a historical study of events that occurred in The Great War. It was necessary for the author to hypothesize on what Stephen Ernest Shortliffe's actions, thoughts, fears, and hopes may have been during the time he served in France and Belgium. Therefore, those sections of the book where he is quoted are actually thoughts and words created by the author. I tried to imagine what S.E. Shortliffe was thinking at the time of an event. Whether any of those thoughts ever entered the mind of S.E. Shortliffe, no one will ever know. It is all pure speculation. Fictional content will also be found in the letter written to Ernie's parents, and the stories of the furlough in Doullens and the events leading up to his re-joining his battalion in Frevillers, France, on October 14, 1917.

Three years prior to commencing *Bullets, Bombs, and Bayonets*, I contacted the Freeport and Islands Historical Society with the hope that additional information might come to light concerning my Shortliffe ancestors. Dorothy Outhouse, a Freeport genealogist and historian, informed me that although there were no longer any Shortliffe families living on Long Island or Brier Island, Stephen Ernest Shortliffe's name was inscribed on a commemorative WWI memorial situated on the grounds of the Freeport United Baptist Church. She also related that my great-uncle's war medals and two photographs were displayed at the local Royal Canadian Legion. To my great surprise one of the photographs showed S.E. Shortliffe in his regimental uniform in an oval, dark-wood frame. This surprised and excited me as I had often wondered if the photograph still existed and where it might be.

Two years later, my sister Olivia and I visited Freeport, home of the Shortliffes from 1875 to 1923. Our guide for the day was Dorothy Outhouse. Our tour ended at the Royal Canadian Legion where I was reunited with the very familiar photograph. Dorothy and I have kept in contact since my visit to Freeport, and in July 2014, as good luck would have it, Dorothy ironically came into possession of a piece of Shortliffe memorabilia — a five-inch bronze Memorial Plaque (also called a Dead Man's Penny). These medallions were distributed to Canadian families after WWI in recognition of the ultimate sacrifice made on the battlefields of the Western Front. Without the generosity of Dorothy Outhouse, I would never have become the custodian of that bronze medallion which states: "He died for Freedom and Honour — Stephen Ernest Shortliffe."

Following two years of research, it was time to personally experience the sites from the data collected. Uppermost was to satisfy my inquiry as a young boy and my quest as an adult to honour my great uncle. I enlisted the assistance of Fernand Verstraete of the Memorial Museum Passchendaele 1917 as my guide and so began my pilgrimage with visits to towns and villages, battlefields, and cemeteries in Nord-Pas-de-Calais, France, and West-Vlaanderen, (West-Flanders) Belgium.

One particular cemetery visit will forever be etched in my mind.

On May 21, during a solemn walk through Canadian Cemetery No.2, which is situated northwest of Neuville-Saint-Vaast and within a short distance of Vimy Ridge, something quite unusual occurred. Among the 3,000 Commonwealth soldiers buried in this particular CWGC cemetery, approximately 650, are Canadian burials; troops killed in the Battle of Vimy Ridge on April 9, 1917.

After I'd spent some time viewing many of the names engraved on the headstones, at the end of the day it was time to leave for my hotel in Ieper (Ypres). As we were departing, I hesitated at the end of a row of headstones, and for some inexplicable reason, I turned and approached one particular grave. Engraved on the white Portland stone marker was the familiar maple leaf, identifying the soldier buried there as Canadian. This particular headstone marked the grave of Private M.J. McLeod of the 85th Battalion, who died on April 9. It seemed surreal that I should be focused on this one gravesite. After a few minutes I prepared to leave, but not before placing a small Canadian flag and poppy on the soldier's grave, and taking a photograph of the headstone.

After our visit to the military cemetery in Neuville-Saint-Vaast, my battlefield guide Fernand, suggested we take a different route to Ieper, along the scenic and historic countryside of France. Before our departure, we made a brief stop at the Abbey of Mont St. Eloi, then on to a tiny hamlet near Ecoivres, within sight of Mont St. Eloi and Vimy. It was here that we spotted a centuries-old French church. Its proximity to the battlefields of Vimy suggested it probably had been visited several times by General Julian Byng and General Arthur Currie's Canadian Corps between 1917 and 1918. My first thought upon seeing the church was how much history had occurred on those grounds. Within a few minutes of our arrival we found out. What was discovered in the late afternoon of May 21, 2012, were written testaments of Canadian soldiers who had indeed been there. Chiselled into an exterior foundation wall were names — Canadian names. Despite some obscured by graffiti, six cinder blocks contained names that were legible. One of those names was that of Private M. McLeod.

(Ross photo)
The headstone of Private McLeod, Canadian Cemetery No. 2, Neuville-Saint-Vasst

(Ross photo)
Private McLeod's name found chiselled into the church foundation near Vimy Ridge.

Private Malcolm J. McLeod was probably positioned in the vicinity of the church with the 85th Battalion in the spring of 1917 while waiting for the Vimy battle to begin. While there he decided to join others who had left their names for posterity by chiselling the first initial of his name and surname into one of the foundation blocks, using his knife or bayonet. Casualty records show that Private McLeod participated in the Battle of Vimy Ridge on April 9th, 1917 where he died instantly from artillery shell-fire. The grave of Private M.J. McLeod of Margaree, Nova Scotia is situated in Canadian Cemetery No. 2, Plot 1. C. 19, Neuville-Saint-Vaast.

Another name found on the church foundation was that of twenty-one-year-old Private W. D. Boag, 4th Canadian Infantry Battalion (Central Ontario). William David Boag, using a form of calligraphy, carved his inscription on July 3, 1918. A little more than a month later, August 9, he was killed by machinegun fire on the second day of the Battle of Amiens in the Somme. Private William David Boag, son of Henry and Alice Boag of Burwash, Ontario is buried in the Bouchoir New British Cemetery, Plot II. A. 27, the Somme.

(Ross photo)
The engraving of the name W.D. Boag can be easily seen on the church foundation.

(Ross photo)
The church in Ecoivres that bears the names of a number of Canadian soldiers from World War One.

In August 2015, I was excited to find a descendent of Private William David Boag. The family member was Linda Boag Moores. I was pleased to provide Linda with information and two photographs pertaining to her ancestor, Private W.D. Boag.

My time in France and Belgium presented an opportunity to see and visit many memorable and historic places such as Vimy Ridge Memorial, Beaumont Hamel, Grange Tunnel, Tyne Cot Cemetery, Passchendaele New British Cemetery, Menin Gate Memorial, Hill 60, Cryer Farm, and as previously mentioned, the ancient church near Ecoivres, to name a few.

What I eagerly awaited was my pilgrimage to Bellevue Spur and Passchendaele.

On an overcast, foggy morning on May 23, 2012, I was picked up at the Ariane Hotel in Ieper and driven along s'Graventafelstraat northward through the vast agricultural heartland of Flanders. My guide, Fernand Verstraete, was taking me to a location where the 3rd Canadian Infantry Division, which included the 43rd Battalion (Cameron Highlanders of Canada), had launched their attack on Passchendaele, October 26, 1917. On arrival, we made our way on foot along a narrow farm road, which separated large tracts of land, to a spot overlooking a vast field of loam, sand, and clay. It was here, I was told, that the 43rd Battalion and Lance Corporal S.E. Shortliffe would have advanced northward across the open fields, through knee-deep mud. While they attacked, they themselves were attacked by machine guns, shrapnel shells, heavy artillery fire, and asphyxiating gas. I was looking at an area of land where my great-uncle had been struck and killed by an enemy artillery shell ninety-five years ago. My grandmother's words echoed in my brain — *He was my brother Ernie. He died in the war after being hit in the stomach by an artillery shell.*

As far as my eyes could see, were field upon field, farm houses, barns, and small clumps of trees on the crest of Bellevue. There was no mistaking this battleground, once a killing field, with its infamous gradual undulation, rising slowly to a height of land called Bellevue Spur. Almost a century later, this height of land continues to look down upon Flanders fields. I couldn't help but compare the present-day farmland scene to the photos, newsreels, and descriptions of Bellevue when it was a quagmire of mud and clay, millions of water-filled, rat- infested shell craters, and endless rolls of barbed wire; a desolate place of death and despair.

To my knowledge I am the only descendent of Stephen Ernest Shortliffe to make a pilgrimage to Passchendaele and stand on the sacred ground where he lost his life on October 26, 1917.

Later that day I was honoured to place a wreath at Menin Gate Memorial during the Last Post Ceremony. This ceremony has taken place in Ieper (Ypres) every day at 8:00 p.m. since November 11, 1929, except for four years when under enemy occupation in WWII.

The events chronicled in this book will be familiar to many readers. Some will be less well known but are equally important to the overall history of Canada's participation in the First World War. *Bullets, Bombs, and Bayonets* is a tribute to the 60,661 Canadian soldiers who died and the 172,000 who were wounded on the Western Front during the War to End all Wars. It also acknowledges the sacrifice made by the 43rd Canadian Infantry Battalion, whose many brave soldiers perished during the Battles of the Somme, Vimy Ridge, Avion, Méricourt, Cambrai, Amiens, and Passchendaele.

Two decades before the outbreak of the First World War, Canada's third Prime Minister John Abbot described war as "the science of destruction." Years later, Abbot's characterization would be proven correct in both pictorial and oral accounts of the carnage and mass destruction, which impacted most of northern France and Belgium from 1914 to 1918. Often destruction was linked to ruthless revenge. A perfect example was the Belgian city of Dinant. On August 23, 1914, the Imperial German Army torched 1,000 buildings within the city. As German troops razed Dinant, they also executed 674 civilians. These killings were carried out because it was suspected a number of Dinant's population were active participants or supporters of a non-military partisan resistance against the German army. Over the course of the war, 60,000 Belgians perished and 1.5 million were displaced.

On August 4, 1914, England went to war in defense of Belgium, a neutral country of 7.5 million people. Once war was declared, military leaders were confronted with challenges not encountered since the days of the Napoleonic wars. The greatest test facing the United Kingdom was the rapid mobilization and deployment of a strong and well-trained expeditionary force. Twelve million men and eighty thousand women (women served as nurses and ambulance drivers) throughout the British Empire answered their leaders' call-to-arms. Canada alone deployed 424,589 troops to Europe to fight a war that eventually cost the lives of 908,371 British and Commonwealth troops — lives extinguished, fighting for small sections of foreign soil.

Hopefully readers will now have an understanding of what *Bullets, Bombs, and Bayonets* is all about and why I undertook this project on May 12, 2010. The initial intention was to produce a book on the First World War, based on the participation of S.E. Shortliffe and the 43rd Battalion, and to make it available primarily to family and friends. As time went by, however, the target market transitioned from family and friends to a larger realm of readership. Through it all, I have found authoring a book to be educational, stimulating, and significantly satisfying, although at times I questioned whether I would ever see an end to manuscript rewrites. During times when I felt drained of creativity, unable to compose a literate sentence or paragraph, I would pause, regroup, and call upon my imagination, emotion, and inner spirit to help me move forward and complete *Bullets, Bombs, and Bayonets*. At the end of the day — I did my best.

Let the story begin.

PART ONE
Canada at War

Chapter One

On August 4, 1914, Great Britain declared war on the German Empire in response to Kaiser Wilhelm's invasion of Belgium. As a result, the Dominion of Canada and all British Commonwealth nations were automatically at war. During the next four years, the lives of one in sixteen Canadian citizens would be directly impacted by the conflict in Western Europe.

England's pronouncement on August 4 was followed shortly thereafter by an official Canadian declaration from Governor General Prince Arthur Duke of Connaught, on August 5. This was quickly followed by speeches and demonstrations of support, parades, flag waving, and the inevitable long lines of young men eager to fight for "King and Country." Large groups of men in Edwardian suits, many of whom were veterans of the South African Boer War, assembled in front of Ottawa's Parliament buildings to excitedly cheer the news. United in a single voice, they proclaimed unconditional support for their country's involvement, calling upon all fit and able males to volunteer. The majority of Canadians (most of whom were of British heritage) felt it was their absolute, unconditional obligation to support Mother England in her battle against tyranny and aggression in Western Europe. Every parliamentarian was expected to give his unequivocal support for Great Britain. One of the very first to do so was Sir Wilfred Laurier, Canada's seventh Prime Minister (1896-1911): "It is our duty to let Great Britain know and to let the friends and foes of Great Britain know that there is in Canada but one mind and one heart and that all Canadians are behind the Mother Country."

In 1914, few dared to raise a voice in protest of sending Canada's young men to the battlefields of Europe, however, by 1917 discontent was beginning to slowly emerge. In August of that year, the government passed the Military Service Act, which soon gave rise to a small, but extremely vocal, anti-war movement. Calling themselves "Conscientious Objectors," these activists pointed to the relentless propaganda that spewed forth from the mouths of patriots and militarists who had predicted a quick and successful conclusion to the war, perhaps as early as Christmas 1914. History has proven that the theory of a short, successful war was highly optimistic and unrealistic. As Canadians eventually came to discover, World War I dragged on for over four years. Kaiser Wilhelm II was somewhat more confident than the British, as he declared the German Infantry would march home to Deutschland before the leaves changed color in the fall.

World War I, aka "The Great War," "The Glorious War," and "The War to End All Wars," was an important game-changer for Canada. By war's end, the country would be seen as a strong, independent-thinking, proud nation with continued ties to Great Britain; but with less of a colonial attachment. When Canada entered the war, it had a full-time army of only 3,111 members, and a part-time militia numbering approximately 50,000. Of that total, 7,000 men had fought alongside the British Army during the South African Boer War from 1899 to 1902. The United Kingdom and its Dominions, which included Canada, fought Afrikaners in Transvaal, Johannesburg, and Pretoria. Twelve years later, citizen-soldiers from Canada would once again find themselves fighting and dying in a foreign land. This time the battles would take place in Western Europe, with names such as Neuve Chapelle, the Somme, Vimy Ridge, Hill 70, Mons, Lens, Avion and Passchendaele. Of all those battlegrounds, Passchendaele epitomized the futility of a war fought in mud and water.

In July 1914, Belgium was a sovereign and neutral nation of 7.6 million people. On August 4, it became a battleground that would eventually involve several countries from around the world, including Canada. Sons and husbands left behind family and friends to rid the citizens of France and Belgium from the scourge of a tyrannical aggressor. The First World War was a product created by the actions of one man; an extremist in Serbia. It was in the city of Sarajevo where Archduke Franz Ferdinand, heir to the Austro-Hungarian Empire, and his wife, Sophie, Duchess of Hohenberg, were both assassinated by Gavrilo Princip on June 28, 1914.

One month later, tensions had reached a boiling point, resulting in the full mobilization of the Austrian Army on the Serbian border on July 31. Two days later, Austria declared war against Serbia. The Austrian declaration started a chain reaction, which resulted in Germany, the most influential and powerful member of the Triple Alliance (Germany, Austria-Hungary, and Italy), declaring war on Russia on August 1, and against France two days later. There was a concern expressed by Kaiser Wilhelm II to his generals that the French might attempt to reclaim the provinces of Alsace and Lorraine, west of the river Rhine. These former French provinces had been lost to the Germans during the Franco-Prussian War, fought July 19, 1870 to May 10, 1871. The Kaiser had no need to worry as they were heavily fortified and sufficiently manned, therefore not in jeopardy of being reclaimed by France. Belgium, on the other hand, held the key to the Kaiser's imperialistic ambitions to crush France, and ultimately occupy the crown jewel — Paris.

On August 2, 1914, the Kaiser sent a message to Albert, King of Belgium, claiming France was assembling its armies in preparation for an invasion of Belgium, in order to launch an attack on Germany. He therefore requested Belgian permission to allow German troops to cross into neutral Belgium from Luxembourg to thwart an impending French attack. King Albert adamantly rejected the Kaiser's request and suggested French mobilization along the frontier was nothing more than a blatant fabrication.

The armed forces of Belgium, on August 3, numbered 117,000 troops in the field plus 90,000 men stationed in the fortress cities of Liège, Namur, and Antwerp. Belgium's Compagnie des Aviateurs, which comprised sixteen planes and 175 airmen, were ordered to destroy all road bridges in the city of Liège, as well as railway bridges and tunnels on the frontier with Germany. The next day, the German

Second Army, under the command of General Otto von Emmich, invaded Belgium and advanced towards Liège. Although well armed and heavily fortified, Liège was significantly undermanned. By August 7, General Erich Ludendorff's 14th Brigade had occupied most of the high ground north of the city of Liège. From that particular advantage point, the Germans then proceeded to launch attacks against the Belgian forts, resulting in the deaths of between 2,000 and 3,000 defenders. Despite major setbacks, Belgian troops displayed heroic and persistent determination in successfully repelling several attacks, especially along the River Meuse where they killed approximately 2,000 German soldiers during ten days of intense fighting. As of August 15, enemy soldiers and artillery had entirely destroyed and captured their initial objectives and were now preparing to move on. Prior to leaving, the Germans rounded up and slaughtered many of the local residents, before burning their homes to the ground.

The decision by England to come to the aid of Belgium was based on a pact signed by all of the European Great Powers on April 19, 1839. Known as the Treaty of London, it recognized and guaranteed total neutrality and independence for Belgium and her citizens. Germany, by its deliberate action of hostile invasion, had contravened that treaty, thereby lighting the fuse on a powder keg that would produce a war of such magnitude that its horror and terror would reverberate around the world.

Compared to Great Britain's population, Canada's 7.2 million people was by far much smaller, but her contribution to the war effort was very significant. This was demonstrated by the more than 600,000 citizens between the ages of eighteen and forty-five who were mobilized for war. (British Army recruitment policy actually stated that soldiers must be between the age of nineteen and forty-two to serve in the trenches on the Western Front.) During the 1,558 days of the war, 60,661 Canadian soldiers gave their lives in the line of duty, an average of 39 Canadians killed every day. In addition, an estimated 150,000 to 200,000 Canadian Expeditionary Force troops, in the European theatre of war, suffered wounds with varying degrees of severity. Ten thousand to 15,000 were incapacitated as a result of "shell shock." In total, as many as 6.8 million

United Kingdom, French, and Russian (Triple Entente) soldiers died in the Great War. Half of those deaths were a direct result of combat, the other fifty percent were from unrelated causes such as accident, infection, disease, (for example, the Swine Flu of 1918), self-inflicted injuries, and prisoner-of-war internment conditions.

Passchendaele, the primary focus of this story, had once been a quiet, quaint, and friendly Flemish village, situated 160 feet above sea level, in West-Flanders, on the highest section of a geological formation called a "ridge." Looking south from Passchendaele, one had an unobstructed view of the flat valley with its narrow roadways, lush farmland, forested areas, and neat, self-contained villages. Ypres, the commercial hub, lay eight miles to the south. For centuries, this city had played an integral part in commerce and municipal government. Numerous produce and dairy farms within its 700 square-mile, flood-prone area required protective measures to prevent a disastrous event, such as excessive water, from wiping out a lucrative agricultural industry. In most cases, West-Flanders was only three feet above sea level. Because of this, it was necessary for Belgian farmers to construct an elaborate, extensive irrigation and flood protection system by expanding existing streams and digging beeks (ditches), in order to direct all excess water from the fields to the canals.

Passchendaele Ridge was a six-mile long, crescent-shaped escarpment, which pointed in the direction of the Belgium coast, forty miles to the west. In Canada, where mountain ranges extend to thousands of feet above sea level and hills several hundred feet, Passchendaele Ridge was an anomaly in the fact that it was an undulation of the earth's crust, or in other words, a hill or knoll of less than 300 feet in height. On Belgium's Western Front, these heights of land took on great prominence because of the flatness of West-Flanders, which stretched for miles in all directions, thereby giving tactical advantage to occupying forces on the ridges and crests. These heights of land were strategically crucial when it came to militarily controlling the Ypres Salient. Messines Ridge (elevation 260 feet), which extended north-east to the Gheluvelt plateau and Passchendaele Ridge are two excellent examples of hills that provided the enemy with defensive advantage.

Chapter Two

"Gentlemen, we may not make history tomorrow, but we shall certainly change the geography."

General Herbert Plumer, British Second Army

In their attempt to wrest control of Passchendaele from the grip of the Imperial Germany Army, the British developed an ambitious plan to take the ridge and liberate Passchendaele village. It took three years and three major battles to achieve that objective. In total, 245,000 British and Commonwealth troops became casualties before Passchendaele was officially declared a victory. The name, "Battle of Ypres," was adopted despite the fact Ypres had only been occupied by the Germans for one day during the four years of the war — that day being October 7, 1914. The British Army, under the supreme command of General Douglas Haig, Chief of Staff, declared the primary objective of the British Expeditionary Force (BEF) was to capture, occupy, and hold Passchendaele. In order to successfully achieve this goal, a massive and well-coordinated battle plan was implemented . It was known as the Third Battle of Ypres, and it commenced on July 31, 1917.

The First Battle of Ypres had been fought between October 19 and November 22, 1914. It was on that last day, November 22, that the Germans began shelling Ypres with incendiary bombs. The Second Battle of Ypres followed in the spring of 1915, beginning on April 22, and ending with the Second Battle of Bellewaarde on September 25 of the same year. During those five months, troops from Great Britain, the Colonies, and France engaged the Germans in six major combat operations. The first was the Battle of 's Graventafel, which commenced at 5:00 p.m. on Thursday, April 22. That operation lasted until the following day, with the first stage fought on Pilckem Ridge, north of the Ypres Salient.

It was during this battle that poison gas was first deployed by the Germans. They released 168 tons of chlorine gas over a four-mile front, held by the French 45th Division. Dug-in along this front were soldiers from Morocco, Algeria, and North Africa, along with men of the 87th Division from Brittany, France. Within ten minutes, 6,000 French soldiers perished from the effects of the chlorine gas. Those who managed to survive quickly abandoned their positions en masse, leaving a large, gaping, undefended hole in the front-line. Canadian troops were called upon to seal that gap. Showing remarkable courage and intestinal fortitude, Canadian infantrymen held rags saturated with urine over their faces, desperately hoping to neutralize the deadly respiratory effects of the hypochloroic acid. The urine-moistened cloths proved an effective antidote to the gas. As a result, Canadian soldiers were able to secure and defend the gap from further attacks until May 3.

That first use of chlorine gas in 1915 was a terrifying experience for the multitude of soldiers who died, choking on massive clouds of the yellow-green vapour.

Those who survived would forever be haunted by the memory of that gas attack. Captain Hugh Pollard, a witness to the French massacre, described in his book, *The Memoirs of a VC*, the following account:

Dusk was falling when from the German trenches in front of the French line rose that strange green cloud of death. The light north-easterly breeze wafted it toward them, and in a moment death had them by the throat. One cannot blame them that they broke and fled. In the gathering dark of that awful night they fought with the terror, running blindly in the gas-cloud, and dropping with breasts heaving in agony and the slow poison of suffocation mantling their dark faces. Hundreds of them fell and died; others lay helpless, froth upon their agonized lips and their racked bodies powerfully sick, with tearing nausea at short intervals. They too would die later — a slow and lingering death of agony unspeakable. The whole air was tainted with the acrid smell of chlorine that caught at the back of men's throats and filled their mouths with its metallic taste.

(Ross photo)
The Brooding Soldier Memorial in St. Julien near Ieper (Ypres) commemorates the more than 2,000 Canadian soldiers who died in April 1915 in the Ypres Salient during poison gas attacks.

In addition to the Battle of 's Graventafel, there were five other relatively short battles; namely: St. Julien from April 24 to May 4; Battle of Frezenberg, May 8 to 13; First Battle of Bellewaarde on May 24 and 25; the Battle of Hooge on July 30 and 31, where German flammenwerfers (flamethrowers) were used for the first time, and finally the Second Battle of Bellewaarde on September 25, 1915. Two years after those combat operations had ended, British, French, and Commonwealth Forces would once again find themselves fighting the German Army for much of the same territory. For an exhausting and casualty-filled 103 days, the Battle of Passchendaele, known in German as Dritte Flandernschlacht — (Third Flanders Battle), raged on.

On July 31, 1917, at 3:15 a.m., the first Battle of Passchendaele got underway in the Ypres Salient. Tens of thousands of troops, supported by medium and heavy artillery, slugged their way through the mud under the vilest and demoralizing conditions. Most soldiers had never heard of the word "salient" and fewer had ever fought in one. Simply put, a salient was the shape of a battlefield, a bulge, surrounded by combat troops at the front and on two sides. The most vulnerable salient was one in which there was a pronounced, deep bulge, creating a significant threat of becoming sealed off at the base. Should this result, soldiers would find themselves isolated with limited or no route of escape.

Two weeks in advance of July 31 and Zero Hour, the British field artillery bombed enemy positions. These concentrated bombardments caused a tremendous number of enemy casualties, as well as further contributing to the huge amount of devastation resulting from millions of previously exploded artillery shells. The village of Passchendaele and surrounding Flemish countryside had been transformed from picturesque to grotesque. It had become a scene of shell craters indenting the landscape filled with bodies, their remains being ravaged by thousands of marauding, insatiable, battlefield rats. Limbless stumps, once trees, were scattered among twisted steel. Endless piles of rubble marked the spots where buildings once stood. A residual smell of chemical gas and the omnipresent mud added to the ghoulish and ugly atmosphere of the salient.

The battle was about winning Passchendaele. Attack en masse. Advance in stages. Secure the captured ground. Move on. Climb the crests and charge the enemy. The sacrifice would be great, the achievement remarkable, and the ultimate reward — bittersweet. During the Third Battle of Ypres, 582 men from England and the British Commonwealth died each day, fighting to win Passchendaele. Many left this world from the sharp sting of a bullet, vaporized by a bomb, or on the pointed end of a steel bayonet.

Philosopher and writer Voltaire once said: "All murderers are punished unless they kill in large numbers and to the sound of trumpets."

World War I exemplified the magnitude by which man could eradicate millions of people. All that was needed was a simple call-to-arms and the introduction of modern weaponry. World War I weapons and munitions were manufactured for one purpose, to kill or maim an adversary. Some weapons performed better than others, some in different capacities. The Germans feared two weapons in particular, the Vickers and Lewis machine guns. On the other hand, however, Allied troops paled at the familiar sound of the infamous Maschinengewehr 08 (MG-08), a machine gun that could spit out 400-600 rounds of bullets every sixty seconds.

War is hell, not a sporting event organized for someone's entertainment. Despite the terrifying and gruesome accounts of lives being snuffed out on the battlefields of Western Europe, these stories failed to have a negative impact on the enthusiastic Canadian youth. Nothing could dissuade them from leaving home and going off to war. A naive perception of what constituted combat, and a vastly overblown expectation of honour and glory, was all that was needed to send pubescent boys under legal enlistment age to a local recruitment office. Part of the underage-soldier problem lay with the military, which feared it might not meet its manpower quotas, and thereby would be unable to replenish the beleaguered and under-strength battalions on the Western Front. Many adolescent lads lied to get into the army, fabricating surnames and hometowns. Others simply reinvented their birth dates. Approximately 20,000 underage boys remarkably qualified for duty with the Canadian Army after having passed the process of attestation and medical tests. These adventure-seeking volunteers would become known as "Boy Soldiers." By all accounts, at least 2,500 of these illegally-enlisted lads gave their lives for King and Country on battlefields somewhere in France and Belgium. Although representing approximately five percent of the total number of soldiers who served in Europe, not all boy soldiers received a free trip to wartime adventure. Approximately 1,700 were discovered to be under eighteen years of age. Those wannabe candidates were attached to a "Young Soldiers' Battalion" and shipped to England to train and wait until they became of legal age.

Private John Henry Foster "Jack" Babcock of Frontenac County, Ontario, was one of those boy soldiers. John Babcock enlisted at age sixteen and spent his war years in an army camp in England, training for front-line duty. As fate would have it, the war ended with Private Babcock still in England, and still too young to serve his country. Babcock was to be the last surviving member of Canada's First World War army. He passed away on February 18, 2010 at the age of 109 years.

The youngest volunteer to serve overseas in a Canadian uniform was Robert Clarence Thompson of Hillier, Ontario. At the time of his enlistment, Thompson was a high school student at Prince Edward Collegiate Institute in Picton. Having enlisted twice while fourteen years old, no one was more persistent at becoming a soldier than Robert Clarence Thompson. Both times, he was found to be underage. One year later, a third attempt on March 16, 1916 proved successful for the determined young man when he became a member of the 155th Canadian Infantry Battalion in Belleville. At the time, Thompson's Attestation documents showed his age as nineteen, although he was actually fifteen. His true age came to light in October 1917, while he was serving in France. He was immediately shipped home to Canada. Upon his arrival in Toronto, Thompson re-enlisted on November 22, claiming his birth date was December 12, 1898, and therefore attaining an age of nineteen years. Two weeks later, Thompson and his unit were sent to Halifax to assist the city and its people after the Halifax Explosion of December 6, 1917. After their work was completed, Thompson and his unit returned to Toronto where he was promoted to sergeant-major, and he returned to France where he served with the CMR (Canadian Mounted Rifles). He was now truthfully sixteen years old. Robert Clarence Thompson died in 1950 at the young age of forty-nine.

One of several underage Canadian soldiers who fought and died in World War I was Private Harry Pope, born in Smith Falls, Ontario, the son of Alfred and Catherine Pope of Montreal. At the time of his enlistment, Private Pope gave his date of birth as July 15, 1897, which would have made him eighteen years of age at the time. He was killed on January 8, 1916, while performing work on a communication trench line. It was noted in the battalion casualty records that Pope was actually fifteen years old when he was killed. Harry Pope, who served with the 3rd Canadian Infantry Battalion (Toronto Regiment) and 1st Infantry Brigade, 1st Canadian Infantry Division, is buried in the Wulverghem-Lindenhoek Road Military Cemetery, Belgium.

Soldiers who perished in France and Belgium were originally buried in shallow graves, marked by plain wooden crosses. Sometime later, their remains were exhumed and identification of each soldier was undertaken, followed by reburial ceremonies in an Imperial War Graves Commission Cemetery (IWGC). In 1917, the IWGC adopted three principles by which the commission would be guided in the care and remembrance of all British Commonwealth troops who died on the Western Front, during the years 1914-1918.

The first principle stated that every soldier would have his name commemorated on a headstone of identical color, size, and shape, which would be placed in an Imperial War Graves Commission Cemetery. Those soldiers killed on the battlefield, whose bodies were never recovered and therefore had no known graves, would have their names inscribed on the wall of a memorial dedicated to all those missing in action.

The second principle stated that all those who fought in the war would be afforded equal and universal treatment in death, with no special consideration, based on rank or social standing, as to where a soldier was to be buried within the grounds of the military cemetery.

The third principle was highly contentious and the most difficult for families to accept. This particular principle disallowed the repatriation of bodily remains to their homeland. There were two reasons why repatriation was not permitted. First, it was to protect Red Cross workers from exposure to potentially serious health issues associated with the exhumation of soldiers' bodies. Secondly, the policy was adopted to discourage financially-independent families from repatriating their relatives' bodies for reburial in their home country, while those of less influence and wealth would be denied the same opportunity. Despite strict enforcement by the Imperial War Graves Commission, attempts were sometimes made to circumvent the system, though only a few families were ever successful.

One person, who through perseverance ultimately succeeded, was Anna Durie, mother of a Canadian officer killed on December 29, 1917, who was laid to rest near Lens, France. Anna Durie's son was Captain William A. P. Durie, of the 58th Canadian Infantry Battalion (Central Ontario). In 1919 she made a formal request to the Imperial War Graves Commission to have Captain Durie's remains repatriated to Toronto; but to no one's surprise, her application was denied. Six years later, in August 1925, with the covert assistance of paid accomplices, Anna exhumed her son's body and transported it to Toronto; where a few days later, a full military reburial ceremony took place in St. James Cemetery. A number of Captain Durie's former comrades were in attendance and participated in the ceremony. The IWGC was oblivious to the fact that Captain Durie's body was missing from its original burial site in France, that is until officials saw the published reports in the local Toronto newspapers.

At least one repatriation has been officially sanctioned. In the year 2000, a formal request was delivered by Canada to the Commonwealth War Graves Commission (formerly the Imperial War Graves Commission), asking permission to repatriate an unknown Canadian soldier, buried in the Cabaret Rouge Cemetery near Souchez, France. The request was eventually granted and the soldier's remains flown to the nation's capital, Ottawa, where he was accorded full military honours during a reburial ceremony at the National War Memorial's Tomb of the Unknown Soldier. Unlike the non-repatriation policy established by Great Britain and her colonies in 1917, France and Belgium never adopted an identical policy. The remains of many French and Belgian soldiers were exhumed and returned to their families for burial in local cemeteries; the cost borne by each family.

Headstones, with the familiar Maple Leaf carved on the front, identify Canada's war dead buried in British Commonwealth military cemeteries throughout France and Belgium. In Belgium, there are 348 CWGC World War I Cemeteries; 168 contain the graves of at least one Canadian soldier. Tyne Cot Cemetery, forty-nine acres, is situated on the western slope of Passchendaele Ridge; it is the most frequently visited and best-known military cemetery. It is also the largest WWI British Commonwealth cemetery in the world; the final resting place for 11,954 soldiers, 8,367 of which are unknown burials. Tyne Cot contains the graves of 9,000 soldiers from the United Kingdom, 966 Canadians (554 unknown burials) as well as troops from Australia, New Zealand, South Africa, Newfoundland, the Isle of Guernsey, and the British West Indies. In addition to the British Commonwealth graves, the bodies of four German soldiers are buried beneath two square headstones behind the Cross of Sacrifice, in front of Tyne Cot Memorial. This memorial to the missing lists the names of 34,000 British and Commonwealth servicemen killed in the Ypres Salient, who have no known grave. Similar memorials are located in Ypres (Ieper) at Menin Gate Memorial (54,000 names), Vimy Ridge Memorial (11,258 names of Canadians killed in France, without a grave) and numerous other memorials situated throughout the Western Front.

(Ross photo)
Tyne Cot Cemetery, situated on the western slope of Passchendaele Ridge, contains the graves of 900 Canadian soldiers who were killed in the Battle of Passchendaele, October-November, 1917.

(Ross photo)
Canadian Cemetery No.2, situated on the grounds of the National Vimy Memorial Park at Neuville-Saint-Vaast, was established on April 9, 1917, as a final resting place for those Canadian soldiers who died during the Battle of Vimy Ridge.

Tyne Cot British Military Cemetery, with its solemn Cross of Sacrifice, stands out among the hundreds of long rows of white Portland headstones, set against a backdrop of neatly manicured lawns with colourful flowers adorning each grave. The leaves of elms and maples gently rustle in a soft breeze; the only discernible sound within this peaceful place. The 11,954 final resting places at Tyne Cot are both a lasting reminder of those who gave their lives in battle as well as a tribute to the person primarily responsible for the establishment of Tyne Cot and all other World War I British Commonwealth military cemeteries that are visited today. Sometime in October 1914, while visiting a cemetery in France, a forty-five-year-old British Red Cross volunteer stumbled upon the graves of several British soldiers, which were only identified by a plain, wooden cross. After thoughtful consideration, Fabian A. G. Ware concluded that it should be the responsibility of the Red Cross to take on the work of identifying and registering the names of all fallen soldiers, including the location of each grave.

In May 1915, Ware developed a system to catalogue the names and grave sites of all those who had died in World War I, and from this evolved what became known as the "Graves Registration Commission," later named the "Imperial War Graves Commission," and ultimately what it is known as today, the "Commonwealth War Graves Commission." The mandate of the Graves Registration Commission was to specifically search for the remains of those who had perished on the Western Front (except No-Man's Land where bodies were mutilated beyond recognition), registering each soldier's identity, rank, combat unit, and the exact location of his grave. By October 1915, 31,000 graves had been registered and by spring of the next year, that total had risen to approximately 50,000. Fabian Ware, later to be promoted to the rank of colonel, was concerned about the future upkeep and care of the thousands of gravesites once the war ended. It was because of his deep concern for those who had given their lives in the service of king and country, that he undertook the task of petitioning Edward, Prince of Wales for his support. On May 21, 1917, Sir Fabian Ware was notified that approval had been granted for the establishment of the Imperial War Graves Commission. A century later, the fruits of Fabian Ware's labour and dedication continue to be seen by all the hundreds of thousands of people, young and old, who make a pilgrimage to the sacred battlefields of WWI and visit the Commonwealth War Graves Commission cemeteries. It is there in the military cemeteries, where the heroic young men of Canada have found a final resting place that is as beautiful, as it is serene.

Chapter Three

"In war there are no unwounded soldiers."

José Narosky

Plans for a third major combat operation, in the Ypres Salient, in 1917, actually began two years earlier. It was in 1915 when large-scale improvements commenced on the Hazebrouck-Ypres rail line, plus the construction of new main roads. This work was intended to greatly improve the overall efficiency for transporting weapons, ammunition, and troops to the battlefields. On January 7, 1916, as the plan was moving forward to the initial implementation stage, the chief of staff of the British Expeditionary Force, Field Marshall Sir Douglas Haig, was in the midst of entertaining his staff of army generals at a lavish chateau. At the conclusion of the evening's social gathering, Haig convened a meeting in which he asked each general to produce a detailed plan, similar to the one originally introduced the previous year. His instruction to the generals, was to specifically include a strategy by which the British Expeditionary Force (BEF) would be able to successfully advance from the Ypres Salient against German positions entrenched along the Gheluvelt Plateau, including the high ground of Messines and Passchendaele Ridges.

On January 14, General Douglas Haig asked General Herbert "Daddy" Plumer, commander of the British Second Army, and a veteran of the South African Boer War, to prepare a strategy that would see the British attacking three German-held positions.

The first objective was Messines Ridge, six miles south of Ypres; the second, Lille, twenty-three miles to the south-east; and the third, Houthoulst Forest, eleven miles north of Ypres. General Haig also called in British Fourth Army Commander, General Henry Rawlinson to draw up a strategy for an assault on enemy positions in the Ypres Salient, scheduled to begin on February 4, 1916. Even before the ink was dry on General Rawlinson's strategy plan, Haig was forced to heed the advice of his generals, to forego the combat operation in February, because of previously scheduled major battles, the most significant being the Battle of the Somme, planned for July 1, 1916. That battle alone was expected to extract a considerable toll on men, resources, and morale.

As it happened, the Battle of the Somme continued until November 18, with casualties numbering into the thousands, including the largest single-day count of 57,000 on July 1. Three Canadian infantry divisions participated during the months of September and October. A total of 24,000 Canadian soldiers were killed, wounded, or taken prisoner during the course of that battle.

Exactly twelve months after the planned offensive to capture Passchendaele had been mothballed, Field Marshall Haig summoned General Rawlinson on February 9, 1917, to give his opinion on General Plumer's Messines battle plan. Plumer, who only days earlier had submitted a proposal to the chief of staff, stated that Messines Ridge could be successfully taken in one day of fighting. The general, however, insisted that the capture of Gheluvelt Plateau become part of the plan, especially if the British hoped to continue their advance northward. At a later meeting, between Haig, Rawlinson, and Plumer, the field marshal accepted General Plumer's plan in principle, however, he also insisted on making some additional changes to the original submission. Once Haig had finished, he ordered an amended memorandum be drafted, which would become the basis for the second largest military operation of 1917.

In May, the general again convened a meeting of his army commanders, this time held in the French town of Doullens, in the region of Nord-Pas-de Calais. Together they worked on a specific timetable for the Flanders offensive, including a comprehensive list of objectives. Three of those goals included capturing Passchendaele, liberating Belgian territory from the Germans in the salient, and wearing down the enemy physically and mentally, in the hope of shortening the war.

Phase I of General Herbert Plumer's Messines plan called for an assault on German-held positions at Messines Ridge on June 7, 1917. It was imperative that the armies of Great Britain and France capture that particular ridge, because if they failed to do so, the city of Ypres, which had been held by the British during much of the war, would continue to be vulnerable and at the mercy of the Imperial German Army. Failure to achieve this objective would result in the enemy easily thwarting all attempts, made by the British, to attack eastward from the salient. The Messines sector included a group of hills known as the Messines-Wytschaete Ridge. They were geographically located midway between Armentieres and Ypres; the village of Messines being situated on the southern elevation of the ridge. This area commanded an excellent view of Lys and the valley below. To the north-west of Messines was Wytschaete. The village, situated on the highest point of the ridge at an elevation of 260 feet, afforded the German Army a clear view of Ypres and the British forces. Enemy strategic policy dictated that the battle be primarily defensive; one that would maintain lightly-held forward areas, combined with counter-attack strength formations positioned in reserve. General Plumer and the British Second Army, decided to utilize an additional nine infantry divisions from the II ANZAC Corps, hoping to advance a distance of 4,000 yards, and thereby capture the first line of German defence on Messines Ridge.

Field Marshall Haig, although in agreement with the overall plan, decided at the last moment to make yet another adjustment to Plumer's strategy. The plan amendment added a second line of defense at the rear of the ridge to include the village of Wytschaete, thereby allowing the British an opportunity to advance down the slope an additional 3,000 yards.

Before starting the Battle of Messines, the British decided to introduce mine warfare as part of their assault tactic on the German lines. As a result of that decision, British tunnelling companies excavated more than four and a half miles of tunnels, some over one mile in length and as deep as 300 feet. Galleries, which split off from the main tunnels, were built to provide access to charge chambers, where tons of ammonal and gun cotton were prepared for detonation. A land mine of significant size and lethal potential was located at St. Eloi. That particular land mine, comprising 47.6 tons of explosives, was the largest amount to be deliberately detonated at any one time. It took thirty soldiers, working three shifts a day for three weeks, and carrying fifty pounds of explosives in backpacks, to load each chamber and connect the detonators.

Mine warfare played an integral role in combat planning, not only at Messines, but also at the Somme, on July 1, 1916 and the Battle of Vimy Ridge, in April 1917. In the very early days of the war, 900 experienced coal miners from England and Wales volunteered to serve with the British Army to construct systems of underground tunnels, also referred to as "subways." Tunnels allowed the British Expeditionary Force to move men from support to the front-line trenches, without the fear of enemy artillery fire killing and wounding the troops along the way. Mining had become so important and widely used by the English, that after two years, the number of miners involved in the construction of subterranean passageways, galleries, and chambers had expanded to 25,000 workers. Canadian Corps Commanders, having witnessed the devastating impact land mines had on their adversaries, decided to follow the British lead and organize two tunnelling companies of their own. The 1st Canadian Tunnelling Company and 3rd Canadian Tunnelling Company were formed using experienced underground miners from the coal fields of Nova Scotia and the gold camps of Northern Ontario.

Tunnellers, or "Clay Kickers," as they were sometimes called, were constantly exposed to dangerous situations, working below ground. Soldiers had to use utmost care when dislodging and removing soil and rock from unstable and highly unpredictable areas under excavation. Many times, the lives of engineers, pioneers, sappers, and helpers hung in the balance. Underground fatalities often occurred as a result of suffocation and drowning, due mainly to tunnel cave-ins. There was always the constant threat of asphyxiation caused by chemical gasses seeping into the caverns or carbon monoxide exposure created by excavation machinery operating in poorly ventilated subways and galleries.

There were many times, during which German and British underground workers toiled at their jobs, separated from each other by only a few feet of rock and clay. On a few occasions they simultaneously detonated the explosives in each of their respective chambers, causing multiple fatalities and tremendous destruction to both sides. Other instances found adversaries breaking through a wall into an opponent's tunnel, where they engaged the enemy with small-arms fire, grenades, and bayonets.

In most cases it was more advantageous to incorporate the use of the camouflet in underground warfare. This was an explosive charge intended to destroy an enemy tunnel, however, the charge lacked the power to create a huge crater above ground. Despite lacking the power to produce craters, camouflets still posed serious dangers to all those in a tunnel. This was especially true if a tunnel had not been properly tamped or backfilled. The purpose of tamping a tunnel was to prevent the extreme force of a camouflet explosion from redirecting itself back down the tunnel towards the men who had earlier set the charge. An improperly backfilled camouflet usually resulted in tons of flying rock, debris, and shock waves. The aftermath was soldiers buried under rubble or killed by concussion.

In order to assist the tunnellers in moving these underground systems forward at depths ranging anywhere from twenty feet to 300 feet, specialized excavation equipment was occasionally called into service. One piece of mining equipment that was commonly used was the Stanley Heading Machine, introduced by the British in March 1916. The Stanley Heading Machine or SHM, was an essential piece of equipment when it came to tunnelling. It featured a five-foot diagonal cutting arm, which could slice through large sections of ground at a rate of two feet per hour. Work parties followed closely behind the Stanley Heading Machine, removing rock and muck to a dumping area, in large canvas buckets and pushcarts. Although the machine proved successful in the Douai Plain near Vimy, it was frustratingly useless in the thick, blue clay of the Ypres Salient. One exception was at Wytschaete, where soil conditions were conducive to deep tunnelling operations. The Canadian 1st Tunnelling Company encountered a similar problem in 1917 with another British-built mining machine named the Whittaker. This piece of equipment also had to be eventually removed from service and replaced by manual labour, in the form of clay kickers using picks and shovels.

June 7, 1917, at 3:10 a.m., the St Eloi land mine and its 95,000 pounds of ammonal and 300 pounds of gelignite were exploded. A total of ten detonators was used, each in a stick of gelignite bound together with twelve other sticks and embedded in a fifty-pound can of high explosive, consisting of powdered aluminum, ammonium nitrate, and TNT. When the charge was detonated, the earth heaved and shot towards the heavens in the shape of a gigantic mushroom, illuminating the night sky with a brilliant red and yellow fireball. Clouds of black, acrid smoke; thick, lung-choking dust; and the sickening smell of explosives and death enveloped St Eloi. Tons of steel, wood, and concrete smashed down upon the earth, impaling and crushing those who, only moments earlier, had survived the cataclysmic explosion. Large sections of the German front and support lines no longer existed; obliterated, as were the men who had once occupied them. Within twenty seconds of the detonation and explosion, British field artillery began a series of creeping barrages. This was soon followed by an infantry assault spearheaded by the tank corps, which drove on past the enemy's first-trench system. Resistance was limited. The British, Australian, and New Zealand troops continued to advance at a steady pace up the ridge.

Two hours after the St Eloi land-mine explosion, Ulster regiments, from the 36th Division, had completed their second objectives. By 7:00 o'clock that same morning, soldiers from New Zealand successfully captured Messines and at 9:00 a.m. Wytschaete fell to the British. General Plumer could bask in the glow of self satisfaction, having accomplished what he had promised...delivering Messines and the entire ridge to General Douglas Haig and the British Expeditionary Force by the end of the first day. The British and ANZAC forces, which had anticipated strong resistance from the Imperial German Army, were amazed how quickly they captured what remained of enemy positions. They confronted shell-shocked, confused, and terrified young Germans, weeping uncontrollably; their arms held high above their heads in surrender. The 7,200 German survivors who were taken prisoner that day, were the fortunate ones. More than 10,000 of their comrades remained entombed in their trenches, tunnels, and dug-outs on Messines Ridge.

In victory came the spoils of battle. The British Expeditionary Force became the beneficiary of sixty-seven guns, ninety-four trench mortars and 294 German machine guns.

Although the Canadian Corps did not actually participate in the June 1917 Battle of Messines, they did play an important role one year earlier. In the spring of 1916, the 3rd Canadian Tunnelling Company was assigned responsibility for the construction of a subway called the "Berlin Tunnel," located south-east of Ypres, directly below the German tunnels and mine chambers at Hill 60. Originally excavated to a depth of eighty-eight feet, the tunnel had been painstakingly advanced a considerable distance by the Canadian sappers before encountering unstable ground. Halted by soil conditions, the Canadians paused to consider their options. It was determined they were close enough to the German front, and therefore should terminate their advance. After doing so, they excavated a large charge-chamber and prepared it for detonation. When work finally resumed, the 3rd Canadian Tunnelling Company collectively focused on increasing the size of one charge-chamber, but while they were in the process of doing so, a sudden rush of water, sand, and clay flowed in upon them. After successfully sealing the leak and stabilizing the ground nearby, they resumed digging. Instead of constructing one large chamber, as previously planned, the Canadians proceeded to dig several smaller chambers where they loaded 53,500 pounds of ammonal and 7,800 pounds of gun cotton slabs.

Once the Berlin Tunnel had been completed, the Canucks turned their attention to yet another tunnel under an enemy position on Hill 60, called "Caterpillar," which was situated north of a main railway line. Again the 3rd Canadian Tunnelling Company encountered bad ground. The men immediately proceeded to backfill the gallery and move in an alternate direction; a route that took them through more stable clay beneath the German second line, towards Caterpillar. Upon the men finishing their work, the chamber was made ready for detonation on September 20, 1916, with 70,000 pounds of ammonal explosive. Six weeks following Caterpillar's completion, the 1st Australian Tunnelling Company relieved the Canadians and proceeded to extend the depth an additional ninety-four feet, where it eventually connected with the Berlin Tunnel. Both subways had now been fully loaded with huge amounts of explosives. Although charged and ready to fire, the explosives were not used immediately. As a result, the British were required to vigorously defend both mines from enemy attack, in order to prevent them from being captured by the Germans, as well as ensuring the chambers did not become flooded. The two mines, at Hill 60, were held in abeyance from September 1916 until activated during the Battle of Messines in June 1917.

On June 7, the simultaneous explosion of these two gigantic mines at Hill 60 produced such a thunderous, ear-deafening noise that it was reportedly heard as far away as London and Dublin. The noise, debris, and chaos created by the exploding Caterpillar land mine, far exceeded anything previously experienced by combat troops. The volcanic-like eruption that resulted from the explosion shook the ground nine miles away, lifted soldiers off their feet, and tossed them to the ground. A sudden rush of turbulent, hot air sped towards the British lines with the force of a Pacific cyclone. Wood, steel, and soil plummeted from the sky to the ground, landing inside and beyond the newly created Caterpillar crater, a massive hole, fifty-feet deep and 270 feet in diameter. Enemy casualties numbered in the thousands, many horrifically entombed alive in their trenches and tunnels, and sealed off from rescue. A total of ten officers and 677 other ranks from the Imperial German Army 204th Division, died defending Hill 60 from the British Expeditionary Force.

Hill 60 was considered an important victory for the British and ANZAC forces. Their soldiers captured 7,354 enemy troops and a large cache of military hardware, including 218 machine guns, sixty trench mortars and forty-eight heavy artillery guns.

(Ross photo)
This steel-reinforced German pill-box with walls almost three feet thick can still be found on Hill 60, site of fierce fighting during the Battle of Messines, in June 1917.

As it has been noted, during the two-year period, 1915-1917, the Messines Sector had been honeycombed with a network of tunnels and galleries, leading to chambers of explosives, dug by both combatants for the sole purpose of mine warfare and its subsequent death and destruction of the enemy. In addition to those previously noted, twenty-four other mine chambers had also been excavated by the Royal Engineers and loaded with one-million pounds of ammonal high explosives. The majority of these land mines were located within a nine-mile radius of Ypres; Ploegsteert being the most southerly. Of those twenty-four mines, one at Petit Douve Farm was discovered by the German Infantry and destroyed. Four others, near Ploegsteert Wood named "Birdcage," were held in reserve and never discharged.

Each of these land mines was said to contain between 26,000 pounds and 34,000 pounds of high explosives. Military records that showed the exact location of each of the charged mines, were somehow lost between 1917 and the end of the war. It wasn't until June 17, 1955, during a violent thunderstorm, that the location of one of the mines was finally located. During the raging storm, a bolt of lightning struck a tree in a farmer's field, triggering a thunderous explosion and producing a giant mine crater. The exact location of the three remaining land mines still remains a mystery to this day. It is felt they are buried somewhere under a field, near the site of the 1914 Christmas soccer match between British and German soldiers, at Ploegsteert.

Chapter Four

"War is only a cowardly escape from the problems of peace."

Thomas Mann

The first twelve days of June 1917 were bloody ones for the British Second Army, which suffered a staggering 24,562 casualties. This was approximately the same number as the Germans sustained, although the enemy reported an additional 10,000 soldiers missing-in-action. Messines had been the opening salvo in an impending battle that would pit Sir Douglas Haig against General Erich Ludendorff in a major confrontation, on the southern face of Passchendaele Ridge.

In mid-July, German heavy artillery shelled Allied forces with thousands of rounds of bombs, in advance of the Battle of Passchendaele. They also introduced a new and deadly weapon into the war; "mustard gas." This particular toxic agent was the most debilitating of all gases used in WWI, especially when it came in direct contact with a soldier's flesh, or was inhaled into the lungs or brought into the digestive tract. Exposure to mustard gas produced hideous, painful blisters, both externally as well as internally. In many cases, exposure was lethal, especially if a soldier was in contact with large quantities of the gas. German bombardments of the British, over a period of three weeks, caused 14,726 casualties, of which 2,500 were gas-related. In retaliation, before the start of the Third Battle of Ypres, British Field Artillery batteries blasted the enemy night and day for two straight weeks. It was during this "softening up" period that the British Expeditionary Force concentrated their artillery firepower on the heavily fortified bunkers, pillboxes, trenches, dug-outs, and tunnels on Passchendaele Ridge. By the time the British had concluded bombing these German installations, 4.3 million artillery shells had been utilized, including 100,000 trench mortar bombs, containing phosgene gas mixed with chlorine gas. This mixture of phosgene and chlorine gas made a deadly weapon ten to twelve times more lethal.

Despite the number of combat operations, which had occurred along the 420-mile front-line, from the Swiss border to the Belgian North Sea, the Western Front had remained relatively static since May 25, 1915. The Flanders section of Belgium consisted of a front that began in the small coastal city of Nieuwpoort. It then moved south to Diksmuide before bulging out around the Ypres Salient. From here, it snaked south again to the coal mining areas of Lens, Lille, and Loos, before finally crossing the Artois countryside around the City of Arras and the River Somme. Ypres had been under British occupation since mid October 1914. North of Ypres, the Imperial German Army controlled Passchendaele village, including the lower elevated portions of the ridge to the east, as well as the flat stretches of ground further north. The city of Ypres, together with a small section of Flanders Plain, comprised part of the salient that extended a few miles into the German defensive positions. This bulge, or salient, left the British rear section exposed to constant harassing artillery fire directed at them from the surrounding elevations.

The start of the Third Battle of Ypres, originally scheduled for July 25, was postponed for three days. German infantry divisions had endured significant artillery fire, which had exacted a heavy toll on their weapons; a decision was made to withdraw their big guns and reposition them in a more secure sector, out of range of the British field artillery. A further delay was imposed by General Sir Douglas Haig, who explained his reasons in Despatches:

This postponement enabled a portion of our own guns to be moved farther forward, and gave our airmen the opportunity to locate accurately the enemy's new battery positions. Subsequently a succession of delays of bad visibility, combined with the difficulties experienced by our Allies in getting their guns into position in their new area, decided me to sanction a further postponement until the 31 July.

On July 31, 1917, at 3:50 a.m., the Third Battle of Ypres (Battle of Passchendaele) was officially launched in a rainstorm. This would be the first of four wet days in succession, and typical of the weather during the next three months of combat.

On the opening day, the British Expeditionary Force (BEF) watched as twenty millimetres of rain inundated the land. This downpour only added more water to what already existed. Large ponds and small-size lakes covered the land; by-products of a decimated drainage system built to prevent flooding. The once lush Belgian countryside now became a target of the big guns — the fifteen and eighteen-pounders, 4.5 howitzers, and 3.5 mortars. General Hermann von Kuhl, a witness to the ferocity and accuracy of the British shelling, described the massive bombardments:

A hurricane of fire, completely beyond anyone's experience broke out. The entire earth of Flanders rocked and seemed to be on fire. This was not just drum fire; it was as though Hell itself had slipped its bonds. What were the terrors of Verdun and the Somme compared to this grotesquely huge outpouring of raw power?

The British plan had set out clear, identifiable objectives to be met in the early stages of battle. The British Fifth Army would advance and capture the high ground, east of Ypres, where a flank could be organized for future operations. It would also secure a waterway crossing called "Steenbeek." The French Army, under the command of General Anthoine, would focus its attention north of Ypres, between Ypres and Diksmuide.

By 9:00 a.m., all objectives north of the Ypres railway line were under British control, except for a single, strong point north of Frezenberg, known as Pommern Redoubt. After an hour of heavy fighting, this position fell into the hands of the British Expeditionary Force. Later that day, the British 39th Division captured St. Julien, while fighting continued to rage for several more hours south of the Ypres railway line on both sides of Menin Road. As daylight faded, troops of the British Fifth Army consolidated the capture of the German defense system south of Westhoek and by doing so also claimed possession of the ridge. This acquisition of the high ground denied the Germans an unobstructed view of British troop activity in the Ypres Salient. During the night of July 31, and for the next forty-eight hours, the Germans counterattacked in an effort to dislodge the British Expeditionary Force from the high ground between Menin Road and the Ypres railway, as well as Frezenberg and St. Julien. All attempts failed. A total of 6,100 enemy soldiers were taken prisoner, including 133 German officers.

Most days in August 1917 it rained. Relief arrived on September 7 and for ten days the salient finally enjoyed warm, gentle breezes and brilliant sunshine. The change in weather couldn't come soon enough for the soldiers, who had hunkered down in the mud and water-filled trenches, while enduring the misery of 127 mm of relentless rain in August. That amount was five times greater than what fell in the same period in 1916.

The height of land, called Passchendaele, provided Field Marshall General Erich Ludendorff and German 4th Army Commander, General Frederich Sixt von Armin with an excellent position from which to observe and study their adversary, as they moved within the confines of Berlin Wood, Waterloo Farm, and Abraham Heights. The village of Passchendaele, except for its name, ceased to exist in 1917. It had been pummelled and pulverized by millions of shells. Homes, businesses, and even the local church in the village square had been demolished, replaced by concrete bunkers, tunnels, pillboxes, barbed wire, and networks of winding trenches. The villagers; those who had survived the initial bombings, had long since fled, displaced by the war. What remained of Passchendaele was for the occupiers to defend and the attackers to capture.

The gentle slopes of Passchendaele Ridge had been heavily fortified with thousands of feet of stacheldracht (barbed wire). The wire was attached to six-foot steel posts, twisted into the soft ground and positioned in patterns crisscrossing No-Man's Land. The heavy belts of wire-strands, with razor-sharp barbs spaced close together, were once used by farmers to keep livestock in and trespassers out. The barbed wire now provided protection for those manning the bunkers, pillboxes, and front-line trenches. To increase the effectiveness of the wire, a method was developed by the Germans whereby the enemy unwound and attached the barbed wire to a second post, then doubled it back to add a thicker concentration of flesh-tearing barbs. Subsequently, the wire was arranged in such a manner that it drew assault troops into perfect target range for enfilading (flanking) machine-gun fire. The result was the slaughter of British Expeditionary Force soldiers unable to defend themselves from the soft-core, lead projectiles fired from steel-reinforced, concrete pillboxes and blockhouses.

Large 8 x 10-foot, rectangular blockhouses contained as many as five MG-08 machine guns, each operated by a four-man crew of elite maschinengewhres (machine-gunners). Arranged on a battlefield in a pattern similar to five dots on a dice, a blockhouse represented the middle dot, and it provided a curtain of machine-gun crossfire, which could decimate waves of attacking troops. These blockhouses or machine-gun bunkers were designed with up to as many as three compartments, all connected to an enemy trench system by rear entrances. A ventilator shaft was situated in the middle of the structure. The outer dots represented the smaller, but deadly, pillboxes. These structures, which in most cases contained only one compartment with a single entrance, connected to a fire trench. Built of reinforced concrete, the three-foot-thick walls and roofs were almost indestructible. Depending on the contour of the land, some pillboxes were constructed with openings called "loop holes" on two sides of the structure. Mostly there were no loop holes, but instead the Germans mounted their machine guns on platforms and positioned them over a doorway or on a corner of the pillbox.

(Ross photo)
This is one of two German blockhouses still to be found in Tyne Cot near the entrance to the cemetery. A third was used as a base for the Cross of Sacrifice.

(Ross photo)
A British pill-box situated on the former battlefield of Passchendaele.

Neither belligerent possessed a lack of weaponry in the Battle of Passchendaele. The British Expeditionary Force had an inventory of 3,091 heavy artillery guns and 406 Royal Flying Corps (RFC) aircraft. The artillery weapons and aircraft were an integral part of the nine combat infantry divisions under the command of forty-seven-year-old General Hubert Gough, of the British Fifth Army. General Gough was the youngest and least experienced of all the British Army commanders, and therefore it came as both a surprise and a disappointment to many, that he was promoted by Field Marshall Haig to be the commander of the British Expeditionary Force. Most of those associated with the military and government presumed Haig would appoint the older, experienced, and cautious veteran — General Herbert Plumer.

General Gough's adversary in the Battle of Passchendaele was General Friedrich Sixt von Armin, of the German Fourth Army, who under his command had thirteen infantry divisions and 600 aircraft.

Within days of assuming command, General Gough planned an ambitious and aggressive attack against the Germans, along Menin Road between Zillebeke and Boesinghe. At that point, he proposed to dispatch his troops south, across numerous swollen streams and ditches, while advancing in the direction of Passchendaele only a few miles to the north. On paper, the plan appeared reasonable. Unfortunately, it failed miserably when the time came to actually execute it. The British attack simply ground to a stop, halted by extreme weather and exceptionally determined German resistance. The only combat force to exhibit any degree of success was not the British; it was the German infantry. Enemy soldiers diligently and effectively employed several massive and sustained gegenangriffs (counterattacks), and were rewarded with strategically important ground on the higher elevations.

Marginalized by his failure to generate a positive result in the war against Germany, General Hubert Gough found himself out of favour with his superior, General Douglas Haig. Gough's burning ambition to be successful was overshadowed by the lack of a definitive plan, which when implemented would meet, or perhaps even exceed, Haig's expectations. As the days and weeks passed, the general found himself more and more ostracized from the inner circle of Haig and his generals. Eventually the end came, like death from a guillotine axe.

Hough was ultimately replaced by a pot-bellied, white-haired general, who had successfully planned and implemented the recent Messines campaign — Herbert Plumer, commander of the British Second Army. Shortly after Plumer assumed command of the British Expeditionary Force, the clouds evaporated and the rain stopped falling on the salient battlefield. The sun appeared and gentle breezes swept across West-Flanders, drying the ground. Troops could now dig new trenches, build badly needed roads, and best of all, exchange their kilts and trousers for khaki summer shorts. Life had become somewhat more tolerable on the Western Front, at least in the short term.

Although this brief respite from the rain in September was greeted with wide, boyish grins and deep sighs of relief, it did not produce a hiatus from the reality of war and its killing. Many British Empire soldiers fell, victims during short assault missions and trench raids against heavily defended German positions.

One particular attack, on September 15, 1917, was led by a young British second-lieutenant, named Bernard Noel Cryer, of the 7th Battalion, London Regiment. Taking advantage of the nice weather, Cryer and a small raiding party conducted a surprise attack on an underground bunker behind the German second line, east of Hooge, near Menin Road. This bunker had been used at times as an Advanced Dressing Station (ADS) for first aid care, and as an enemy defense position. Lieutenant Cryer and his men stormed the bunker and after a few minutes of gunfire and hand-to-hand combat using fixed bayonets, ten enemy soldiers were left dead and thirty-six taken prisoner. Lieutenant Cryer received accolades from the men and officers of his regiment after they learned of this success, however there was little time to celebrate.

The next day, on September 16, the Germans launched a counter-attack, in an effort to retake their bunker from the English. The British were steadfast in their determination not to relinquish control of the underground facility. They were successful, but at a cost. During the attack, Second-Lieutenant Bernard Cryer was killed, but his body was never recovered. One assumes he was killed by a high-explosive shell and vaporized. In honour of the young British lieutenant, the bunker was given the name, "Cryer Farm." The last to occupy Cryer Farm were Canadian troops during the Battle of Passchendaele in October. The Cryer Farm underground bunker still exists, hidden from public view on private property not far from Ypres (Ieper).

(Ross photo)
Battlefield guide, Fernand Verstraete inspects one of the chambers of an underground bunker known as Cryer Farm, once occupied by the Germans near Passchendaele.

The Battle of Menin Road Ridge began at 5:40 a.m. on September 20, 1917. It was a morning clouded in thick mist, which made visual observation of the battlefield almost impossible. British, Australian, and New Zealand soldiers began their advance along an 8.3 mile (14,550 yard) front, moving steadily behind lines of creeping barrages. There was, on average, one large artillery gun for every fifteen feet of frontage. The barrages lasted three minutes, then lifted and moved forward 110 yards. This pattern was repeated until the objective had been realized or the field artillery had been ordered to cease firing. By mid-morning, the majority of all objectives had been captured and secured. However, the Germans, who had retreated, consolidated their positions and began an aggressive counterattack in retaliation. The enemy soon discovered they were unable to make any definitive headway, despite penetrating and briefly occupying a few key positions on the British Second Army front. Five days into the battle, on September 25, the German Infantry Divisions launched another sizeable attack and this time, they were successful in recapturing their pillboxes at the south-western end of Polygon Wood; albeit at a cost of many lives.

Within a few hours, the British Second Army, with the assistance of ANZAC troops, had also consolidated their positions. These forces followed up with a further attack on those same enemy placements at Polygon Wood, resulting in all gains achieved by the Germans only one day earlier, being wiped out. Casualties for the five days of fighting totalled 3,148 British Expeditionary Force troops killed in action and 3,243 taken prisoners. Overall, during the sixteen days of intense combat fighting between September 20 and October 3, Great Britain, Australia, and New Zealand suffered a total of 31,850 casualties.

Broodseinde, situated a short distance northwest of Zonnebeke and 1.8 miles south of Passchendaele, was the site of an important battle primarily designed to capture the Gheluvelt Plateau and Broodseinde Ridge. It was speculated that once General Plumer's troops successfully achieved their objective of capturing both Gheluvelt and Broodseinde, they would move east and prepare for an assault on Passchendaele Ridge soon thereafter.

In the meantime, the defensive-minded Germans became increasingly agitated over the substantial amount of territory now under the control of the British Expeditionary Force, in particular, the hills near the town of Zonnebeke. On October 4, German commanders made a decision to switch from a defensive to offensive strategy, and thereafter would conduct a massive assault on British positions. Ironically, on the same day, twelve infantry divisions of the British Second and Fifth armies badly mauled the Germans in combat along an eight-mile front. The enemy incurred a tremendous number of casualties in both killed and wounded as well as having 5,000 soldiers surrender.

In the meantime, Australian troops were occupying a small section of Passchendaele Ridge, until driven back by a fierce and sustained counterattack. The Australian troops were battle-weary and bruised from their October 4 encounter with the Germans at Passchendaele and were looking forward to a break from front-line duty. They were given five days to rest and regroup before being ordered back into combat to capture Poelkapelle, together with ten divisions from the French First Army, British Second Army, and the British Fifth Army.

The fighting at Poelkapelle was a horrific slaughter. More than 13,000 Allied casualties were counted, many of them killed in action. All the many accomplishments amassed by the Australians, utilizing some of the heaviest firepower and hand-to-hand combat, were disappointingly negated by the Germans. The New Zealanders, on the other hand, made a gallant effort on October 9, and again on October 12, to breach enemy lines in an effort to identify German defense weaknesses. All endeavours were met with failure, stonewalled by thickly laid, impenetrable, barbed wire and artillery fire similar to the bombardments encountered by the Aussies, eight days earlier.

The capture of Passchendaele was an obsession that occupied the thoughts of British Field Marshall Haig 24/7. As he perceived it, Passchendaele was within his grasp; it was only a matter of time. It took much persuasion from his commanding officers to convince Haig otherwise. The massive number of casualties already inflicted on British and Commonwealth forces during the Third Battle of Ypres would be, in the general's opinion, an inconceivable waste of men and resources should Passchendaele fail to fall to the British Expeditionary Force. General Haig finally came to the realization that British and Commonwealth troops had reached their limit of endurance. There was little assurance that a Passchendaele victory would prevail in the near future.

After considerable soul searching and contemplation, Generals Gough and Plumer were summoned to a meeting with Haig at his chateau. The meeting's main topic was a proposal to have forty-one-year-old, Lieutenant-General Sir Arthur William Currie to be the saviour of the British Empire. It would be the Canadian general's job to capture Passchendaele, thereby restoring General Douglas Haig's reputation as a great military leader and a smart strategist.

While Generals Currie and Haig heatedly debated the Canadian Corps' participation in the assault on Passchendaele, the Australians were at the same time having success forming a line from Broodseinde village, northward, for almost a mile down the slope towards Tyne Cot, where the New Zealanders were entrenched. Days earlier, the Aussies and Kiwis had joined forces to take a 125-foot height of land, called Abraham Heights. After capturing Abraham Heights, the ANZAC troops continued their advance beyond 's Graventafel and Berlin Wood, to a location that afforded a clear and unobstructed view of Ravebeek and Passchendaele Ridge, named "Waterloo Farm." In the days preceding the war, Ravebeek was a small stream, flowing down from Passchendaele into Flanders plain, where it gently meandered through luxurious, agricultural and dairy fields until it was eventually absorbed into the Yser Canal, and then ended its journey several miles away, on the Belgian coast.

Chapter Five

"There is nothing that war has ever achieved that
we could not better achieve without it."

Havelock Ellis

By October 1917, the formerly picturesque Ravebeek had been transformed into an ugly, putrid, stagnant, stinking body of water, littered with bloated and decaying bodies of both soldier and animal. The Ypres Salient was a vile place; a hell on earth. Moving troops, weapons, and supplies beyond Waterloo Farm was an on-going, logistical nightmare because of the mud and rain. Battle-fatigued soldiers of the ANZAC and British infantry divisions stood knee deep in water in trenches, while they waited for the Germans to attack. Every man looked at the sky and prayed for the rain to stop. At Waterloo Farm, the New Zealanders had to contend with non-stop explosions from whiz-bangs[1] and 77mm shells, not to mention numerous canisters of asphyxiating gas. Enemy machine-gunners eviscerated several of the soldiers as they attempted to cut their way through heavy rolls of barbed wire, strung along and across 's Graventafel Road. Machine-gun fire simply sliced through the advancing troops, as they pressed on. The determination by troops of the British Expeditionary Force to move onward relentlessly was met with monumental resistance from the enemy, and as a result both sides incurred large numbers of casualties. By now, General

---

1   A fast, low-trajectory shell named for the whizzing sound it made.

Douglas Haig was entirely convinced only the Canadian Shock Troops could finish the job and capture Passchendaele.

Lieutenant-General Sir Arthur W. Currie met with General Douglas Haig and members of the War Ministry, who presented Currie with a proposal, which would utilize the Canadian Corps (with British Infantry support) as the lead players in the Battle of Passchendaele. Currie argued vigorously against the idea, with much of what he said framed in expletives to forcefully make a point with his conservative English assemblage. Currie ferociously opposed sending his men to fight and die for a height of land that had failed to capitulate after almost three months of combat. However, despite his protestations, General Currie failed to convince General Haig to have a change of heart. Even though Currie implored the British to, "Let the Germans have Passchendaele — let them rot in the mud," he possessed little leverage to alter made-up British minds. Even though a major contributor to the war effort, Canada was a colonial entity of Great Britain, and England called the shots. The Canadian Expeditionary Force was part of the overall British Expeditionary Force and therefore under the ultimate authority of the BEF Chief of Staff, General Douglas Haig. This was an indisputable fact, one General Currie accepted, albeit reluctantly.

Although Arthur Currie may have lost the battle with Haig, he hadn't lost the war. Through General Currie's "tunnel vision" determination and intractable persistence, he was able to extract major concessions from Haig, particularly in two areas. The first was to allow Currie sufficient time to properly train and prepare his soldiers for battle. The second concession was for the sole benefit of his men; that once the Passchendaele operation had ended, all the survivors were to be immediately transferred out of the Ypres Salient, to a quieter sector. No matter what his thoughts may have been at the time, Douglas Haig had no choice but to acquiesce to General Currie's demands. Haig was totally cognizant of the fact that his reputation was intertwined with the outcome of the Passchendaele battle. As Chief of Staff of the British Expeditionary Force, Haig was also aware that British Prime

Minister, David Lloyd George personally disliked him, and on many occasions had referred to him as "Butcher Haig."

(Ross photo)
An unearthed artillery shell sits resting against a Passchendaele (Passendale) New British Cemetery wall at Mosselmarkt, on the former Bellevue battlefield. An estimated 331,000 pounds of unexploded artillery and gas shells are removed each year from the fields of West-Flanders.

As the hour approached when all four Canadian Infantry Divisions would begin arriving in the Ypres Salient, Canadian Corps Commander Arthur Currie contacted General Haig with yet one more request. This appeal was for a substantial number of medium and heavy artillery guns, together with sufficient ammunition to sustain a heavy bombing schedule lasting at least sixteen days. Currie was assured that the Canadian Corps would receive ample ammunition for 587 artillery weapons. But when the time arrived to move the guns into position, only 350 actually made it through the mud. Many of the larger guns simply disappeared, swallowed up by the salient mud; unable to fire a single round. In addition to the number of guns supplied by the

British, the Canadian Field Artillery batteries were also the recipients of several weapons left behind by the New Zealanders after being relieved by the Canadians. Once the Field Artillery moved into position on October 18, they immediately commenced a two-day, opening salvo, firing 2,800 tonnes of shells. The artillery guns were loaded and fired so rapidly and for such an extended period of time that a number of eighteen-pounder gun cannons overheated, melting some and warping others. A significant number of the artillery shells that fell on Flanders' plain during those two days in October, 1917 failed to explode. Today, these century-old shells are still being unearthed by Flemish farmers. Rusted, clay-caked ordinance is routinely found by Belgian farm tractors during the spring planting season. Once discovered, they are carefully removed from where they were found and placed alongside the roadway to await arrival of a special bomb squad disposal unit.

Plans for the Canadian Corps' role in the Battle of Passchendaele were quickly coming together as they prepared for a follow-up to their success at Vimy Ridge. It was time for the arrival of the Canadian Infantry. One of the soldiers making his way to West-Flanders and the Ypres Salient would be Private Stephen Ernest Shortliffe, 43rd Canadian Infantry Battalion (Cameron Highlanders of Canada), 9th Canadian Infantry Brigade, 3rd Canadian Infantry Division.

PART TWO

Vimy Ridge and Other Battles

Chapter Six

"In war there is no prize for runner up."

General Omar Bradley

Stephen Ernest Shortliffe was born on Christmas Day 1892, in Freeport, Nova Scotia. Freeport was a busy seaport of approximately 1,000 people living on the west end of a twelve- mile island. It rested between the turbulent waters of the Bay of Fundy and the much calmer St. Mary's Bay. Stephen Ernest was the seventh of ten children born to Sophia Mae (Outhouse) and Isaac Lee Shortliffe, who were married on October 26, 1875. Forty-two years later, on the exact day and month, their son would be killed in the First World War.

By the time Ernie arrived into the Shortliffe family, there were already five siblings; James Melbourne (b: 1879), Mabel Elizabeth (b: 1881), Delbert Llewellyn (b: 1885), Eva May (b: 1887), Olivia Maude (b: 1890), the author's maternal grandmother Velma Una (b: 1898 -October 26), and Ruby Wilma (b: 1901). Two of the ten Shortliffe children died in infancy; Mary Ethel at age thirteen-months and Estella Blanche, aged three.

One assumes Ernie was a typical young boy of that era, spending many hours fishing from harbour wharfs or sitting in a dory, hand-lining for mackerel, Pollock, and flounder. Like most young people, he probably spent time with friends; rolling wooden wagon wheels, riding his bike, and playing games in the Freeport school yard. When it came to school, Freeport was no different from most small Nova Scotia fishing communities in the early years of the twentieth century.

Some parents, such as Sophia and Isaac Shortliffe, encouraged their offspring to get a good education and seek careers away from local fishing, farming, and ship building. For many of the young men in Freeport, however, there was no choice. They were needed to supplement the family income with a job, not attend school. Many boys dropped out at grade eight or even earlier, looking for employment at one of the local lumber mills, or fish-processing plants.

As it so happened, the Shortliffe children took different career paths, which ultimately led them into academic and medical occupations. James Melbourne, the eldest, was a graduate of Acadia College in Wolfville, Nova Scotia and Yale University in New Haven, Connecticut. Upon graduation he would go on to become Professor of Economics at Dartmouth College, Colgate University, and Harvard University. Brother Delbert became a teacher of mathematics at a school in Stonewall, Manitoba and eventually moved to Edmonton, Alberta teaching at Victoria High School. It was there he developed the math course curriculum for the Alberta Department of Education and while involved in this project is said to have interacted with the renowned mathematician Albert Einstein. Sisters Velma Una and Olivia Maude also became teachers in small, one-room elementary schoolhouses; the author's grandmother in the village of Little River, on Digby Neck and Maude in Milford, Nova Scotia. Ernie Shortliffe's other sisters sought careers in the United States. One of his sisters, Mabel Elizabeth, became a nurse and later served with the United States Army in France during World War One.

Unlike his older brothers, who chose academic careers, Stephen Ernest eventually found his chosen occupation in banking. Bidding farewell to family and friends in the summer of 1912, he set off on an eighteen-hundred mile journey to Manitoba. There he was reunited with his brother Delbert and Delbert's wife Mayme, who were living in the small town of Stonewall, Manitoba, sixteen miles north of Winnipeg.

Stephen Ernest Shortliffe. c. 1912

Ernie, as he was known, began working as a bank teller on August 21, 1912 in the employ of the Bank of Hamilton, located on the corner of Main Street and Centre Avenue in Stonewall. The Bank of Hamilton was founded in 1872 and opened its local branch in 1900, but its existence would be short-lived; it merged with the Commerce Bank (later known as the Imperial Bank of Commerce) in 1924.

Two years after leaving Nova Scotia, Ernie Shortliffe, now a bank clerk, was sitting at his desk on August 5, 1914, when he learned Canada was at war with Germany. The day before, England, on behalf of her colonies and dominions, had declared to defend and liberate Belgium from the invading forces of Kaiser Wilhelm II. The authority to invoke war was contained in a document called the Treaty of London, signed in 1839. The treaty stated that Belgium would not attack any warring nation and no warring nation was to attack Belgium. England's decision meant her colonies; Australia, New Zealand, India, and Canada, would be part of the conflict as well. No prior consultation had taken place. The Government of Canada, under Prime Minister Robert Borden, responded by introducing and passing legislation known as the War Measures Act, giving sweeping powers to the government of the day. This included immediate suspension of all civil rights within The Dominion of Canada.

Like many young men of his age, Ernie knew that somewhere in time he would have to make the decision to volunteer overseas. At the moment he was a member of a highly respected Stonewall Militia Unit, the 79th Cameron Highlanders of Canada Regiment. Militia membership in Canada was very popular, especially since the end of the South African Boer War in 1902. In August 1914, there were at least 50,000 weekend warriors registered; whereas Canada's full-time army numbered only 3,111 soldiers.

At the beginning of the war, there was an abundance of exuberance, unbridled enthusiasm, and patriotic fervour captivating the minds and hearts of young Canadians everywhere. Thousands answered the call of the Canadian Expeditionary Force. Robert Borden showed Canada's willingness to assist Mother England in the war against imperialistic aggression by immediately committing 25,000 soldiers to the war effort. Recruitment centres opened across the country to an overwhelming response from young and older men eager to go and fight in numbers far exceeding Borden's most optimistic expectation. Within two months of the start of war, Canada's commitment of 25,000 troops was not only achieved, but had been surpassed by 7,000 additional volunteers.

During the same period, the Princess Patricia's Canadian Light Infantry (PPCLI) had undergone basic training and been deployed to France, arriving on October 3, 1914. The PPCLI was the first of 260 Canadian battalions to be organized during the war and sent to England, however, many were dissolved soon after arrival and troops were allocated to reserve battalions before being sent to other Canadian Expeditionary Force units in France and Belgium.

In the spring of 1915, fresh from English training camps on the 300-square-mile plateau of Salisbury Plain and its famous landmark, Stonehenge, the Canadian Expeditionary Force (CEF) found itself in northern France preparing for a set-piece battle against the Imperial German Army in the small town of Neuve Chapelle. The Canadians, under orders of the British Army, were given the task of preventing the Germans from reinforcing a particularly important section of town.

A successful and heroic operation was completed by the CEF. This combat action allowed General Douglas Haig, commander of the British First Army, to push through enemy lines and eventually establish a new allied front. The operation, which took place March 10-13, 1915, resulted in approximately 11,200 British and Commonwealth casualties. Many were Canadian troops. As the war in Western Europe steamrolled ahead, Ernie Shortliffe continued to work at the Bank of Hamilton while training with the 79th Cameron Highlanders of Canada Regiment on weekends.

Although the vast expanse of the Atlantic Ocean separated Canada from the war in France, stories of major battles and loss of Canadian lives were making their way into the daily life of families at home. Reports by war correspondents gave glowing accounts of battles and triumphs with pictures of smiling Canadian faces waving from the back of a lorry. Seldom were the words "defeat" and "casualties" ever mentioned in print, especially within the same sentence. The early days of war were portrayed as a time of adventure and camaraderie, while fighting a despicable enemy in olive-green wearing leather pin helmets. (Steel helmets for infantrymen did not make an appearance on the front until early 1916)

Nothing described the horror of war better than black and white, scratchy images of newsreel documentaries filmed by cameramen embedded with the Canadian Expeditionary Force. This relatively new medium generated great interest and thought-provoking questions as to the merit of sending a whole generation of young Canadians to war, many of whom would never return. Movie theatres became the venue for silent images of war as audiences stared intently at soldiers clambering out of trenches and rushing across battlefields littered with barbed wire, shell craters, and lifeless bodies. Viewers gasped in disbelief as they watched Canadian soldiers dropping to the ground, cut down by enemy machine gunfire and shrapnel. Action, drama, and tragedy were there for all to see on 28mm Pathé celluloid. Motion picture film dramatically changed the way people viewed the war by giving them access to stories (often heavily censored) recorded by newsreel photographers.

One such incident took place in April 1915. The first use of chemical gas by the Germans took place during an assault on Pilckem Ridge, and resulted in the deaths of 2,000 Canadian soldiers. Canadians read accounts of several disturbing events such as the increased escalation of casualties on the Western Front including the death of a twenty-two-year-old lieutenant by the name of Alexis H. Helmer.

(Ross photo)
Essex Farm Advanced Dressing Station where Lieutenant
John McCrae composed "In Flanders Fields."

Lieutenant Helmer of the 1st Brigade Canadian Field Artillery lost his life on May 2, 1915 during the Second Battle of Ypres. Witnessing his tragic demise was his good friend, Lieutenant- Colonel John McCrae, author of the renowned poem, "In Flanders Fields," which he wrote on May 3 to commemorate the memory of his friend and all who died on the Western Front. McCrae, a surgeon with the Canadian Medical Corps was attached to an Advanced Dressing Station situated at Essex Farm, not far from Ypres. Lieutenant McCrae died in France on January 28, 1918 from pneumonia, complicated by meningitis.

Another story making headlines was that of British nursing sister Edith Cavell. The Germans executed her on October 12, 1915 for assisting soldiers escaping from Belgium. This tragic story provoked indignation and outrage against the German Empire throughout Canada and Great Britain. It resulted in a greater determination to crush Kaiser Wilhelm's army decisively.

As the weeks, months, and years passed, Canada experienced a drastic, declining enlistment rate. This forced Robert Borden's Conservative government to take action in order to convince those aged between eighteen and forty-five to volunteer for duty. Canada's military combat strength had to be sustained to ensure a final "Road to Victory." Proponents, who once preached adventure, patriotism, and loyalty to the Crown, as the reasons to enlist, now had doubts as to whether this war was worth the sacrifice.

Canada was a relatively young country with strong and loyal ties to the British monarchy. It was not surprising that seventy percent of the 400,000 men who volunteered to serve in the Canadian Army, were of British descent. By the end of 1915, most of the eligible men born in Canada, including those who were unemployed, already had been recruited as part of the first quota of 50,000. The second phase of recruitment began in December 1914 and produced 150,000 combat soldiers before the end of the following summer. Once these targets had been met, the government redirected its focus to farming, mining, fishing, manufacturing, and office workers to fulfill Borden's New Year's pledge of 1916; to reach a total war-effort contribution of 500,000 soldiers. Borden's Canadian troop commitment was an ambitious one, considering the population at the time was only 7.2 million people. In order to reach half a million soldiers, it would be necessary for the government to enact special legislation on August 28, 1917, called the "The Military Service Act." This legislation immediately imposed a mandatory draft, commonly referred to as "conscription," on all eligible men who had not previously enlisted on a voluntary basis to serve in the Canadian Army.

Conscription would become a bitter pill for farmers, trade unionists, and anti-war organizations to swallow as they vehemently opposed the implementation of this particular law. The loudest outcry, however, came from the French-speaking communities in Quebec; the most vociferous opponents of conscription. Francophone Quebecers were enraged that Prime Minister Borden would renege on his promise to never institute obligatory service in the Canadian Army. The day conscription was declared law, hooligans embarked on a two-day rampage in downtown Montreal; breaking store windows, ripping up rail lines, rioting, and destroying property. During the protest, one person died and four Montreal residents were injured. In a further incident, during the Easter weekend of 1918, a twenty-three-year-old man, Joseph Mercier, was arrested by Quebec City police in a downtown bowling alley. His crime: failing to produce his conscription registration papers.

The arrest of Mercier precipitated mass demonstrations as protesters stormed army registration offices. Protestors looted and tossed thousands of files onto the street. Opponents of conscription across the entire country strongly believed enough had already been done to support the war effort and that Canada's interests were not being served by the continued deployment of troops to the Western Front. Despite protests and loud rhetoric, conscription remained a fact of life, and it was enforced. Those objecting to the draft were eventually offered a concession by the government, allowing them to file an exemption claim and appeal under the Military Service Act. Approximately ninety-five percent of the conscientious objectors filed an appeal, however, after the dust had settled, 47,000 out of 119,490 draftees actually saw combat overseas and that was mostly in the final months of the war in 1918.

Recruitment poster urges Manitobans to enlist with the 179th Battalion.

On January 12, 1916, the 179th Canadian Infantry Battalion (Cameron Highlanders of Canada) was officially authorized and formed in Winnipeg, Manitoba under the command of Lieutenant-Colonel James A. Cantile. Three weeks later, the new battalion had absorbed the 79th Cameron Highlanders Drafting Detachment from Stonewall, Manitoba. The 179th Battalion was one of three Cameron Highlander Regiments to be mobilized for service during the war in Europe; the first being formed on December 18, 1914 under the command of Lieutenant-Colonel R. M. Thompson, and known as the 43rd Canadian Infantry Battalion. In the summer of 1917, the final regiment of Cameron Highlanders, the 174th Canadian Infantry

Battalion, was dissolved shortly after arriving in England and its troops were reassigned to the 43rd Canadian Infantry Battalion. The same fate awaited the 179th Infantry Battalion on October 21, 1916.

The 43rd Canadian Infantry Battalion (Cameron Highlanders of Canada), consisting of thirty-five officers and 1,020 other ranks, sailed from Montreal to England on May 29, 1915, aboard the S.S. Grampian, a 485-foot former luxury liner. Upon their arrival, the troops were transported to a training camp situated at Lower St. Martin's Plain, in Shorncliffe, England. They were stationed there for a brief time before being relocated again to another camp in East Sandling, thirty miles southeast of London. During their time at East Sandling, the 43rd Battalion was called upon to supply reinforcements to the many Canadian infantry battalions suffering from manpower shortages. The 16th Canadian Scottish Battalion was strengthened and reinforced by 386 soldiers from the 43rd Battalion. This was only one of several reinforcement drafts involving the 43rd Battalion and other battalions within the Canadian Expeditionary Force.

As reassignment of soldiers to other battalions continued, the Cameron Highlanders of Canada sadly watched their ranks shrink to a critical level. The dissolution of the 43rd Battalion was becoming a real possibility. Fortunately, a decision to discontinue the transfer of men from the 43rd Battalion arrived before that happened. With a halt in the relocation of battalion soldiers to other units, a program of rebuilding the 43rd began, utilizing manpower resources from the Cameron Highlanders Overseas Drafting Detachment in Winnipeg. This decision breathed new life into the 43rd Canadian Infantry Battalion, saving it from extinction.

After replenishing its ranks and completing its training in East Sandling, the 43rd Battalion departed for France on February 21, 1916. They joined the 9th Canadian Infantry Brigade, which was part of the 3rd Canadian Infantry Division. Over a period of more than thirty months, the 43rd Battalion would participate in several combat operations, including the Somme, Vimy Ridge, Avion, Lens, Hill 70, Passchendaele, and Drocourt-Quéant.

On May 9, 1916, seventy-seven days after the 43rd Battalion arrived in France, twenty-three-year-old Stephen Ernest Shortliffe joined a long line of young men outside Minto Armoury in the west end of Winnipeg to volunteer in the Canadian Army. Minto Armoury (also called Minto Barracks), an army training facility built in 1914-15, was an impressive red brick and white stone, Tudor-style building. Its fortress motif made it appear medieval, especially with its turret-like corner towers and low-arched entranceways. Once inside this huge armoury, Ernie stood in a drill hall partitioned into sections. Recruits were interviewed, processed, examined, inoculated, vaccinated, and congratulated on becoming new members of the 179th Canadian Infantry Battalion (Cameron Highlanders of Canada) CEF.

Ernie Shortliffe had started the enlistment process. He completed a set of attestation papers in the presence of a recruitment officer named J.M. Dill, who hastily filled in the information and asked Ernie to read and sign the document. The Oath of Allegiance was administered by a Justice of the Peace. Ernie was then directed to a medical officer, Captain C. A. McKenzie, who conducted an examination of his heart, lungs, feet, and eyes. His height was recorded as 5 feet 9 inches (minimum height requirement: 5 feet 5 inches) and his expanded chest size was 40 inches (minimum expanded chest size: 34 inches). Shortliffe's eyesight was determined to be good, as he was able to see clearly from both eyes. One item noted by Captain McKenzie was the presence of a scar on his left forefinger, no doubt the result of a razor-sharp, fish-filleting knife from Ernie's earlier employment at a Freeport seafood-processing plant. Recording this scar was important should it be needed on the battlefield for body identification.

Upon completion of the examination, S.E. Shortliffe was given a Certificate of Medical Examination, indicating he was fit to serve in the Canadian Army. The commander of B Company welcomed Ernie and the other enlistees into the 179th Battalion. Ernie had now become Private S.E. Shortliffe, Regimental No. 860029.

Private S.E. Shortliffe was promoted to the rank of lance corporal on October 22, 1917.

Three weeks after enlisting in Winnipeg, Shortliffe and the other recruits, together with the battalion commander, Lieutenant-Colonel John Young Reid, boarded a Canadian Pacific Railway train for the 120-mile ride to Camp Hughes; six miles west of Carberry, Manitoba. Camp Hughes was a state-of-the-art training centre, with 1,037 acres of flat, rolling fields. It was designed with extensive trench systems, front lines, and support lines as well as "enemy lines." Training exercises consisted of combat manoeuvres, long marches traversing swamps, obstacle courses, and practice at grenade and rifle ranges, leaving little time for anything else. Conditions in the field during summer training were less than ideal at the best of times. Wet weather and Manitoba's notorious hordes of mosquitoes exacted a toll on a soldier's body and mind. Despite the environmental nuisances, soldiers were focused on a single objective: To become the best-trained battalion at Camp Hughes.

Preparing for combat duty on the Western Front meant training under realistic battlefield conditions, including live ammunition, rain, and mud. Boot camp at Camp Hughes was not without its casualties. Between July 13 and September 12, 1916, while Private S.E. Shortliffe and the 179th Infantry Battalion were undergoing rigorous battlefield training at Camp Hughes, six soldiers died. The cause of death of five of those soldiers was given as illness; one illness being spinal meningitis. The sixth soldier, forty-eight-year-old Private William R. Perkins of the Canadian Provost Corps, died from unknown causes. With Perkins being a member of the military police, one can only speculate whether his demise was from natural causes or perhaps from a confrontation with an enlisted man.

Private Perkins, together with Privates Walter Barringer, John James Davidson, John H.R. Messenger, Percy Smith, and Lance-Corporal James E. Kendall are buried in Camp Hughes Cemetery, on the site of the former WWI training facility, approximately sixteen miles from where Camp Shilo, Manitoba is now situated.

When Camp Hughes, a training complex, first opened in 1909, it was known as Sewell Camp. Six years later, it was renamed in honour of Major-General Sir Sam Hughes, Minister of Militia and Defence. In 1914 Sam Hughes had been the driving force behind the construction of Canada's first WWI training camp at Valcartier, Quebec. That facility could accommodate 33,000 trainees at any given time. Despite the perception of influence and power associated with Hughes, he was often ridiculed as being "Sir Sham Shoes," a snide reference to his reputation of being cheap, especially when it involved spending money on Canada's small, full-time army. His penny-pinching measures could be extreme. For example, Hughes issued a directive to army staff to procure combat boots for his troops, but the soles had to be made from cardboard, not leather. Another ill-conceived decision was to equip the army with the Ross Rifle, the MacAdam Shield Shovel, and the Colt machine gun. All three were either replaced or abandoned because of inferior quality. The Ross rifle, in particular, was known to be unsuitable for the muddy and wet conditions of trench warfare. Despite this fault, the rifle had a reputation as an exceptionally accurate firearm and therefore was used by most snipers throughout the war.

In November 1916, Robert Borden finally tired of his minister's antics and confrontational attitude and forced Sir Sam Hughes to resign from his cabinet. Hughes' resignation from cabinet did not remove him as a sitting member of Parliament, therefore he continued to direct inflammatory accusations and insults against anyone he chose, including General Sir Arthur William Currie. Sam Hughes and his vendetta to tarnish the reputation of Arthur Currie carried on long after the war ended.

In 1910 when Sewell Camp was first utilized, a total of 1,469 soldiers from the Canadian artillery, cavalry, and infantry units were trained there. Within five years the camp needed renovation to accommodate 10,994 trainees. By the time Private S.E. Shortliffe arrived on May 30, Camp Hughes had grown even larger. It was now the size of a big city with thousands of white, bell-shaped tents to house soldiers from twenty-seven battalions. In the summer of 1916, Camp Hughes was a bustling community with its own recreational centre, in-ground heated swimming pool, six movie theatres, hospital, post office, prison, and several retail stores. The portrait studios were busy taking photo portraits of proud, young men dressed in uniform. Between the years 1914-1918, at least 38,000 troops of the Canadian Expeditionary Force (CEF) trained at Camp Hughes.

As the days of summer drew to a close, Ernie Shortliffe and the 179th Canadian Infantry Battalion were ending their training and preparing to leave for England. Prior to that, soldiers were granted Harvest Leave, to allow time for visits with their families before heading off to war. While other ranks were away on furlough, a number of NCOs remained at Camp Hughes, to attend advanced training school, in the hope of one day becoming fully-commissioned officers.

September 26, 1916 was the final day at Camp Hughes for the 179th Infantry Battalion (Cameron Highlanders of Canada) and seventeen other infantry battalions. They assembled for parade and inspection by the Governor General of Canada, Prince Arthur, Duke of Connaught. At the conclusion, 922 men of the 179th Battalion including Stephen Ernest Shortliffe, in ceremonial attire and led by Lieutenant-Colonel Reid, marched to the nearby railway siding for the long ride to the port of Halifax, Nova Scotia.

Upon arrival in Halifax, Private Shortliffe and his comrades boarded the 580-foot passenger cargo carrier, S.S. Saxonia, bound for Liverpool, England. The Saxonia had been a luxury liner built in 1900, for the Cunard Ship Company by Clydebank Engineering and Ship Building Company. It cost 1.6 million dollars. Equipped with twin-screw propellers, it could cut through the water at speeds of up to 16.59 knots. The S.S. Saxonia had made its maiden voyage on May 22, 1900, carrying 1,960 passengers from Liverpool to Boston. On October 4, 1916, recently refitted as a troop-transport vessel, it left for England carrying thirty-two officers and 890 infantrymen from the 179th Battalion, as well as additional numbers of recruits from sister battalions.

Chapter Seven

"Kill one man and you are a murderer, kill a
million and you're a conqueror."

Jean Rostad

On October 13, after 2,633 miles and nine agonizingly long days at sea, the Saxonia finally dropped anchor into the dark, green waters of Liverpool Harbour. Everyone on board was thankful to have survived the turbulent and sometimes unforgiving Atlantic Ocean. Its monstrous waves had swept over the convoy of ships for days. There had also been the threat of an attack by German U-boats, seasickness, boredom, and homesickness. The men's nerves had been on edge for the greater part of the voyage.

Once the gangplank was lowered, Private S.E. Shortliffe and the men of the 179th Battalion left the ship and assembled for roll call and inspection before proceeding, in quick-time, to the Liverpool railway siding. When all the troops were confirmed to be on board, a black and red locomotive huffed and puffed its way down the tracks, picking up speed for its destination, East Sandling.

Eight days after their arrival in England, officers of the 179th Infantry Battalion received notice their battalion would be officially dissolved as of October 21. All soldiers would be reassigned to other reserve battalions for additional training before joining a new combat unit in France. Out of 922 soldiers from the 179th Infantry Battalion, 487 (fifty-three percent), including Private S.E. Shortliffe became members of the 17th Canadian Reserve Battalion in England. While attached to the 17th Reserve Battalion, the Canadians received occasional weekend passes. These were opportunities to visit the English countryside or take the train to London, where a soldier and his pay cheque were often quickly separated from each other. Soldiers were always warmly welcomed by shopkeepers, pub owners, and especially ladies of the night. These women were well aware that Canadian soldiers were paid much more than their counterparts in the British and ANZAC forces. Canadian soldiers, earning $1.00 a day ($1.10 on the Western Front), were viewed by many Commonwealth soldiers with envy and resentment. On more than one occasion, these emotions led to brawls in and outside English watering holes. The exchange of insults resulted in soldiers spilling out of the pubs to defend their honour and that of their battalion. Excited crowds of British spectators cheered enthusiastically. The numerous confrontations, leading to fisticuffs, resulted in a general perception that Canadian soldiers were troublemakers and bar-room bullies. Despite this notoriety, the majority of British Expeditionary Force officers held the Canadian infantryman in high esteem. For the most part, they respected and admired Canadian bravery, tenacity, loyalty, and fighting ability.

In the fall of 1916, England was like Freeport in mid-winter. There were several days of thick fog mixed with rain, wind, and the occasional wet snow. Private S.E. Shortliffe and his comrades had pretty much adapted to England's climate, but the incessant rain and fog did tend to get on one's nerves after awhile. Just after Ernie had finally acquired a taste for warm beer and fish and chips wrapped in newspaper, he was told he would be among 219 officers and ordinary regulars from the former 179th Infantry Battalion to leave East Sandling for the Western Front in France. There they would join the 43rd Canadian Infantry Battalion (Cameron Highlanders of Canada) in Bois de Bruay.

On November 14, 1916, Private S.E. Shortliffe sailed across the English Channel to Le Havre, France. There, he found himself among thousands of British Expeditionary Force troops in transit to battlefields in North-western France. Partial gridlock best describes the painfully slow movement of men, vehicles, and machinery to the front-lines.

Without patience, discipline, and exceptional organizational skill, none of them would have ever reached their final destination.

The weather was extremely wet; a bitterly cold wind slapped at the faces of the troops with stinging hail and rain. Eventually, the horrendous deluge of rain flooded the roads, bringing the movement of ammunition, food, weapons, and medical supplies to a complete standstill. Motorized transportation experienced identical problems to those of the horse-drawn limber (wagon). For much of the day, both were hopelessly mired in the clutches of deep mud. Teams of horses and hundreds of soldiers could be seen pushing, pulling, and lifting the supplies onto more stable ground. After spending several days bivouacked along a major French roadway, the 219 reinforcements from the 17th Canadian Reserve Battalion, along with Private S.E. Shortliffe, set off on a journey that would take them to the 43rd Infantry Battalion camp, sixteen miles northwest of Vimy Ridge.

The 43rd Canadian Infantry Battalion arrived at Camp Bruay, in Nord-Pas-de-Calais from the Somme valley, on October 24. After the Battle of the Somme, the three Canadian Infantry Divisions, who had been part of that major operation, made their way slowly to a place, described by General Sir Julian Byng, as "a quieter combat zone."

The 43rd Canadian Infantry Battalion (Cameron Highlanders of Canada) at Camp Bruay, near Vimy Ridge.

Upon arrival, soldiers were flabbergasted to learn they were within only a few miles of the infamous Vimy Ridge, an escarpment successfully defended by the Imperial German Army, since 1914. Exhausted Cameron Highlanders needed a respite from battle. The Somme had taken a huge toll, emotionally and physically, on the entire battalion. They were afraid a similar calamity could occur, if called upon to launch an assault against Vimy Ridge. These veterans of the Somme spoke from personal experience. The 43rd Battalion had fought in two battles at the Somme; one small and one major operation. The first, on September 20, saw D Company, led by Lieutenant C. G. Carey, capture a 200-yard section of the Zollern Graben Line, while undergoing a severe rifle/grenade bombardment. Casualties climbed until the few remaining soldiers in Lieutenant Carey's company were forced to retreat from ground they had taken earlier. They turned and headed back over No-Man's Land, to their jumping-off trench.

The second battle between the 43rd Battalion and the German Army took place on October 8, 1916, when the Cameron Highlanders attacked the heavily defended Regina Trench at 4:50 a.m. Led by bagpipers, the Highlanders crossed No-Man's Land and advanced directly into razor-sharp barbed wire and a hail of machine gun fire. The uncut wire presented the Cameron Highlanders with a significant challenge, one that ultimately stopped the soldiers "dead in their tracks." Only a few troops reached Regina Trench, and that small number was unable to hold on.

October 8 was a devastating day for the 43rd Battalion. Casualties numbered three officers killed, two wounded, and four missing. Ordinary regulars killed were nine, with 121 missing and 224 infantrymen wounded. Most, if not all, of those missing, were in fact killed in battle. If it had not been for the fact that some of the men from the 43rd Battalion were held back from battle in transport lines, the battalion would probably have been completely wiped out.

When the 43rd Canadian Infantry Battalion marched from the Somme Valley to the Vimy sector in the latter part of October, the battalion numbered only 257 men. That number should have been closer to 1,000. Overall, in the Battle of the Somme, approximately

24,000 Canadians were killed and wounded, out of a total combat force of 60,000 men. Most left the Somme battered, weakened, and disillusioned.

On the last day of November, reinforcements from the 17th Canadian Reserve Battalion had almost reached their destination in Bruay. The previous evening, officers and men had spent the night sleeping among the ruins of abandoned homes and an archaic Catholic church. After getting a relatively good night's sleep, the men awoke before dawn, had a breakfast of cold rations, and continued their trek in an easterly direction towards Camp Bruay. On the afternoon of December 1st, Private S.E. Shortliffe, along with 218 of his comrades from the 17th Canadian Reserve Battalion, reported for duty with the 43rd Canadian Infantry Battalion (Cameron Highlanders of Canada) CEF.

Chapter Eight

"When war is declared, truth is the first casualty."

Arthur Ponsonby

One day after arriving at Camp Bruay, soldiers of the disbanded 179th Canadian Infantry Battalion immediately began a four-day, intensive training program, preparing themselves for eventual deployment to the front-line. Instructions covered a multitude of subjects, but basically focused on trench warfare, the use of gas masks, and small-box respirators. Soldiers were also taught how to neutralize the effectiveness of enemy barbed wire without being detected by German sentries, as well as methods of attacking, defending, and counterattacking. One subject many soldiers found disgusting was how to control the gag reflex. Only a small number of the 219 reinforcements had ever seen a dead person, let alone witnessed death on a battlefield or smelled the foul stench of a rotting, grotesque-looking corpse. In the mind of the military, psychological conditioning was essential as it played an integral role in desensitizing soldiers against the barbaric and terrifying aspects associated with the hells of war. Most coped, but a significant number simply sank into the dark hole of depression.

Training manuals in the Great War were written for and by the British military, and were used extensively by the Canadian Expeditionary Force to train their troops. That being said, most instructors were Brits. Two particular skills would receive special attention; marksmanship and hand-to-hand combat. In addition, rigorous exercise was mandatory. Canadian infantrymen were reputed to have outstanding mental and physical abilities and could outsmart and outfight equally determined and trained opponents.

At the conclusion of the third day of training, on December 4, a number of new reinforcements were selected by each of the four company commanders. These soldiers were to participate in a reconnaissance mission in advance of a planned trench raid by the 43rd Battalion, on December 14. Trench raids were thought of as a sort of sporting exercise ever since the Princess Patricia's Canadian Light Infantry had conducted its first successful raid against a German line in February 1915. Now, platoons competed against each other to determine which unit could accumulate the most enemy kills or capture the greatest number of prisoners during a raid.

During the coming days, Private S.E. Shortliffe and his comrades were introduced to the underground tunnel. Tunnel systems were built primarily to move large numbers of infantry troops from rear positions to the forward trenches. They also offered protection to soldiers from enemy artillery shelling, prior to being ordered into battle. Julian Byng, current commander of the Canadian Corps, had been responsible for establishing at least a dozen tunnel and trench systems when he was a general in the British Army. Now, General Byng ordered the British Engineering Corps to design and build "subways," networks of tunnels. These tunnels were narrow, claustrophobic, subterranean passageways connecting larger areas where troops ate, slept, and awaited orders to emerge and engage the enemy. Once the order was heard, soldiers climbed steep sets of stairs into the trench lines, then over the parapets into a hail of machine gun fire. Tunnels were known to easily accommodate anywhere from one to four infantry battalions of soldiers, together with food, water, ammunition, medical dressing stations, communications, and battalion headquarters. Activity within the tunnels could easily be carried on under No-Man's Land or extended directly below the German lines. On numerous occasions, Canadian troops were only a few feet away from the enemy, who were excavating their own tunnels, galleries, and charge chambers. It goes without saying that tunnels were an extremely important concept employed extensively by both combatants in the Vimy-Arras sector of Nord-Pas-de-Calais.

Reconnoitring missions into No-Man's Land, or what some made reference to as the "dead zone," were important for the gathering of information on enemy positions and approximation of troop strength. These covert operations were on-going by both combatants, even though No-Man's Land was considered by the Germans as a neutral zone. Canadian commanders dismissed the idea of a buffer zone not being occupied, therefore, on numerous occasions, Canadian Corps troops were entrenched only a stone's throw from German lines.

No-Man's Land was like a scene from Dante's Inferno — parched, blackened, colourless, smoke- filled, and repugnant. One could almost imagine a loud, booming voice emanating from No-Man's Land declaring: "Abandon all hope, ye who enter here." No-Man's Land was definitely not a place of joy. However, on one particular Christmas in 1914, it was.

(Ross photo)
Ploegsteert, approximately fifteen km south of Ypres (Ieper) was the site of a 1914 Christmas soccer match between British and German troops.

This strange, historic event took place on a Belgian farmer's field in Ploegsteert, a few miles from Ypres. On Christmas day, after the British and German soldiers listened to each other sing carols, an eerie quiet fell upon the battlefield. Without warning, soldiers from both sides slowly rose from their trenches and an unofficial truce was declared. They waved and walked towards each other to meet in No-Man's Land. There, in that disgusting, narrow stretch of hell, they wished each other Merry Christmas — shook hands and exchanged gifts of cigarettes and rum. Afterwards, an impromptu game of soccer was played, prior to the two archenemies returning to the job of killing. For one brief moment in time, hatred, fear, and mistrust were replaced by celebration and peace in No-Man's Land.

In the late afternoon of December 6, the Cameron Highlanders were relieved in the front-line by troops of the 58th Canadian Infantry Battalion (Central Ontario). Once the 43rd Battalion had relinquished its position to the 58th, A Coy (Company) and D Coy moved to the support line in the right sub-section, which was occupied by the 60th Canadian Infantry Battalion (Quebec). In the meantime, Private S.E. Shortliffe and fellow members of B Coy, along with troops from C Coy, were relocated to a support line in the left sector. After leaving the Somme Valley, the 43rd Battalion had maintained forward positions near the town of Neuville-Saint-Vaast, approximately seventeen miles south of Camp Bruay. From this town, in Nord-Pas-de-Calais, by means of deep tunnels, the 43rd continued to advance towards the German lines at La Maison Blanche, to the trenches of Claudot, Guillermot, Sapper Avenue, and Territorial. The 9th Brigade line was located 1,200 yards east of Neuville-Saint-Vaast in a No-Man's Land mine field named "The Crater Line." It was there, in No-Man's Land, that the 43rd and 58th Battalions rotated troops between front, support, and reserve lines until February 11, 1917, when the 43rd Infantry Battalion (Cameron Highlanders of Canada) was ordered to La Folie Wood.

Except for an earlier reconnoitre mission, Private S.E. Shortliffe and his comrades spent most of their time at combat instructional school in Transport Line, where they were paid a visit, on December 8, by the battalion's second-in-command, Major William K. Chandler, who observed part of the training. In addition to teaching, battalion officer/instructors were also involved in preparing twenty-eight ordinary regulars, a scout, and Lieutenant Nutter from A Coy, for an impending trench raid. On December 12, one hundred of the two hundred and nineteen men who had arrived at Camp Bruay as reinforcements, were taken from Transport Line and ordered to relieve the 58th Canadian Infantry Battalion in the front-line, shortly after midnight.

Measures were taken to pre-empt any attempt by the Germans to breach the Canadian sector, however, there was no contact whatsoever between the enemy and the 43rd Battalion patrols.

The party selected to carry out a raid on the German lines was advised that it would take place on the evening of December 14, commencing at 6:00 p.m. The men, after reaching the enemy barbed wire, were to place and detonate a number of ammonal tubes with the intention of destroying a portion of the massive wire placements. This would allow easier and quicker access to the German-occupied sector.

The raiding party carefully eased its way across the terrain, occasionally being forced to take cover behind crater rims, to avoid being seen by German sentries as night flares lit-up No-Man's Land. After finally reaching the belts of barbed wire, the raiding party encountered an unexpected problem with the wooden, ammonal plugs. The plugs could not be removed from the tubes, so fuses could not be inserted to create the necessary detonation and explosion. Frustrated, the raiding party abandoned the mission and returned to the battalion lines. The aborted raid was rescheduled for the following night.

The explosive device used to destroy enemy barbed wire was for all practical purposes known to most soldiers as an "Ammonal Tube," but it also went by other names such as "Pipe Bomb" and "Bangalore Torpedo." Ammonal tubes measured approximately two and half inches in diameter. The length of the tube itself could be extended, depending on the depth of the barbed wire that had to be destroyed. A pointed, wooden plug was inserted into the front end of the tube, as well as a flat plug placed at the opposite end. A hole was drilled through the flat plug, allowing a fuse to be inserted, which when lit, ignited ammonal ingredients, resulting in an explosion. The ammonal composition of the pipe bomb was identical to what was generally used in other bombs, including hand grenades and artillery shells — ammonium nitrate and aluminum powder.

After having dealt with the frustration of the previous ammonal tube failures, it was now time to try again, but even this later attempt proved unsuccessful. This time, it was partly the fault of the Canadian Field Artillery gunners. They mistakenly interpreted an enemy bomb explosion, assuming the raiding party was detonating its pipe bombs as a signal for the artillery to lay down a bombardment of shells upon the German lines. As Canadian bombs fell all around them, Lieutenant Nutter and his raiding party feverishly worked to fire-off the ammonal tubes, but once again the fuses failed and consequently so did the entire operation. The lieutenant gathered his men and retreated to their line, where they waited until satisfied the enemy had no intention of retaliating for the bombs dropped earlier.

Leading his party of men once again, Lieutenant Nutter left at 11:50 p.m. to recover all unexploded pipe bombs attached to the German barbed wire. Lieutenant Geddes and his party of sixteen infantrymen also returned to a location where numerous pipe bombs had been left two days earlier and successfully recovered all the explosive devices. After returning to their combat units, company officers convened a meeting in which they approved plans for another attempt to blast enemy barbed wire, on December 17. Shortly after the decision was made, word came down the line that the mission was cancelled. It was not unusual, in the theatre of war, to abruptly delay or suspend planned operations, even at the last minute.

Fighting trenches on the Western Front were wet, muddy, cramped, odoriferous, and not to mention, rat and lice infested. The time a soldier spent in a trench was usually an average of three consecutive days; occasionally, infantrymen were known to be subjected to longer stays; several weeks or longer, depending on the circumstances. Usually a soldier lived 15% of his time on the front-line, 10% in support, 30% in reserve and 20% in rest areas behind the lines. The remaining 25% was allotted to time at field hospitals, travelling to combat zones, billets, furloughs, and training. During daylight hours, enemy snipers more or less controlled the routine movement of troops within the field work (trench) area. Consequently, soldiers led a very stressful and perilous life between the sand-bagged walls of their trenches. Thus, the majority of activities took place after dark, e.g.: reconnaissance patrols and movement of troops and supplies, in addition to construction, expansion, and rehabilitation of trenches.

Fighting the war in France from a trench in Nord-Pas-de-Calais presented unique challenges and a multitude of risks, only some of which were being shot, bayoneted, or bombed. The fact that life-saving drugs, such as antibiotics and penicillin would not be discovered until 1928 by Louis Pasteur, often meant serious wounds resulting from weapon fire or accidental injury could easily end in amputation or even a soldier's death. Abdominal wounds were almost 99% fatal, while 50% of soldiers, suffering a major head injury would succumb to their wounds. Water-soaked trenches were the breeding grounds for dysentery, cholera, and typhus, due to poor sanitary conditions and improper hygiene. In addition, these conditions also contributed to parasitic problems such as ringworm, round worm, and tapeworm, not to mention the many other sicknesses transmitted to soldiers by rats, fleas, and lice.

One such illness, found to have been transmitted from insect to man, was known as Pyrexia of Unknown Origin (PUO), also called "Trench Fever." Between the summer of 1915 and the end of the war, an estimated 450,000 reported cases of PUO affected troops of the British Expeditionary Force, including numerous Canadian soldiers. The term "Trench Fever" originated with British troops when they first became ill in Flanders, during the summer of 1915. The symptoms of this unrecognized disease included headache, dizziness, muscle pain in the joints and lower back, stiffness in the thighs, severe pain in the legs, and a relapsing fever, caused by some sort of bacterial infection.

The relapsing fever of PUO appeared similar to malaria fever. In the beginning it was treated with quinine, however, this had no effect on changing the course of the illness. By the end of 1916, it had been determined that Pyrexia of Unknown Origin or Trench Fever was transmitted by body lice. The louse was the most common, bloodsucking insect found. Lice were in the trenches, on the blankets, and on soldiers' bodies. These obnoxious bugs were most prevalent during the cold, winter months; hence, flies and mosquitoes were ruled out as carriers of the disease. The wartime scourge, known by the French as "Typhus Mineur," by the Germans as "Wolhynian Fever," and by fifty-nine divisions of the British Empire as "Trench Fever- Pyrexia of Unknown Origin," would continue unabated until the end of the war. Failure to find a cure caused a tremendous drain on manpower resources throughout most of WWI.

During the early morning of December 19, the 43rd Battalion was transferred from front-line duty to Divisional Reserve Camp. Later that morning, Lieutenant-Colonel William Grassie performed an inspection of the 219 reinforcements; their battalion was to be officially attached to one of the four company combat units. That evening, Private S.E. Shortliffe and his fellow reinforcements were treated to a special meal and social, hosted by officers of the 43rd Battalion.

Even as Christmas approached, the 43rd Battalion continued with their combat-training program each morning, commencing at 9:00 a.m. and lasting until late afternoon. The exception was December 23, when bagpipers and drummers led the Cameron Highlanders past a reviewing stand, in a pouring rainstorm, for a ceremonial salute and inspection by Brigadier-General F.W. Hill, commander of the 9th Canadian Infantry Brigade. After remarks to the officers and other ranks, Brigadier-General Hill joined 43rd Battalion Commander Grassie and company officers for a meeting at battalion headquarters. The officers discussed training and combat preparedness. The focus on special training for machine gunners and bombers, fuelled speculation of a possible spring offensive at Vimy Ridge. That scenario had already been discussed on November 21, 1916, during a meeting between Canadian Corps commanders and their counterparts from the British First Army. It was at that time a suggestion was made, to have the British Expeditionary Force conduct the next major operation on the Western Front, near the city of Arras. It was anticipated that the event would be of a magnitude greater than the Battle of the Somme.

The day before Ernie's twenty-fourth birthday, B Coy gathered for a special Christmas Eve service at 9:30 a.m., in the YMCA hut, led by the battalion chaplain, Captain Pringle. At the end of the service, the men sang a few Christmas carols before stepping out into the cold, crisp December air. It was now time to relieve the 58th Canadian Infantry Battalion at the front in the support line; the place where Ernie and his friends would celebrate his birthday.

During Christmas of 1916, soldiers from both sides of the war seemed to take a short hiatus from killing, especially on Christmas Day. On that day, a severe cold spell arrived, bringing with it snow and rock-hard, frozen ground. The wintry weather would last into the early part of January before changing to rain. With the rain came the floods, and with the flooding, severe erosion of the trenches. Weeks after occupying a support line at the front, three Coys from the 43rd Battalion were relocated during the early hours of December 31, to Brigade Support. B Coy was one of the three Coys transferring at 4:00 a.m. to a position on the immediate right of the 60th Canadian Infantry Battalion (Quebec).

The third year of the Great War was about to begin.

Chapter Nine
JANUARY 1917

"God is not on the side of the big battalions, but
on the side of those who shoot best."

Voltaire

Happy New Year!

It was hardly a joyous occasion for those unfortunate enough to be stuck in a wet, cold, and foul-smelling hole-in-the-ground, determined to stay alive, while fighting a war. Even an optimist would have realized there was little hope of a swift end to the bloodshed in 1917. Troops of the United Kingdom continued to perish on the battlefields, attempting to capture a few yards of blood-soaked soil, as they had done in the recent Battle of the Somme. January 1917 would be remembered as a month during which Canadian troops suffered the most, enduring snow storms and daytime-low temperatures of -7 degrees Fahrenheit. It was also the month in which a possible spring offensive would become a priority for discussion and debate, as insisted upon by General Arthur William Currie, commander of the 1st Canadian Infantry Division.

General Currie, together with his British and Canadian counterparts, paid a visit to the battlefields of Verdun-sur-Meuse at the special invitation of the French Army. French officers shared their individual and collective experiences from the Bataille de Verdun.

One of the longest-running combat engagements of WWI, the encounter was fought from February 21 to December 18, 1916. In the Battle of Verdun, the combined casualty totals for both French and German armies were estimated to be 700,000 combatants. The French related the strategy at Verdun as being based on a pre-assault program, involving numerous combat rehearsals, prior to the actual battle itself. The army introduced the implementation of two incredibly large waves of assault troops against the Germans, supported by artillery fire and combined with intensive, indirect harassing fire. The French also incorporated two significant features in their attack plan. The first was to use platoons supported by specialist units, and second was the sharing of tactical information, including maps and photo reconnaissance with front-line troops. The latter allowed for the empowerment of NCOs and other ranks to make spur-of-the moment decisions during the heat of battle, should a commanding officer be immobilized or taken prisoner.

Based on the analytical information regarding the Verdun battle, the French, British, and Canadian commanders agreed to move forward with further discussions in order to facilitate future combat actions. Further discussions would involve paying special attention to the necessity for medium and heavy artillery, harassing fire, and company-platoon flexibility. General Currie, 1st Canadian Infantry Division Commander, although initially sceptical of such a plan, eventually agreed. Canadian Corps Divisional Commanders could learn and benefit from the French Army's experience at Verdun. The outcome of the meeting resulted in a plan being drafted for General Henry Horne, of the British First Army, requesting his approval for a major spring offensive.

The 43rd Battalion's first casualty of the New Year occurred on January 5. An ordinary regular was wounded on the front-line by gunfire, during the relief of the 58th Canadian Infantry Battalion in sub-section C-2. Two days later, as the 43rd Battalion rifle sections were practicing rapid fire; spraying the German positions with numerous rounds of bullets, the enemy responded by shelling the Cameron Highlanders for two hours, using their 15cm schwere Feldhaubitze 13s (long barrel Heavy Field Howitzer guns). Not wanting to be denied the last shot, the 43rd Battalion's Field Artillery carpet bombed No-Man's

Land and enemy lines beyond, resulting in a score of German soldiers being killed and wounded.

The war game "Harass Your Enemy" continued in several sectors along the front lines, with the Cameron Highlanders of Canada undergoing severe bombardments during four separate days: 9, 18, 19, and 21 of January. On the last day, German Field Artillery gunners stepped up the frequency and volume of shelling along the front and support lines, creating extensive damage to Canadian positions.

Livens Projectors, mortar-like weapons used to discharge shells containing asphyxiating gas, are seen here, being prepared for firing.

As if the constant noise of exploding shells wasn't enough to drive soldiers squirrelly, there were always the frequent gas alerts to keep one from daydreaming in the trenches, although the first gas alert of the New Year did not take place until January 10 at 4:40 p.m. The warning system, used to alert the men to incoming gas, was usually one of two types. The first, a bell, was improvised by using the casing of a spent artillery shell. This device worked well to prepare troops, provided there was no great amount of noise at the time, to muffle the sound of the alarm. Despite striking the bell forcefully with a metal bar, it seldom produced a warning heard above the roar of artillery guns and explosions. On those occasions, troops were alerted by means of an air horn called the "Strombos"; an alarm that could be heard for eight miles.

Gas-attack alerts were common occurrences during World War I. Although the common perception is that the German Army was the first to use chemical gas, it was actually the French who deployed tear-gas grenades in August 1914. It would not be long after that when the Germans deployed chemical weapons in significant quantities, beginning with a non-lethal gas that caused sneezing and severe irritation to eyes and nose membranes. Hundreds of shells containing this particular irritant were released on October 27, 1914 against the French Army at Neuve Chapelle. Three months later, on January 31, 1915, the Imperial German Army used benzyl bromide in shells against the Russians on the Eastern Front, at Bolimow; because of the extreme cold weather, the ingredients did not vaporize; therefore no gas was produced. The Germans eventually corrected this particular problem. A colourless liquid compound, called "Bromacetone" (chemical formula: CH_3COCH_2Br), was added and used against the French at Nieuport, on the Belgian coast, in March, 1915.

Throughout the war, both sides employed a variety of chemical gasses, with most producing devastating effects on all those exposed to their toxic fumes. Chlorine and phosgene gasses, in addition to being extreme irritants to soldiers' eyes, also attacked the lungs before moving to the nervous system. Of the two, phosgene was ten to fifteen times more deadly; it attacked a soldier's blood vessels and the alveolus (the anatomical lung structure), directly. Both gasses were referred to as "asphyxiating gas." The infamous mustard gas, also called "Yperite," created its own hell upon the bodies of soldiers. It formed festering blisters on the skin or in the lungs, wherever the blistering gas made contact. It should be noted that mustard gas was combined with phosgene gas almost every time it was deployed. A third classification was arsenic gas; an extremely poisonous chemical weapon that immediately attacked the white cells in a soldier's lungs, poisoning and killing the victim. Chemical weapons such as these were used throughout the war, albeit on a lesser scale in the waning months of World War I. It is estimated that the British Expeditionary Force (which included Canadian Expeditionary Force troops) suffered 188,000 casualties directly related to chemical weapons.

Sunday, January 12, saw a thick, grey fog shroud the entire front, forcing the cancellation of an important practice scheduled between the men of the 43rd Battalion and fighter planes from the Royal Flying Corps (RFC). It was agreed to reschedule the practice to another day, when the weather would be much more favourable. Three days after the cancellation, Private S.E. Shortliffe was removed from active duty because of a chronic high fever, body pains, and acute respiratory problems. After sick parade, Ernie was dispatched to the 3rd Canadian Infantry Division, #10 Field Ambulance where he remained under the care of medical staff for one week. Major T.M. Leask, the medical officer in charge of #10 Field Ambulance diagnosed Shortliffe's illness as PUO (Pyrexia of Unknown Origin). PUO was only one of a number of illnesses affecting soldiers on the Western Front. There was also a strain of E-Coli toxin; a dysentery- producing bacteria named "Shigella," which was said to have killed as many troops as did enemy bullets. Five days after Private S.E. Shortliffe was discharged from the field ambulance hospital, it was reported that a severe outbreak of mumps had occurred in Ecoivres, Mont-Saint-Eloi, and Camp Bray. As a result, all meeting areas were declared off-limits to army personnel, unless authorized.

On January 27, eight NCO reinforcements from the former 184th Overseas Battalion (Winnipeg), arrived at Camp Bruay, adding manpower to the 43rd Battalion. Like so many infantry units deployed to Great Britain, the 184th Battalion was also disbanded shortly after its arrival in England. The men were absorbed into the 11th Canadian Infantry Reserve Battalion. Three days after joining the 43rd, a number of the NCOs were assigned to Lieutenant Geddie. With the addition of scouts Buchan and Lough, they crossed into No-Man's Land under the cover of darkness, successfully severing the belts of German barbed wire, in advance of another attempt to raid enemy forward lines.

In the first month of 1917, the 43rd Infantry Battalion reported twelve wounded and four killed in action. Among the dead were: Private Thomas Ambrose, killed on January 7 in the Crater Line, Private William Lorne Milton, January 8, Lance-Corporal Robert Patterson, January 11, and Corporal William Michie on January 30.

Chapter Ten
FEBRUARY 1917

"Mankind must put an end to war before
war puts an end to mankind."

John F. Kennedy

Once a comprehensive analysis of the Battle of Verdun had been completed, divisional commanders and their officers worked to finalize detailed plans for an assault on Vimy Ridge. Final approval was expected sometime in early March. In the meantime, the Cameron Highlanders remained within a short distance of German troops; separated by roll upon roll of rusted, barbed wire, piles of rubble, and unclaimed bodies. February on the front-line was predictably cold and depressing. Housecat-size rats scurried, faster than normal, across the icy plain and along the duckboard floors of the front-line trenches. Soldiers cocooned themselves, doing whatever was necessary to keep warm and preserve precious body heat. Small bonfires provided some limited relief from the cold, while extra wool socks and mitts helped to keep feet and fingers from becoming frostbitten. Most soldiers wrapped themselves in woollen blankets over their greatcoats and sleeveless leather jerkins. A leather jerkin provided only minimum heat retention, even though it was a favourite item of uniform. The primary reason for its popularity was the freedom of movement it provided, especially when engaged in hand-to-hand combat. In addition, the jerkin was much less likely to become entangled on barbed wire than the cumbersome greatcoat.

Soldiers on the front-line were trained to react quickly to an enemy raid, in order to prevent a section of trench being breached. Defending a Coy trench line meant using all means available to repulse the enemy; from small arms fire, to hand grenades, and machine guns. These weapons included the Lewis machine gun, the Enfield .303 rifle, and the Mills hand grenade. Approximately seventy-five million of these hand grenades were manufactured for exclusive use by the British Expeditionary Force during WWI.

There was also another killing device — the Mark III bayonet was utilized in close quarters to terminate the lives of enemy soldiers. During assaults and trench raids, the bayonet was an integral tool for soldiers, as it helped to conserve precious ammunition and reduced the chance of being shot in the back by wounded combatants. The Germans were also enthusiastic fans of bayonets, which they called the "S98/05," and which were nicknamed by the British as "butcher-blade bayonets."

It was not surprising that soldiers who witnessed barbaric and senseless cruelty would develop a distrust and deep-seeded hatred for their enemies. This was especially evident in those who fought at the Battle of the Somme. They had witnessed the execution of their comrades on the spot, after they had surrendered to their German captors. These veterans of the Somme also recalled seeing terrified soldiers torched and burnt alive, while fighting in the ruins of buildings and in the trenches, by Kleinflammenwerfers (flamethrowers), which spewed ribbons of fire as long as fifty-four feet. There were also rumours of German troops committing horrible atrocities, such as gouging out eyes of villagers, slicing off hands of young men, raping women, pillaging, and crucifying Allied troops in No-Man's Land.

Despite war's cruelty and frequent inhumanity, there were rare times when all belligerents took a break from killing. As mentioned, the unofficial Christmas truce at Ploegsteert in 1914, was one example; at other times, during morning breakfast, a brave, fearless soul would stand and hold aloft a wooden board, which was a signal to cease firing. As long as the board was visible, it was supposedly safe for troops to leave their trenches to retrieve water and food. The moment the board was withdrawn from sight, the killing resumed.

After several failed attempts to conduct raids on enemy positions, on February 2, two battalion lieutenants, Nutter and Verner, selected twenty-two Cameron Highlanders to plan an attack on part of a German trench line named La Maison Blanche. As the party approached the German-held territory, it suddenly came under intense enemy rifle fire and stiff resistance from those defending the line. Using grenades, the Highlanders inflicted a degree of damage to a section of La Maison Blanche trench, before falling back to the Canadian lines with one German prisoner in tow. One day after Lieutenants Nutter and Verner held their successful trench raid, German heavy artillery retaliated by pounding the 43rd Battalion position. In response, the 9th Infantry Brigade's Canadian Field Artillery and Canadian Trench Mortar Battery fired numerous rounds of shells, including several eighteen-pounders, eventually quietening down the Germans.

Aside from February 4, the Western Front remained relatively quiet up until February 9. The lull in enemy activity, between the 4th and 9th, gave the 43rd Infantry Battalion a window of opportunity to move their men to Divisional Reserve at Camp Bray. Private S.E. Shortliffe and his comrades enjoyed a few days of rest, hot baths, and haircuts, as well as mandatory inoculations and vaccinations. While at Divisional Reserve, Lieutenants Nutter and Verner were dispatched to join the battalion's A Coy in Rhine Trench, on February 7. They relieved Lieutenants Smart, Simpson, and Morgan. Lieutenant Morgan and Lieutenant Simpson returned to Rhine Trench a few days later, this time accompanied by Lieutenant Barraud, who had re joined the 43rd Battalion after spending time in Blighty (England), recuperating from serious wounds sustained in earlier combat.

On February 11, the 43rd Infantry Battalion, with the exception of A Coy, left Divisional Reserve at Camp Bray and moved some distance away into billets situated in Auchel, France. Auchel was to become the 43rd Battalion's training location, along with eleven other battalions from the 3rd Canadian Infantry Division. Operation orders issued by

Captain J.C. Kemp, on behalf of Brigadier-General F.W. Hill of the 9th Infantry Brigade, set-out the protocol to be instituted for the transfer of the Cameron Highlanders of Canada and the other regiments to Auchel, commencing at noon, from Camp Bray. The 43rd was led by company scouts, followed by bagpipes, drums, and brass sections, then signallers, runners, B Coy, C Coy, D Coy, and finally one company of troops from the 58th Battalion. Transport Section met the 43rd Battalion at the first crossroad and continued on from there, in timed intervals of five minutes. Private S.E. Shortliffe and his buddies were relieved to be making the trip with a lighter load; most of their equipment and supplies had been packed and transported earlier to Auchel, by truck and general purpose limbers. The route to Auchel travelled by the 43rd Battalion started with a north-westerly march to the main road at Mont-Saint-Eloi via Estrée, Cauchie, and Cauchin Legal, before moving to the crossroads above Ranchicourt. The battalion proceeded from Ranchicourt northeast to another crossroad at Houbain, before finally arriving in Ruitz at 4:45 p.m. Here, the men were billeted for the night.

On February 11, just before the battalion's arrival in Ruitz, then Auchel, two advance billeting parties departed the quartermaster store. The parties were organized by Lieutenant Robert Shankland with the assistance of Private Hunt, from battalion headquarters. They consisted of a regimental tailor and one soldier from each of Coys, B, C, and D. The three soldiers acted as custodians of the stacks of blankets and supplies once they arrived at the billet location, as well as guides to Ruitz. A second billeting party, made up of Major Hossie and Private Seddon from battalion headquarters, together with Privates Fortune and Johnson from the quartermaster store, accompanied trucks loaded with tons of supplies for Auchel. There they were met by Captain J.A. Hope of the 9th Canadian Infantry Brigade. Before leaving Divisional Reserve, a number of NCOs were ordered to ensure that none of the tents, stoves, or building materials had been removed. The supplies would be needed by the next contingent of soldiers. Officers conducted a final inspection of the trenches, billets, baths, laundry facilities, latrines, horse areas, and parade grounds, to confirm the area had been left clean. Private S.E. Shortliffe would spend St. Valentine Day; Wednesday, February 14, 1917, in Auchel.

On Sunday, the 18th members of the Cameron Highlanders of Canada came together at 2:30 a.m. for Divine services, before returning to their billets to catch a few hours sleep. They were heading off for a day of lectures at Army Instructional School. This particular training facility, in Auchel, was elaborate in comparison to other camps. It contained detailed mock-ups of German trench systems, defence fortifications, plus actual man-made hills and ridges designed and built by army engineers. All were prominently marked with brightly coloured tape and flags. At Auchel, each company was given a practice schedule; troops then practiced attacking a mock-up of Vimy Ridge. The real Vimy was waiting for its next major battle. Training moved ahead and the Highlanders displayed more skill and confidence with each passing day. On February 19, a draft reinforcement of 110 men, from the 3rd Canadian Entrenching Battalion, arrived to enhance the strength of the 43rd Battalion.

Sunday Divine services were held twice on the morning of February 25, at 8:00 a.m. and again at 10:15 a.m. Following church services, a troop inspection and a medal ceremony took place. Military Medals (MM) were presented to soldiers of the 43rd Battalion, in recognition of personal acts of heroism performed during the Battle of the Somme, a few months earlier. Major-General Louis J. Lipsett, commander of the 3rd Canadian Infantry Division, pinned metals on the chests of seven soldiers. The first, Lieutenant George H. Burns, had been a member of the 43rd Canadian Infantry Battalion since his enlistment in Winnipeg, on October 4, 1915. Born on August 13, 1892 in Moosimin, Saskatchewan, Lieutenant Burns was awarded the MM for his action in treating wounded soldiers while coming under heavy enemy fire, at Courcelette, France. In addition to the Military Medal, Burns was also the recipient of the Italian Bronze Medal for Military Valour. (Lieutenant Burns was later killed in action).

General Lipsett also presented a Military Medal to Sergeant Alexander Buchan, a twenty-six-year-old farm worker born in Aberdeenshire, Scotland. Sergeant Buchan had enlisted at the Minto

Armoury, in Winnipeg, on June 16, 1915. Buchan was killed fighting the Germans, one mile west of Vimy Ridge, on April 13, 1917. General Lipsett also presented Military Medals to Lieutenant Nutter, Sergeant-Major Anderson, Sergeant Burges, Private Lough, and Private Zidar.

The 43rd Battalion casualty list for the month of February reported that Corporal William K. McKay passed away on February 5, from battle injuries suffered days earlier. Besides Corporal McKay, other Cameron Highlanders to die that month included: Private Charles W. Oram, February 1, Private James H. Doig, February 2, Private Hugh Murray, February 5, Private William Peterson, February 6, Private Frederick W. Mattin, February 9, Private Frederick C. Woodworth, February 17, Lance-Corporal Angus Gunn, February 19, and Private James Freeman, February 26.

Chapter Eleven
MARCH 1917

"The whole art of war consists of guessing at what is on the other side of the hill."

Arthur Wellesley, Duke of Wellington

Beyond the dead zone of No-Man's Land, where rusted, twisted wire; shell craters; and decomposing bodies formed a ghoulish landscape, the commanders of Kaiser Wilhelm's Imperial German Army quietly contemplated the timing of the next major offensive. Some generals thought, perhaps, that the Canadian Infantry was more concerned about recovering from the trauma of 24,000 casualties incurred at the Battle of the Somme, than thinking about conducting an assault on Vimy Ridge. The German theory was that General Byng would be reluctant to sacrifice more of his Canadian Corps in a major attack against the heavily fortified, nine-mile long Vimy escarpment. The Germans had successfully defended this escarpment since the first attempt by the French failed in 1915. A number of infantry commanders acknowledged their elevated position, on a height of land overlooking the Douai Plain, to be a significant advantage, but not invincible if faced with a sustained and concentrated set-piece attack. It was necessary for the Germans to obtain as much intelligence data as possible, in order to properly prepare for the eventuality of a massive assault from both ground and air. The compilation of information was derived from various sources, air and ground reconnaissance, interception of communications, and the interrogation of prisoners-of-war; one being a young Canadian defector of German heritage.

Members of the 43rd had now been billeted for fifteen days in Auchel, thirty miles northeast of the city of Arras. Joining the 43rd Battalion in Auchel, were the 52nd Battalion, under the command of Lieutenant-Colonel W.B. Evans, the 58th Battalion commanded by Lieutenant-Colonel H.A. Genet, and the 60th Canadian Infantry Battalion led by Lieutenant-Colonel F.A. de L'Gascoigne. These battalions would later join other units from the four Canadian Infantry Divisions, to fight as one united force under the command of British-born Lieutenant-General Sir Julian Byng. The troops nicknamed themselves "Byng's Boys" as a show of respect for the very popular lieutenant-general. The Canadian Corps would also have the benefit of military support from the British 5th Infantry Division. The British 5th Division agreed to provide not only 42,609 tonnes of ammunition, 245 heavy guns, and four 12-inch howitzers, but also a substantial number of troops, engineers, and labour units, bringing the potential combined combat strength to approximately 170,000 men.

Over a period of weeks, various combat units carried out manoeuvres inside enemy territory; laying mine charges and staging hit and run raids along the German lines. One operation in particular, which took place between 5:40 a.m. on March 1, and 8:15 a.m. on March 3, saw the 4th Canadian Infantry Division, led by Major-General David Watson, ordered to attack enemy positions on Vimy Ridge, known as "The Pimple" and "Hill 145."

This mission proved to be very costly. On the first day of March, Watson's troops vaulted from their trenches and scurried across 750 feet of No-Man's Land, fighting desperately to breach the heavily defended escarpment, only to be met with an enormous amount of machine- gun fire, clouds of asphyxiating gas, and sniper bullets. To make matters worse, Canadian artillery shells were landing far short of their targets, falling amongst Watson's infantry, resulting in numerous casualties. Equipped with gas masks and small-box respirators, the men of the 4th Division fought on gallantly. It was difficult to see the enemy, at the best of times, through their mica eye-goggles. German firepower was overwhelming. Canadian soldiers were being slaughtered. This was confirmed when it was reported that 700 infantrymen, from four battalions of the 4th Canadian Infantry Division, had been killed and wounded in battle, including commanders from the 54th and 75th Battalions. The three-day attack on Vimy, by the 4th Infantry Division, would be regarded as a tragic event for Major-General David Watson and his troops. The 4th Canadian Infantry Division, approximately 20,000 strong, which was organized in England in April 1916, departed Bramshott for France, in August 1916 where they participated in the Battle of the Somme, at Le Transloy, Ancre Heights, and Ancre.

While the 4th Canadian Infantry Division was being prevented from winning a small piece of territory around Vimy Ridge, on March 3, the Cameron Highlanders of Canada and Private S.E. Shortliffe were leaving Auchel for the 52nd Canadian Infantry Battalion (New Ontario) training grounds, in Marles-les-Mines, two miles from Vimy. It was there that Private Shortliffe and B Coy studied and memorized details of scale-model layouts of enemy trench and dugout systems, as well as replicas of machine guns and observation posts. All of the miniature displays, including battlefield topography, were designed and constructed to scale, utilizing aerial photographs and scouting reports. At the conclusion of the session, the 43rd Battalion returned to their billets in Auchel. Forty-two officers of the 9th Canadian Infantry Training Battalion were waiting to provide the Cameron Highlanders with additional instruction on trench and battlefield tactics. While this was taking place, twelve officers and 220 other ranks of C Coy, from the 116th Canadian Infantry Battalion (Ontario County), arrived in Auchel, at 3:30 p.m. They would be joining four other battalions from the 9th Canadian Infantry Brigade, 3rd Infantry Division already in billets, one of which was the 60th Canadian Infantry Battalion (Victoria Rifles of Canada). Two months later, the 60th Battalion would cease to exist as a combat unit of the Canadian Corps. The Victoria Rifles of Canada would be disbanded, as of April 30, 1917 and replaced by the 116th Canadian Infantry Battalion (Ontario County). The same fate would befall the 73rd Canadian Infantry Battalion (Royal Highlanders of Canada), on April 19, of the same year.

The formal order from divisional headquarters, announcing the break-up of the Royal Highlanders of Canada, was received on April 16, 1917. It included a directive to transfer all troops born in Nova Scotia to the 85th Infantry Battalion (Highlanders of Nova Scotia), with the remaining soldiers attached to the 38th Battalion (Eastern Ontario) and the 78th Battalion (Winnipeg Grenadiers).

That event is considered by the author to be of historical significance. Dissolving an entire experienced, infantry battalion, on the Western Front, in order to reinforce other battalions and satisfy political whims, was precedent setting. Battalions selected to supply troop reinforcements were normally disbanded while stationed at training camps in England, such as Shorncliffe and East Sandling. After the dissolution of the battalions, the men were transferred into the Reserve unit system, before being deployed to the front line as needed.

The decision to dissolve the 60th Canadian Infantry Battalion was met with bitterness, shock, and disappointment. The feelings of the battalion's thirty-one officers and 1,048 ordinary regulars were expressed clearly by the adjutant, in the 60th Battalion War Diary, dated April 29, 1917, in Villers-au-Bois:

Church Parade, R.C.s at 11:00 a.m., other denominations 2:00 p.m. After Parade, the Battalion was assembled, and the Commanding Officer delivered a farewell address. The disbanding of a force of fighting men of all ranks, well trained with a perfect organization to carry it through the war, for Political reason, seems most unjust, and shows little feeling, or respect for the officers, N.C.O.s and men, who have been in the trenches for fourteen months and to those who have made the supreme sacrifice with their lives, and who rest in named and unnamed graves throughout France and Belgium. If tried and efficient Battalions are to be broken up like this in the midst of a great war, and on the very battlefields, it will surely be more discouraging than encouraging, to further recruiting in Canada.

Those sentiments were reinforced by Lieutenant-Colonel F.A. L'Gascoigne, commanding officer of the 60th Canadian Infantry

Battalion (Victoria Rifles of Canada), and the officer responsible for organizing the battalion on May 23, 1915. The 60th Battalion, authorized on August 15, 1915, was raised in Montreal and trained at Valcartier, Quebec. On November 6, the troops sailed on the Scandinavian for Plymouth, England. The vessel arrived fifteen days later, with forty officers and 1024 other ranks. After supplemental training at Bramshott, the battalion left on February 22, 1916, for Le Havre, France. In Southampton, they became part of the 9th Brigade, 3rd Infantry Division.

Lieutenant-Colonel L'Gascoigne spoke to the troops for the very last time, on the afternoon of the April 29, 1917. He addressed the rumours concerning the demise of the battalion that had been actively circulating. Now, he confirmed the rumours sadly to be true. L'Gascoigne emotionally praised his troops for their undying loyalty and dedication to him, the officers and the battalion. Next, his comments centred on the reasons behind the decision to disband the 60th Canadian Infantry Battalion:

It is unnecessary for me to discuss the why's and wherefores of the situation, but as you know, the provinces of Quebec and British Columbia were too ambitious, and put into the field, a greater proportion of Battalions than they were entitled to, and more than they could support with reinforcements. The provinces then demanded representation in the field, on the basis of recruiting, and the Canadian Authorities selected the 60th and 73rd Battalions as the two Province of Quebec Battalions to be withdrawn to make room for one Battalion from Ontario and one from Nova Scotia. There is no reason why the 60th should have been selected, except that it was the junior of the four purely Montreal Battalions to be sent to France, and Montreal was not providing its quota of reinforcements. The Authorities here did everything possible to prevent the withdrawal of a trained Battalion like ours, not a substitution by a 'green one', but the Authorities in Canada, with their knowledge of the recruiting situation before them, decided that it was in the interest of recruiting and the war in general, that the Battalions named, should be withdrawn, and we must, therefore, bow to the inevitable and accept their decision as being for the best, and resolve to do our best for the Empire wherever we may be placed.

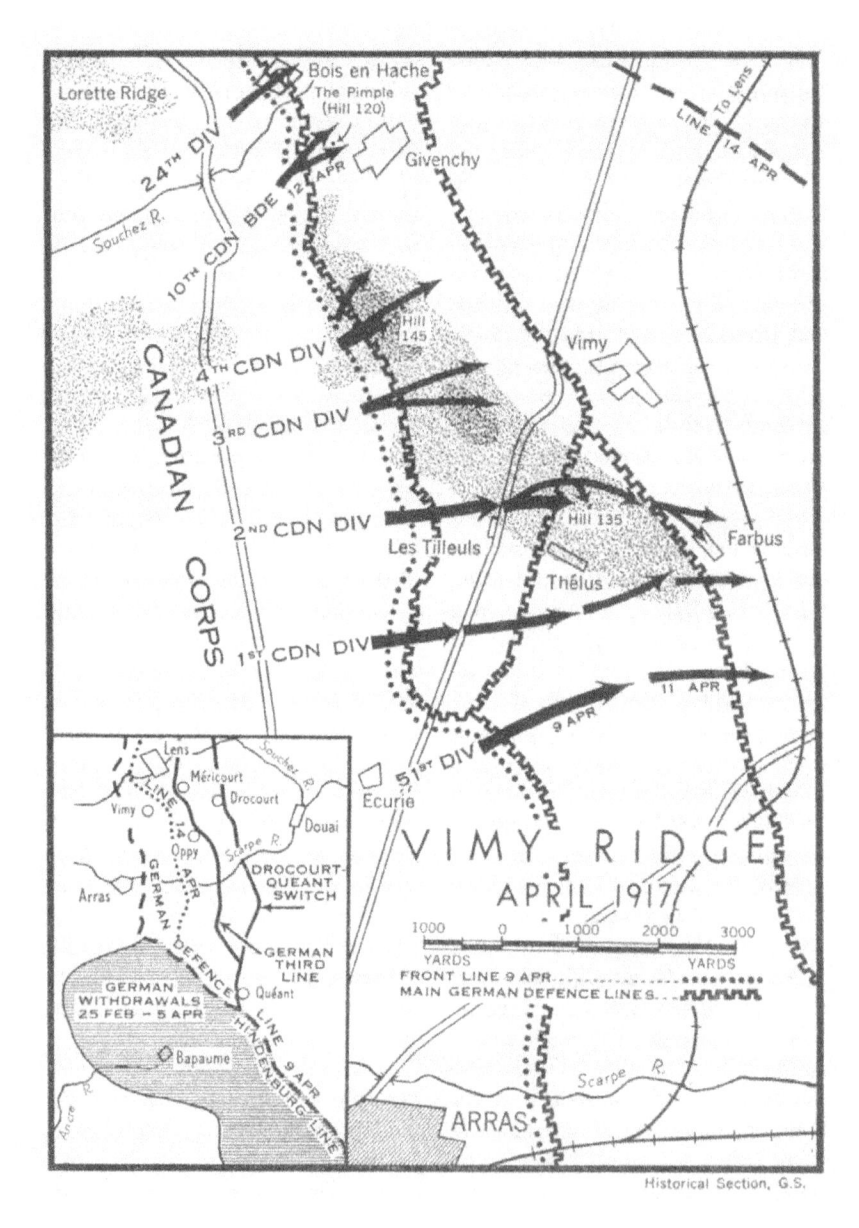

A Battle of Vimy Ridge assault map showing the attack areas assigned to each of the four Canadian Corps infantry divisions, as well as that of the British 24th and 51st Divisions.

On April 30, 1917, the men of the 60th Battalion (Victoria Rifles of Canada) were absorbed into the 5th Canadian Mounted Rifles (Quebec) and the 87th Canadian Infantry Battalion (Grenadier Guards of Montreal). The distribution of manpower was as follows: Eleven officers and 333 other ranks to the 5th C.M.R.s and twenty officers and 715 other ranks to the 87th Battalion. The curtain had come down on the 60th and 73rd Canadian Infantry Battalions.

Meanwhile, on March 5, the Cameron Highlanders of Canada headed to lectures and training at 10:30 a.m., and the 116th Battalion fell-in for parade inspection undeterred by a wet snowstorm. Marching drills followed inspection for the benefit of Major-General Louis Lipsett. The major-general was there to inform Lieutenant-Colonel Grassie and company officers that British First Army Commander General Henry Horne had officially approved the Canadian Corps plan for a spring assault on Vimy Ridge. Also on March 5, Private William Arthur Hicks of the 43rd Battalion was killed in action.

The Vimy offensive called for a massive operation; one that would utilize all four infantry divisions. The main attack was to be conducted on a four-mile wide front, opposite the village of Vimy, on the east side of the escarpment. The first objective, designated The Black Line, would involve the capture of the German forward defensive line by the 2nd Canadian Infantry Division, under Major-General H.E. Bursrall. The Red Line, situated on the northern flank, would involve the 1st Canadian Infantry Division led by Major-General A.W. Currie. It would be the task of the 1st Infantry Division to overrun the highest and most fortified part of the ridge, known as The Pimple, then move on to capture Folie Farm, and Zwischen-Stellung and Les Tilleuls lines. The other two Canadian Corps divisions, specifically the 3rd and 4th, were to assume positions to the south. They would advance to capture the town of Thelus, the wooded area near the town of Vimy, and the Zwolfer-Graben trench, as well as the German second line. The two infantry divisions would receive sufficient ground support from artillery light field guns; creeping barrages were laid down in a pattern of 100 yards. At the same time, well ahead of the advancing infantry, medium and heavy howitzer guns would deploy a series of standing barrages directed at identified enemy defensive positions. The plan called for combat units to leapfrog over one another, in order to maintain consistent momentum during the attack. The heavy artillery batteries would be ordered to pause momentarily, and then reserve units could proceed beyond the division lines. The Canadian Corps were expected to maintain an attack schedule, advancing at least two miles toward the German positions. Should the assault go as predicted, most of Vimy Ridge would fall under Canadian control by no later than 1:00 p.m. on the first day of the operation.

The plan, as approved by General Horne, was incorporated quickly into the training protocol of the Canadian Corps at Divisional Camp, in Auchel. There was a beehive of activity. Battalion commanders conducted high-level meetings at brigade headquarters. Coy officers familiarized themselves with the trenches running along the 7th Canadian Infantry Brigade front-line. In preparation for the spring offensive, nine NCOs, from the 43rd Battalion, pulled out of Auchel for England, on March 7, at 8:00 a.m. They would be taking part in an officer-training program with the expectation of obtaining a full commission rank and future command of a coy or platoon. Meanwhile, at divisional camp, Private S.E. Shortliffe engaged in bayonet practice, marksmanship, and loading and firing trench mortars and Lewis machine guns. Understanding how to use each weapon could be the difference in a soldier's survival on the battlefield, not only for him personally but also for his comrades, who would be depending on him to cover their backs.

March 8 was extremely cold. Strong winds and blowing snow faced the Cameron Highlanders of Canada as they prepared for training manoeuvres, along with their comrades-in-arms from the other battalions of the 9th Canadian Infantry Brigade in the rehearsal area. Officers from the five battalions of the 9th Brigade made their way overland in an army bus, to view the lines and dugouts the troops would be occupying. Later that morning, the 43rd Battalion moved to brigade attack locations within the 8th Canadian Infantry Brigade sector and awaited the start of the scheduled rehearsal. The tactical exercise was designed to introduce the strategy that would be used in the Battle of Vimy Ridge. The ninety-minute exercise involved 4,000 troops of the 9th Infantry Brigade, including field artillery gunners, engineers, pioneers, medical units, and mortar and machine gun specialists. The planned scenario had the 8th Canadian Infantry Brigade failing in its attempt to capture the infamous German stronghold, known as the Zwischen- Stellung Line. The 8th Brigade would retreat to a former German-occupied support line, and there they would be replaced by the 9th Canadian Infantry Brigade. The brigade would follow-up with a full-scale, frontal assault, leading to a successful capture of Zwischen-Stellung. Once this had been accomplished they would push onward, to consolidate their final objective.

The Zwischen-Stellung Line had played an integral role, as part of the vast system of German defences within northern France. The Line had been excavated and built under the direct orders of both Field-Marshall Paul von Hindenburg and General Erich Ludendorff. The system consisted of shell-proof bunkers and machine-gun emplacements, as well as miles of barbed wire, deep tunnels, subways, galleries, charge chambers, trenches, and dug-outs. In February 1917, the German hierarchy decided to remove their infantry from this particular sector and establish a new defensive line, pointing in the direction of Arras and Vimy Ridge.

At 2:00 o'clock on the afternoon of the 8th, three battalions from the 9th Brigade, including the 60th, 52nd, and 43rd, were ordered into jumping-off positions on the observation line, including front and support lines. The 58th Infantry Battalion, which was positioned in reserve line, sent two companies of approximately 300 soldiers to Cenot Cave and Pylones trenches. Brigadier-General Frederick W. Hill, of the 9th Canadian Infantry Brigade, ordered all three forward battalions to move into their assigned areas, as shown on their field maps, in relation to the position of the German support line. Once there, they assembled at 1:45 p.m. to await the commencement of the scheduled exercise. Artillery barrages of live ammo signalled the battalions to attack the enemy front.

At Zero Hour plus three minutes, field artillery batteries began laying down a heavy barrage of shells, 100 yards in advance of the jumping off trenches. Shelling followed every three minutes, until the barrage reached the Zwischen-Stellung Line. At this point, artillery gunners began firing their field guns, the eighteen-pounders, for ten minutes, before shifting their attention to the north-east edge of La Folie Wood. They continued the heavy bombardment until ordered by brigade officers to cease firing. While the shelling continued, the 60th Canadian Infantry Battalion engaged the "enemy" in combat on the left side of Sunken Road. The 52nd Battalion attacked the junction of Old Trench and the Zwischen-Stellung Line, before moving on to La Folie Farm. While this event was underway, the 43rd Infantry Battalion (Cameron Highlanders of Canada) was confronting the opposition on the northern boundary of the 8th Canadian Infantry Brigade. Two companies from the 58th Battalion were advancing simultaneously from their positions at Cenot Cave trench at the rear, immediately behind the Zwischen-Stellung Line, at Prinz Arnolf Graben. The remaining two companies, from the 58th Battalion at Pylones, became observers rather than participants. They viewed the seventy-five minute exercise with brigade and battalion commanders before returning to their billets in Auchel.

During the afternoon of March 9, Major W. K. Chandler, accompanied by a number of officers from the 43rd Battalion, departed from Auchel for a five-mile trip to the 3rd Infantry Division Headquarters in Bruay. Prime Minister Sir Robert Borden met with the officers; they discussed the progress in the war effort to date, and advised him of the major spring offensive planned by the Canadian Corps for Vimy Ridge.

As dawn broke on March 10, the Cameron Highlanders packed their haversacks and left their billets in Auchel. The regiment marched to a nearby railway siding and boarded a troop train at 7:10 a.m. They were billeted five hours later, in Gouy.

The next morning, after a bath and clean-up, Private S.E. Shortliffe attended a Presbyterian church service. Later, he spent part of the day maintaining his combat kit, sharpening his bayonet, and cleaning and oiling his Lee-Enfield rifle. Lieutenant-Colonel William Grassie returned to duty on the same day, after one of many leaves.

The colonel's first priority was to issue Operation Order No.83. The order pertained to the relief of a coy from the 22nd Canadian Infantry Battalion (Canadien-Français) of the 5th Brigade, 2nd Canadian Infantry Division.

The operation, scheduled for the afternoon of March 12, was to take place between Vernon Crater and Lasalle Line with B Coy, from the 43rd Battalion, conducting the relief. Private Shortliffe and his comrades commenced the mission at 5:30 p.m. from Villers-au-Bois. They proceeded quickly to relieve the 22nd Infantry Battalion's B Coy, in the left sub-section at La Folie Wood, as well as sniper positions at Vernon Crater. In the meantime, Lewis machine- gun crews, signallers, scouts, and bombers, who had departed at 11:30 a.m., were arriving at the front lines. Later that evening, at 10:00, battalion headquarters were handed exclusive control of the Quarries Line. 43rd Infantry Battalion Headquarters staff was deployed to trenches at Machine Gun Fort and Cross Street. By 2:00 a.m. on March 13, all coy combat units of the 43rd Battalion had reported in; they were now in position. Unfortunately, during the deployment, thirty-one-year-old, Private Thomas W. Bartholomew was shot and killed. Three companies of Highlanders, including Private S.E. Shortliffe and B Coy were in the front-line positions; a fourth unit, A Coy, was in the support trench. All soldiers, entrenched along the front-line were confronted with endless wet and cold conditions; a stationary weather system covered much of the Western Front throughout the month of March 1917.

On March 15, a large work party, made up of six NCOs and 105 other ranks from B Coy, were joined by men from three other companies, at 9:00 a.m. They repaired the damaged trenches between Vernon Crater and Commons Crater. This particular area had been severely damaged the previous night, at 3:30 in the morning. German artillery shells and seventy-nine soldiers had raided and successfully breached the right side of one company position, using rifle grenades and trench mortars to attack the Canadian lines. After several minutes of intense fighting, the Cameron Highlanders were able to dislodge the Germans from the 43rd Battalion trenches; once again they regained control of the front-line, without loss of territory to the enemy. The German raid did exact a small number of casualties on the battalion; one twenty-eight-year-old Cameron Highlander was killed, Private Steve Solar, one was seriously wounded, and two soldiers were taken prisoner. One hour after the raid had concluded, the wind abruptly switched direction and began blustering across No-Man's Land, into the faces of the 43rd Battalion. The change in wind direction triggered the usual gas alert, but after thirty minutes when nothing had transpired, the stand-down order was given.

As terrifying and exhausting as the war had become on the Western Front, between 1914 and 1917, it could also be extremely boring at times. It was during these quiet periods that soldiers in the fighting trenches spontaneously organized things to help pass the time. Card games were popular with the majority of troops; others got their adrenalin rush from bayoneting rats. The goal was to eradicate rats from the battlefield by exterminating them, one at a time, on the sharp end of a bayonet. In reality, the rat population seemed to increase exponentially with each kill. Ironically, these rodents, considered to be the scourge of the earth, also played a bizarre helpful role. They proved to be an accurate warning system, alerting troops of an imminent artillery bombardment. It was discovered that when an unusually heavy artillery bombardment was about to occur, all the rats would suddenly disappear, until things once again quieted down.

At sunset, a patrol of ten soldiers set out, under Captain Hamilton and Lieutenant Geddes, to raid and inflict damage and casualties on an enemy post, in retaliation for the German attack the previous night. However, the operation was aborted; Canadian artillery shells were landing too close to the troops. Undeterred, the lieutenants made another attempt, eight hours later, during the morning of March 16, at 3:15. With their party of ten and an additional eight soldiers, the Cameron Highlanders entered No-Man's Land, severing numerous belts of barbed wire. The raiding party reached the enemy trenches easily and a firefight ensued. Several enemy soldiers were killed or wounded. At 4:20 a.m. the party returned to the safety of the Canadian trenches.

Daybreak, on March 16, the 43rd, Canadian Infantry Battalion awoke to their fourth consecutive day at La Folie Wood. It was to be a rare day of sunshine and gentle, refreshing breezes from the southwest, rather than the typical rain and wind. At 43rd Battalion Headquarters, Colonel William Grassie finished dictating a strategic plan, called a "Provisional Defence Scheme." The plan elaborated on the defence of the La Folie Section by the Cameron Highlanders of Canada, currently entrenched from Vernon Crater to the La Salle Line. Troops positioned in this particular sector were at a significant disadvantage; numerous crater rims blocked the Canadian line-of-sight in the direction of the German front lines. In addition to the many craters, there were a limited number of accessible entry points into German territory, just a few hundred yards from the Canadian lines. These facts forced the Cameron Highlanders to risk life and limb establishing observation posts along the crater rims, in direct line of enemy sniper and machine gun fire. Fortunately for the Highlanders, the ground did not rise to any great height between Grange and Birkin trenches. This advantage afforded the 43rd Battalion soldiers an excellent view of Neuville-Saint-Vaast, including all the eastern approaches facing the German occupied territory.

Colonel Grassie was emphatic in his communiqué to his officers in which he wrote: "The Outpost Line is not to be surrendered to the enemy under any circumstance without a stubborn fight." The Outpost Line, also referred to as the "Firing Line," was the main line of resistance. The battle areas continued to be quiet off and on for the rest of March 16, allowing time for the assessments of trenches damaged by an earlier heavy bombardment. It was determined that the immediate support line appeared to be in questionable condition, but not as badly damaged as the demolished Sombart and Givenchy Road trenches. Three battalion companies of the 43rd were ordered to hold the front-line and immediate support line, utilizing two Lewis machine guns and crews in both Observation and Firing Lines. In addition, four machine-gun crews, from the 9th Canadian Infantry Brigade, were posted in both the support line and Givenchy Road trenches, together with three light Stokes trench mortars, to protect the 43rd Battalion frontage.

In Colonel Grassie's PDS (Provisional Defence Scheme), he also addressed the possibility of an enemy bombardment of the 43rd Battalion lines at La Folie Wood:

In the event that this may happen, 25% of the infantrymen are to man the trenches, the remainder to move to the artillery shelters where they will standby fully equipped with a sentry posted at both the top and bottom of the stairs. If it should happen that the artillery shelters are not within the immediate area of the Firing Line, then 50% of the men will occupy the Firing Position. The Lewis Machine Guns would be kept in the shelter next to the Firing Line until the enemy barrage subsides. Once the enemy fire appears to have lessened, then a counter attack bombing party of 8 men who have been held in readiness by each of the four companies near Company Headquarters will be deployed to drive the Germans out of any portion of the trench that they may have forced entry. A Support Company from the 43rd Battalion will wait in their shelters until such time as ordered by Battalion Headquarters to move with or without their Lewis Guns to address the situation.

The 43rd Battalion Provisional Defence Scheme, also called on,… *the Firing Line to remain and form part of a garrison. Those behind the Frontline would be collected by an Officer or NCO in charge of the bombing party who will report by runner to Battalion Headquarters on strength and position of the bombing party.*

Once entrenched along the 3rd Canadian Infantry Division frontlines, the 43rd Battalion prepared for the unexpected. In most cases, the unexpected was an assault by canister or artillery shell containing phosgene and chlorine gas, (most times phosgene was combined with the other gas to increase the lethality of the weapon). Mustard gas is known to have been used for the first time on July 12, 1917, near Wieltje in the Ypres Salient. The Germans had reportedly conducted tests using mustard gas weeks before, in the region of Neiuwpoort, on the Belgian coast. Coy NCOs made sure that gas blankets had been lowered to the men in the trenches in the Firing Line; at the same time, they confirmed that everyone was equipped with an operable gas mask and a small-box respirator. All troop movement and conversation were to be kept to a bare minimum. Communication was restricted to written messages delivered between trenches and Battalion Headquarters, using infantry runners or messenger dogs. Under extreme emergency situations, verbal messages were permitted to be communicated by telephone, using a 1916 British codebook. If a German co-ordinated attack against La Folie Wood, succeeded in breaching the left side of the 43rd Battalion, the SOS code would be transmitted, alerting all Canadian troops. Once the alert was issued, troops would form a defensive flank along La Salle Line to Quarries Line, however, if the breach occurred on the right side, then a defensive flank would have to be re-established along Commons trench to Givenchy Road. That scenario would involve Private S.E. Shortliffe and B Coy, who were already dug in and prepared to hold the line with rapid rifle fire, trench mortars, and grenade rockets. Logistically, the 43rd Battalion Headquarters was located at Machine Gun Fort and Cross Street Lines, while the 9th Infantry Brigade Headquarters was established at Quarries Line.

Much of La Folie Sector, on March 17, remained relatively quiet. Shortly after meals at 6:45 p.m., the 58th Canadian Infantry Battalion (Central Ontario), under the command of Lieutenant-Colonel H.A. Genet, arrived to relieve the Cameron Highlanders in the line. The Highlanders moved back into the Support Area. A Coy was moved to Pylones; D Coy relocated to Empire Redoubt; and B Coy proceeded to Support Area, in Neuville-Saint-Vaast. The C Coy reserves were split-up; a number were sent to Pylones Trench in right support and Garrison trench, thereby joining A Coy. The remaining C Coy troops were moved to defensive positions near Neuville-Saint-Vaast and Battalion Headquarters.

Leading up to the Vimy offensive, each day seemed more frenetic than the last, especially with the influx of close to eighty thousand troops. Field artillery batteries, engineers, medical corps, and fighting men from forty-eight battalions of the Canadian Corps arrived. Preparations for the Vimy assault, under the command of Lieutenant-General Sir Julian Byng, were progressing well.

Meanwhile, in German-occupied territory, soldiers were rushing to refortify defence installations; they restocked ammunition, food, water, and weaponry for what they considered to be an imminent major battle. Troops of the 1st Bavarian Reserve Corps, under General Karl Ritter von Fasbender and the VIII Reserve Corps, led by General George Karl Wichura, were working feverishly to increase front-line troop strength and defence lines along the entire north section of Vimy Ridge. An additional infantry unit, Reserve Division 79, was now selected to defend the central section of Vimy Ridge, including Hill 145. A month earlier, the Reserve had just finished a two-year tour of duty, fighting on the Eastern Front. On April 9, 1917, they would meet Byng's Boys, who would fight like hell to capture the ridge.

Work parties were scheduled for March 18, 19, and 20. For three days, soldiers of the 43rd Battalion, under the supervision of the 9th Infantry Brigade, laboured away; they excavated four communication trenches. Two trenches snaked across the plain to connect with the front-lines and two in the reversed direction. As the four trenches were completed, they were given avenue names, beginning with Guillermot ,then Territorial, followed by Claudot, and lastly Sapper. The physically demanding work of excavating trenches and tunnels, with picks and shovels, was undertaken by four work parties including Tunnelling Companies, under the command of Brigade Field Company Engineers. They were also assisted by men of the 123rd Canadian Pioneer Battalion. Deep subterranean tunnels in the Vimy sector had been part of the Great War since 1915. They had been utilized by both the British Expeditionary Force and the Imperial German Army.

The Germans were the first to develop large and elaborate subway systems; they contained headquarters, supply depots, ammunition bunkers, hospitals, water reservoirs, and sleeping quarters for officers and other ranks. The British quickly responded by constructing twelve networks of subways, utilizing the expertise of five tunnelling companies. They carved out underground systems, in some cases more than 300 feet deep and one mile in length. Front lines connected to reserve lines were used for the quick, efficient, and covert movement of British Expeditionary Force troops. These underground systems also contained light-rail lines, to transport supplies, weapons, and ammunition. Tons of high explosives were placed in underground detonation chambers and made ready for inflicting considerable damage and loss of life on the enemy, prior to an all out-assault.

There is no question that tunnels are confining and claustrophobic. In most cases, the tunnelled passageway was only three to four feet in width and six feet in height. The length of these tunnels varied, as did the number of rooms that branched off from the passageways. In many instances, a tunnel system could accommodate between one to three combat battalions; they consisted of sleeping and eating areas, kitchens, supply rooms, and ammunition depots. Medical facilities, including advanced dressing and casualty clearing stations[2], were also located within the tunnel labyrinth.

(Ross photo)
Grange Tunnel served as headquarters for a number of Canadian infantry battalions, including the 43rd Battalion during the Vimy Ridge operation in April 1917.

---

2   A casualty clearing station (CCS) was a short-term medical treatment centre where the wounded would be cared for until deemed fit to return to combat duty, or if their injuries were more serious, transferred to a base hospital.

(Ross photo)
A working and sleeping area once occupied by a Canadian officer in Grange Tunnel, Vimy Ridge.

On March 20, General Byng ordered the Field Artillery commanders to commence a twenty-day bombardment, to begin the next morning. The intensive bombing of German positions on the Vimy escarpment was interpreted by the German high command as a precursor to a major ground assault. Byng ordered heavy shelling initially, followed by a substantial increase in the intensity over the following twenty days. The goal was to demoralize, confuse, and overwhelm the enemy, together with the destruction of German fortifications and heavy weapons. The Canadian Corps had the benefit of being in possession of 245 heavy guns, howitzers, and more than 600 pieces of field artillery. British support troops arrived with 132 heavy guns and 102 field artillery pieces. All that firepower translated into an average of one heavy gun for every sixty feet of assault frontage and one field gun for every thirty feet of front line. Canadian shelling of German positions increased incrementally, peaking six days prior to the official set-piece assault on Vimy Ridge. Unimaginable noise, destruction, and heart-stopping fear permeated the battle ground. The intensity of the Canadian bombing was overwhelming; the Germans called the last six days before the actual battle of Vimy, "woche der leiden," or "the Week of Suffering."

During the pre-assault bombing, the Canadians undertook numerous raids and attacks on German-held territory. Each mission encountered intense enemy resistance, resulting in 1,400 soldiers being killed, wounded, or reported missing-in-action. These operations were designed to be quick and deadly. There were three primary objectives: kill the enemy, take prisoners, and demolish German fortifications, posts, and trenches. Trench raids, in March 1917, were carried out using methods employed years earlier by the Princess Patricia's Canadian Light Infantry (PPCLI) during the Battle of Ypres in 1915. The system, used by the PPCLI, was soon noted and quickly copied by both the French and British. Raiding enemy trenches was not only important for gathering invaluable information, but this type of activity kept their infantrymen focused, mentally stimulated, and skilled at close-quarter combat.

At Zero Hour-8:00 a.m. on March 21, the first hour of heavy artillery barrages commenced. This opening salvo was followed by a second round of eighteen-pounders, between 9:00 a.m. and 10:00 a.m., directed at the enemy position known as Fast Trench. The next target of the Canadian Corps Field Artillery was Fanny Trench, a target that would endure two hours of bombing from 10:00 a.m. until 12:00 noon. The final two-hour bombardment was directed at selected targets, ending at 2:00 that afternoon. The incredible teamwork of Canadian artillery gunners pounded the German trenches, known as Feather and Artillerie, with standing barrages from 4.5 inch Howitzers. However, because of the magnitude of the shelling, officers from the 58th and 60th Infantry Battalions ordered the immediate evacuation of their trenches. This precautionary measure was taken to prevent casualties in an anticipated reprisal by the German heavy artillery units. Within the ranks it was widely expected that the forthcoming enemy retaliation would be equal or even greater than what the enemy had just endured, but to everyone's surprise...the German guns remained silent.

On the morning of March 23, at 10:15, the weather was a dog's breakfast; a combination of heavy rain and thick snow sent chills through the bodies of the men from B and C Coys. Cold and tired, they shuffled from Billet No.19 to an old church situated near the 43rd Infantry Battalion Headquarters at Gouy-Servins. Forty-five minutes prior to departing for the fifty-three- mile trip to Bruay via Verdrel-Bois, the Cameron Highlanders readied their combat kits for delivery to Company Quarter-Master Sergeants Robert Moxam and Ronald Hay. At the quarter-master store, a junior NCO from C Coy would stand guard over the soldiers' belongings until the battalion arrived at its destination. Field Kitchens were the first to leave at 9:30 a.m., just as the men were assembling for Sick Parade and examination by medical officers from the Canadian Mounted Rifles (CMR). The last contingent of troops from A Coy and D Coy, who had been billeted in Divion, would leave Gouy-Servins at 2:30 p.m., to join their fellow comrades in Bruay. Once they arrived in Bruay, they learned that one of their comrades, Private Jonathan Gillespie was missing and presumed killed, on March 22.

As Byng and his divisional commanders reviewed plans, on March 23, for the forthcoming battle, the bombing of German positions raged unabated. As the thunderous roar of exploding artillery shells echoed across the Douai Plain, the men of the 43rd Battalion lined up at the YMCA hut to get a haircut before attending church services in a local Bruay movie theatre. While soldiers were receiving a haircut, shave, and moustache trim, a secret communiqué, addressed to General Byng, was hand delivered. The message from Lieutenant-Colonel J. Briand, on behalf of Major-General Henry Horne of the British First Army, said the following:

If it appears probable that the enemy intends to withdraw from the ARRAS SALIENT at any time between now and Z-Day, the G.O.C. Third Army intends to press the attack to such a depth as his resources permit: he is at present prepared to capture the BLACK objectives at 24 hour notice. Should the above case arise, the Army Commander intends to act in conjunction with the Third Army by bombarding the enemies' lines with all guns available and sending forward strong patrols to the BLACK LINE.

The opportunity of holding and consolidating the BLACK objectives will be seized if conditions are favourable, but if the indications of hostile withdrawal do not extend to the Vimy Ridge, the attack on the BLACK LINE must not be pressed without adequate artillery preparation. In any case, steps will be taken to co-operate with the XVIII Corps to the extent of covering any forward movement on their flank.

General Horne's communiqué confirmed a countdown leading to the Battle of Vimy Ridge was underway. All divisional commanders turned their attention to preparing their troops for a successful spring offensive. Additional training and combat rehearsal programs were instituted. Training resumed for Private S.E. Shortliffe and B Coy on March 26. Under overcast skies and in wet conditions, they rehearsed attacks; B Coy climbed high elevations of land, constructed by Canadian Corps Engineers, to simulate the topography of Hill 145. Rehearsals were followed by periods of trench fighting before ending with grenade and bayonet practice. The training regimen for the Cameron Highlanders of Canada usually started at 8:30 a.m. and continued until the late afternoon. It consisted of practicing marksmanship, marching drills, callisthenics, fixed fighting positions, and running obstacle courses in full combat kit. Obstacle courses tested a soldier's physical and mental toughness to undertake and complete endurance challenges (sometimes as many as three challenges in each session). They were required to carry extra combat weight, including a twenty-pound Enfield rifle and 160 rounds of ammunition. The goal was to develop well-conditioned combat soldiers; in other words, a lean and mean fighting machine.

Following a hot meal of mulligan stew and dumplings in the enlisted men's mess tent, Ernie picked up a day pass for a short visit with his cousin Wilbur Harris Shortliffe, a member of the 85th Canadian Infantry Battalion (Nova Scotia Highlanders), 12th Infantry Brigade, of the 4th Canadian Infantry Division. Private W.H. Shortliffe had enlisted in Digby, Nova Scotia on March 6, 1916. He was attested four days later, in Halifax, by Lieutenant-Colonel Joseph Hayes. Ernie Shortliffe and his cousin Wilbur were two of three Shortliffe men to enlist, serve, and die in the Great War; the third was Private Lloyd Clifton Shortliff (the "e" in Shortliffe was omitted at the time his attestation papers were signed) a member of the 24th Canadian Infantry Battalion (Victoria Rifles of Montreal). Twenty-four-year-old Private L.C. Shortliff (e) of North Range, Digby County, Nova Scotia was killed on September 17, 1916, during the Battle of the Somme. His name is commemorated on the Vimy Memorial at Vimy Ridge.

Private Wilbur H. Shortliffe's combat unit, the 85th Battalion, landed in France, poorly equipped and inadequately trained. No one ever imagined they would be fighting the Germans so soon after their arrival. To everyone's surprise and utter embarrassment, the troops were issued pickaxes and shovels instead of ammunition and rifles. Their orders were to build roads, repair trenches, transport ammunition, and remove the dead and wounded from the battlefields. The Nova Scotia Highlanders were just one of a number of kilted regiments to serve in France and Belgium during WWI. Besides the Nova Scotia Regiment, other Highland Regiments were: the Cameron Highlanders of Canada, the 48th Highlanders of Winnipeg, the Seaforth Highlanders of Vancouver, and the Black Watch Royal Highland Regiment of Canada, also called, "The Ladies from Hell." Unlike the other kilted regiments, the Nova Scotia Highlanders received their kilts after they arrived in Europe.

Ernie's cousin, Private W.H. Shortliffe, a member of C Coy, fought at Vimy Ridge, Passchendaele and in the battle of the Drocourt-Quéant. During that particular battle in the final months of the war, he was struck in the thigh with shrapnel and died on September 2, 1918. The remains of Wilbur Harris Shortliffe are buried with fellow soldier William Snowdon, in Vis-En-Artois British Cemetery, Haucourt, Pas-de-Calais, France.

On Saturday, March 31, one week before Easter, the 43rd Canadian Infantry Battalion assembled at 9:30 a.m. in front of their billets, ready for a twelve-mile march to the town of Villers-au-Bois, southeast of Bruay. An advance party of scouts was the first to depart, followed by bagpipers, drummers, communication sections, and lastly Coys B, C, D, and A. The battalion marched through Barlin, Bois D'Olhain, Verdrel, and Grand Servins, arrived in Villers-au-Bois at 3:30 p.m., and then erected a temporary camp in an open field. The 43rd Battalion remained in camp until the 60th Canadian Infantry Battalion (Quebec) had cleaned and vacated their billets, after which the officers and other ranks settled into their new quarters by 7:00 p.m. and were ready to be fed by the field kitchen cooks.

In addition to the four ordinary regulars who were killed in March, a Toronto-born soldier, Private Milford William Switzer died on March 15, from complications associated with a severe case of pneumonia. He enlisted on September 1, 1915 and one year later fought in the Battle of the Somme, where the 43rd Battalion suffered a tremendous number of casualties at Regina Trench.

Chapter Twelve
APRIL 1917

"In those few minutes I witnessed the birth of a nation."

Brigadier-General A. E Ross

The first days of spring 1917 saw all troop leaves cancelled, as part of a Standing Order issued by the 43rd Battalion's CO, Lieutenant-Colonel William Grassie. The Standing Order addressed procedures and protocols during the forthcoming spring offensive, outlining individual and group responsibilities within the 43rd Battalion. These protocols had been drafted and approved based on the assumption that the Cameron Highlanders of Canada would be participating with the 9th Canadian Infantry Brigade and 3rd Canadian Infantry Division during the Battle of Vimy Ridge. The directive also explained where depots would be located to supply troops with No. 5 and No. 23 Mills bombs, Stokes mortar shells, machine gun and rifle ammunition, night flares, sandbags, and shovels. A Canadian soldier heading into battle also lugged a twenty-pound Lee-Enfield rifle, a steel bayonet in a 'frog' (sheath), 170 rounds of ammo, night flares, at least two hand grenades, and two days of food and water rations.

Communication between battalion headquarters and front-line commanders was critical during the heat of combat. Messages were sent and received using various methods, e.g.: signals, telephone, carrier pigeons, messenger dogs, runners on foot or horseback, and depending on the conditions, motorized and pedal bikes. Runners were part of the Communication and Signal Corps; they were highly respected by trench warriors, who regarded them as very brave individuals. Infantrymen were always amazed by a runner's speed, agility, and stamina, although, with what appeared to be endless energy, runners often succumbed to exhaustion. In order to prevent messengers from totally collapsing, schedules were drafted allowing runners to take turns making trips, thereby distributing the work load equally among all runners.

As previously mentioned, Communication and Signal units also utilized the equine members of the army to carry messengers from the front to infantry headquarters. No matter what the weather, they prevailed through deep mud and water, dodging bombs and bullets. Horses played an important role in winning the war. Thousands lost their lives on the battlefield, including many serving with Lord Strathcona's Horse Regiment. This Canadian Calvary unit saw action in 1915 with the French, and again in March 1917 in the defence of the Somme Valley. The fatality rate for these courageous and dedicated animals was incredibly high; the average life span of a warhorse on the Western Front was only forty days.

The lives of thousands of these beautiful and courageous animals ended, in the majority of cases, as a result of artillery fire, drowning, or exhaustion. Many fine steeds died from disease; others suffered painful deaths from exposure to chemical gasses. Officers and ordinary regulars highly respected and admired the strength and loyalty of the military horse as well as its contribution to troop morale. This unquestionable love for the warhorse was occasionally affected by the reality that in the theatre of war there were also negative things associated with the horse, primarily an abundance of manure and decaying carcasses. Both of these factors were widely known to pose risks of serious illness to the soldiers. Even though there were health implications associated with horses, in April 1917 the importance of the animal to the military far exceeded any threat of illness. This was clearly evident from the words and actions of infantry commanders; they considered the death of a horse to be of greater tactical concern than the demise of a soldier.

(source: Library and Archives Canada)
Pack horses transporting ammunition to guns located in Neuville-Saint-Vaast, near Vimy Ridge. April 1917.

It has been estimated that approximately six million horses served in World War I. By mid 1917, the British had acquired 591,000 horses and 213,000 mules for the war effort on the Western Front, as well as 60,000 oxen and camels. Approximately 81,000 Canadian-bred horses made their way to France and Belgium from 1914 to 1918. Only sixty of these animals are said to have ever returned home. Besides those that died on the battlefield from war and disease, there were thousands slaughtered in abattoirs for their meat or sold to farmers to work the fields. The one animal most closely associated with the Great War, was eventually commemorated through the dedication of memorials and monuments. One monument erected in Hampstead, England bears the inscription, "Most obediently and often most painfully they died — faithful unto death."

Work on the preparation for the assault on Vimy continued to ramp up logistically as well as administratively, in the field. Memos were circulated advising coy and platoon officers to be vigilant during the heat of battle for any troops whom they suspected to be feigning an injury, in order to be evacuated from the combat zone. It was stressed that weapons and equipment were not to be discarded on the battlefield, preventing a recovery later to be utilized by the Germans. Those who were legitimate "walking wounded" and unable to carry their weapons would be permitted to move to the rear and dispose of their armaments at a supply dump facility, for later salvage. If able-bodied soldiers simply dropped their guns and ran, the deserters were to be forcibly restrained by battle police, acting under the direct orders of the Adjutant of the 43rd Canadian Infantry Battalion.

Another aspect in the preparation for battle was the compilation of a combat specialist list. The list prepared for the 43rd Battalion stated name and rank of ten signallers, thirteen runners, one chemical-gas instructor, one bombing instructor, two Lewis Gun instructors, and three trench, tunnel and dugout specialists. The battalion consisted of four companies, each having 125 to 250 men, depending on battalion strength, at the time of battle. Each coy was under the direct command of a lieutenant, captain, or major. In some cases platoon and rifle sections were under the command of NCOs, such as a sergeant-major, sergeant, lance-sergeant, corporal, and on occasion, a lance-corporal. There were four platoons in each coy, consisting of approximately forty men. A platoon was made up of four rifle bomber specialists, four scouts and snipers, and four Lewis machine-gunners. The balance of twenty-eight soldiers, were part of a rifle section.

All appeared quiet, at least for a short while, on Sunday, April 1 in La Folie sector, south of Hill 145. Private S.E. Shortliffe attended a Presbyterian church service at 10:40 a.m. The remainder of the day was spent preparing for deployment into the trenches, to relieve one of the most highly respected fighting regiments on the Western Front, the Princess Patricia's Canadian Light Infantry (PPCLI).

The Princess Patricia's Light Infantry was the last privately-raised regiment of the British Empire (the cost borne by Brigadier-General, the Rt. Hon Andrew Hamilton Gault) and was mobilized for duty within just two weeks of war being declared. This famous regiment was made up of 1,098 officers and other ranks, 1,049 of whom were veterans of the South African Boer War (1899-1902). When the First World War began, Great Britain found itself in desperate need of troops to meet the challenge. A call went out to all the colonies for assistance, which of course, included the Dominion of Canada. On August 6, 1914, Lewis Harcourt, British Secretary of State for the Colonies, personally expressed England's gratitude to Canada for the government's decision to contribute an expeditionary force to the war effort. In the same breath, the secretary of state urged that some of those troops be "dispatched as soon as possible."

Within weeks of the British request, the Princess Patricia's Canadian Light Infantry was sent to Europe. They arrived in England on October 18, 1914, a few short weeks ahead of the 1st Canadian Infantry Division. One month later, on November 16, the PPCLI was attached to the British 80th Brigade. Eventually the Princess Patricia's Canadian Light Infantry was absorbed into the 7th Canadian Infantry Brigade of the 3rd Canadian Infantry Division, on December 22, 1915.

The 43rd Infantry Battalion (Cameron Highlanders of Canada) on their way to La Folie, passing through Porte Baudimont in Arras.

At 7:00 o'clock, on the evening of April 1, the 43rd Battalion made its way to the La Folie front-line and began its relief operation. A heavy wet snow fell, covering the ground and reducing visibility to only a few hundred yards. The relief of the Princess Patricia's in the front line, and the 42nd Black Watch Battalion (Royal Highlanders of Canada -Montreal) in support, were successfully completed at approximately 1:00 a.m. The following morning, an intense heavy artillery bombardment commenced. Shelling continued for much of that day. The heaviest shelling occurred at 10:30 a.m., against the 43rd Battalion's P-line as well as positions located in the rear section. The battalion artillery batteries exerted enormous pressure on the enemy, using eighteen-pounders to pummel the German lines. Preceding the Battle of Vimy Ridge, Canadian field-artillery gunners fired approximately one million shells of various calibres at German defence installations. The most powerful guns did considerable damage to the enemy's fighting trenches and the numerous belts of barbed wire.

The first Cameron Highlander casualties in the month of April were: Private Walter George Clark, Private William James Tate, and Private William Taylor. All three were killed by enemy fire on April 3. Thirty-one other soldiers from the 43rd Canadian Infantry Battalion would die on the Douai Plain before the month ended.

On Wednesday, April 4, at 8:30 a.m., Lieutenant-Colonel William Grassie, in liaison with Lieutenants Verner, Fowler, and Malcolm, devised plans to incorporate three daylight raids. The assaults would be carried out simultaneously, inside enemy occupied territory, on April 5, commencing at 2:00 p.m. The operation against three separate German trenches was to be synchronized so that each raid would start and end at the same time. On the eve of the mission, artillery guns would commence a series of rapid-fire barrages across German lines, starting at 10:50 p.m. on April 4. The barrages would last five minutes in an attempt to draw retaliatory fire from the German guns. Enemy fire, in response to the Canadian bombing, would then be used to assist in identifying and plotting the exact locations of machine gun and heavy artillery positions.

At 11:00 p.m., the 43rd Battalion Field Artillery fired off several rounds of four-inch Stokes mortar shells, containing asphyxiating gas, at the enemy entrenchments. Suddenly, an abrupt change in wind direction reversed the gas into the faces and trenches of the Cameron Highlanders. Fortunately, each soldier was able to pull on his gas mask quickly, thereby avoiding any serious injury. As expected, the Canadian bomb barrage was met with significant retaliation from German trench mortars and heavy artillery fire. After playing "get even" for several minutes, the guns fell silent. The remainder of the night was calm, until the sun rose in the east the next morning.

On Thursday, April 5, field maps were distributed to all those participating in the three raiding parties, along with material outlining the expected objectives. The first and foremost objective was to capture as many Germans as possible, hopefully ones carrying identification papers, field maps, and other pertinent information. It was imperative to identify German combat units entrenched along the Left Sub Section of La Folie sector. It would also be an opportunity for each party to assess the extent of damage inflicted on enemy trenches, dugouts, and casualty count, as a result of the recent Canadian bombardment.

The three companies selected for the raids were B, C and D, with Lieutenant Verner commanding twenty-two Cameron Highlanders from B Coy. It would be Verner's responsibility to lead his men to the enemy front-lines and enter German territory on the right side. Their mission would be carried out within a time frame of fifteen minutes. B Coy was comprised of twenty-two men, including four snipers, a Lewis Machine Gun crew of four, and three gunners in a mine crater providing cover for the other eleven men. C Coy and its group of sixteen, under Lieutenant Fowler, were to enter the enemy front line from Patricia Crater and remain for fifteen minutes. The third raiding party, D Coy, would approach the front-line from the left, with Lieutenant Malcolm and twenty-five other ranks remaining in their designated sector for the same period of time. The three raiding parties were to engage the Germans simultaneously, returning to their line only at the specified time. Before heading out on the raid, each soldier removed uniform badges and combat unit identification. Personal letters and pay books were left with a sergeant for safekeeping until their return.

Thursday, April 5, 1917. Two o'clock in the afternoon! Mark II, eighteen-pounders erupted in a deafening roar. Shrill, screaming howitzers deployed bomb after bomb against the Imperial German Army, driving the enemy underground. The Canadian Field Artillery bombardment was the signal for the three Highlander raiding parties to storm out of the trenches and rush to their assigned entry points leading to the enemy sector. B Coy assembled to the right, immediately behind Birkin Crater and Commons Crater, before entering the German lines, directly between these two large pits. Within a few short minutes of reaching the German lines, Lieutenant J. D. Verner came upon a frightened young German soldier crouched behind the rim of an artillery shell crater. Amidst the chaos of gunfire and bombs, the soldier dropped his Mauser and ran as fast as his legs would take him in the direction of a damaged trench, with Lieutenant Verner in hot pursuit. Before the lieutenant could overtake him, a Stokes mortar shell exploded directly in front of the young German, ripping apart his limbs, and leaving his lifeless, dismembered body scattered about the trench.

Verner located his men. They had stumbled upon four enemy dugouts and were using grenades to destroy the entrances. In the meantime, Sergeant Williams and C Coy wasted no time in blowing up three dugouts and a cache of 100 stick grenades, hidden in two craters, with a Stokes mortar shell. B Coy pulled back from the German lines carrying two wounded Cameron Highlanders at 2:17 p.m.[3]

The day before, C Coy had conducted a scouting mission with Major McLean and Lieutenant Fowler, reaching Patricia Crater unnoticed by sentries in their observation posts. McLean and Fowler's foray into enemy territory gathered important information for use by Lieutenant Fowler and his men. Within the first seven minutes

---

3   Lieutenant Jack Douglas Verner, recipient of the Military Cross, sustained serious combat wounds later in the war and was evacuated to a hospital in Sussex, England. There, on February 16, 1919, he died of his injuries.

of Fowler entering the enemy line, he personally captured two soldiers from the German 2nd Battalion and handed them over at 2:07 p.m. to battalion headquarters, in Grange Tunnel. Fowler and three other ranks continued to bomb several dugouts. While engaging the Germans in the trenches and dugouts, Fowler and his small party came under severe grenade and rifle fire from directly behind, killing one Cameron Highlander from the blast of a grenade. After several minutes of intense fighting, Lieutenant Fowler and his men successfully subdued the enemy in close combat, using bayonets and rifle, before returning to their line at 2:17 p.m.

A third attack group on April 5 was D Coy, under the command of Lieutenant Malcolm who, with his raiding party, advanced between Durand and Duffield trenches, where Lieutenant Malcolm shot and killed a German soldier. Moments later, Lieutenant Malcolm was struck and killed by a hail of enemy bullets. During the same deadly engagement, Private Frank Turnaway, of the 43rd Battalion, single-handedly killed ten German soldiers before he was slain. Turnaway's comrades were able to remove his body from enemy territory before returning back to the Canadian lines. Private Frank Turnaway, eighteen years of age at the time of his death, is buried in the Ecoivres Military Cemetery in Nord-Pas-de-Calais. All three raids were fiercely resisted by the Germans, using their considerable firepower and impenetrable fortifications, while D Coy desperately sought protection from shell craters, hoping to stay alive.

As the mission drew to a close, men began pulling back to their lines. The field artillery laid down barrages of heavy shells once again, to provide support for each of the returning groups. Cover support was also being provided from a battlefield crater by Lieutenant John Eaton of the 43rd Battalion. Eaton, a twenty-year-old law student born in Derbyshire, England, was selected to lead a covering party of rifle and machine gun crews to a forward position located in Patricia Crater. The previous day, a disappointed Lieutenant Eaton had been denied a request to volunteer as a member of the B Coy raiding party. Now he found himself commanding a small group of soldiers in a crater. It may have been a matter of limited battlefield experience, or perhaps it was just carelessness on Eaton's part, that allowed his body to suddenly appear in the gun-sights of a German sniper's Mauser. One shot to the head and Lieutenant John Norris Eaton of Calgary, Alberta was dead. Eaton is also buried in the Ecoivres Military Cemetery.

The operation undertaken by the Cameron Highlanders of Canada, during the afternoon of the 5th, claimed twenty-six casualties. Two battalion officers and nine ordinary regulars were killed and fifteen wounded. In addition to Lieutenant John Norris Eaton, Lieutenant Alexander Malcolm, and Private Frank Turnaway, the other members of the 43rd Battalion who died on April 5 were: Private Walter Benjamin Woodworth, Private John George Sinclair, Private James Strathearn Pollock, Private Richard Redmond, Private Harold Ernest Stewart, Private James Stuart, Private James Campbell, and Private John Walker Brebner. The number of German casualties was estimated to be approximately the same number. Shortly after their return, the Cameron Highlanders received a congratulatory message for a job well done from Canadian Corps Commander, General Sir Julian Byng.

At 10:00 o'clock that evening, the 43rd Battalion was relieved in La Folie sector by soldiers chosen from several battalions, including the Royal Canadian Regiment of Nova Scotia, Princess Patricia's Canadian Light Infantry (Eastern Ontario), 42nd Infantry Battalion (Royal Highlanders of Canada), and the 49th Infantry Battalion (Alberta). This ambitious operation, involving soldiers from five battalions, was completed without incident and within a period of three hours on a cool and dry Good Friday morning, April 6, 1917. Once the relief operation had been completed, the 43rd Canadian Infantry Battalion (Cameron Highlanders of Canada) moved to billets once again in Gouy-Servins.

An Operations Order was issued shortly after breakfast on April 6, by Major-General Louis J. Lipsett, of the 3rd Canadian Infantry Division. He assigned combat roles, in the Battle of Vimy Ridge, to two of the three infantry brigades under his command. The Order directed the 7th Brigade to take a front-line position to the left side of the 8th Brigade while the 9th Brigade, including S.E. Shortliffe and the 43rd Battalion, would be moved to Divisional Reserve. The decision to place the 9th Brigade in Divisional Reserve meant the Cameron Highlanders of Canada and Ernie Shortliffe would not be part of the initial assault on Vimy Ridge.

On the day of the Vimy assault, both the 60th Battalion and 58th Battalion would be located in "A" Assembly Trench, its headquarters established in dugouts close to the junction of Pont Street and Bethune–Arras Road trenches. The 52nd Infantry Battalion (New Ontario) would join the 43rd Battalion in Divisional Reserve at Lamotte Camp. Although relegated to a supporting role for the time being, the Cameron Highlanders would soon see action after the first waves of Canadian troops had secured the escarpment.

In the early morning of April 8 at 6:30, a message was received ordering the 43rd Battalion to proceed with the 52nd Battalion from Gouy-Servins to bivouac tents at Lamotte Camp. Excluded from the move were Lieutenant E.G.A. Smart from A Coy, Major K.C. Campbell and Lieutenant J. D. Verner from B Coy, Major A.D. McLean of C Coy, and from D Coy, Lieutenant C.H. Barraud. These officers were to remain in Gouy-Servins together with surplus officers assigned to Major Campbell. During the late evening of April 8 and early morning hours of April 9, troops from the lead and support waves of the Canadian Corps were given their orders to move forward to their assembly positions.

The 43rd Battalion began a close-formation march beginning in front of their billets in Gouy- Servins, heading in the direction of Lamotte Camp. Before departing, a final inspection was held ensuring that each infantryman was carrying 170 rounds of .303 rifle ammunition, a sharpened bayonet, hand grenades, two cans of rations, full water canteens, one bandolier, a gas mask and small-box respirator, a flare pistol, wire cutters, and a small shovel. It was no small task, even for a soldier in excellent shape, to march great distances carrying weapons and equipment that easily weighed in excess of seventy pounds.

At the request of the French, the ground assault, originally planned for Easter Sunday, April 8, was postponed for twenty-four hours until Monday the 9th. The delay allowed the Canadian Corps to tie up loose ends concerning procedural items, such as the types of signals to be employed during the battle. A red "Save Our Souls" signal (S.O.S.), indicating distress, was to be displayed using a rocket or pistol-fired flare gun called "a Very Light." This device could discharge several flares in quick succession. In the matter of operational objectives, flags, displaying particular distinguishing colours or identifying symbols from each of the three attacking infantry divisions, would be raised aloft and waved after the troops had reached their assigned objectives. Flag colours were to be black and red, yellow with a black maple leaf, and a single red flag. In addition to flag signals, the 2nd Canadian Infantry Division, with the support of an additional infantry brigade from the 5th British Division, would also fire aloft three white flares to indicate that they had successfully captured their objective, Thelus.

Fighter bi-planes, from the British Royal Flying Corps (RFC), were scheduled to fly over the battle zone at Zero Hour plus fifty minutes and again at Zero Hour plus two hours, lending support to ground troops with machine gun fire and bombs as well as assisting artillery gunners in directing shells at enemy targets. The RFC had a total of 365 planes along the Vimy-Arras sector, vastly outnumbering the Imperial German Army Air Service. Despite having air superiority in numbers, the Royal Flying Corps lost a total of 131 aircraft in the first week of April. Julian Byng's Canadian Corps were given the use of six air squadrons, with No. 16 Squadron being used exclusively for artillery support, reconnaissance, and observation. More than 200 fighter pilots from Canada saw action with the Royal Flying Corps (RFC) and the Royal Naval Air Service (RNAS) in WWI. Of those 200, the top eighty-two pilots accounted for 1,519 victories. Four of the top Canadian fighter pilots shot down 236 German planes. They were: Major William George Baker VC (fifty kills), Major Donald Roderick MacLaren (fifty-four kills), Lieutenant-Colonel Raymond Collishaw (sixty kills) and Canada's best known fighter pilot, Lieutenant-Colonel Billy Bishop (seventy-two kills).

William Avery "Billy" Bishop arrived at Filescamp Farm, near Arras, in his Nieuport-17 fighter on March 17, 1917, where he joined No. 60 Squadron. On his very first day in the air over Vimy,

Bishop and his squadron engaged the Germans in a vicious dogfight. Following his initial encounter with the enemy, Bishop went on to shoot down twelve enemy planes as well as surviving a close encounter with the infamous Red Baron, Manfred von Richthofen in April. Two days before the Battle of Vimy Ridge, Billy Bishop was awarded the Military Cross (MC) for shooting down an enemy balloon airship near Vimy.

Billy Bishop later described April 9 in these words:

The shell-fire this morning was simply indescribable. The bombardment which had been going on all night gradually died down about 5 o'clock...for a time almost complete silence reigned over the battlefield. All along the German lines star-shells and rocket lights were looping through the darkness...precisely at the moment that all the British guns roared out their first salvo of the battle, the skies opened and the rain fell in torrents. The ground seemed to be one mass of bursting shells. Further back, where the guns were firing, the hot flames flashing from thousands of muzzles gave the impression of a long ribbon of incandescent light.

Deep below the surface of Vimy Ridge, under the 4.3 mile escarpment, British tunnelling companies had created an extensive network of twelve tunnels (subways) excavated to depths of approximately thirty-three feet. These tunnels were built especially for connecting reserve lines to front-lines, permitting soldiers to move quickly, safely, and unseen. In addition to the miles of tunnels and galleries created by the British, three additional miles of tunnel construction were completed by the Canadian Corps shortly before April 9. Incorporated into these subways, some of which were on four levels, were light railway lines, hospitals, command posts, ammunition depots, water reservoirs, communication centres, and trench mortar and machine gun posts. The geology of the Douai Plain of Nord-Pas-de-Calais not only contained the usual mixture of sand, loam, and clay found in Flanders, but also a firm, chalky soil, which was beneficial in the construction of deep tunnels, galleries, and charge chambers.

Mine warfare evolved in importance mainly because of tunnel systems. In order to protect attacking troops from enemy machine gun fire as they crossed No-Man's Land once the assault started, a total of eight mine charges, containing thousands of pounds of ammonal explosives, were made ready for detonation and placed at the end of subways in charge chambers. Of the eight land mines, three were detonated prior to the assault of April 9; another five mines, including two specialized charges, were fired at the commencement of the Battle of Vimy Ridge. One of the two most powerful explosions created a gigantic, deep hole, which was given the name "Montreal Crater." In addition to the eight land mines fired, another eight were left unexploded and undisturbed for eighty-one years. In February 1998, one of those charges was discovered seventy feet below Vimy Ridge. This WWI land mine, dating back to April 9, 1917, was disarmed by British military explosives and munitions expert, Lieutenant-Colonel Michael Watkins of the Royal Logistics Corps. On August 11, 1998, Colonel Watkins was fatally injured when part of an excavation he was using to access another mine chamber within the tunnel system, collapsed and buried him.

The set-piece combat engagement, painstakingly planned for months, would involve a nominal strength of 170,000 soldiers; 97,184 Canadian and 72,816 British. British troop support was critical to a victory, especially when it came to artillery firepower. Canadian divisional artillery formations numbered only eight field brigades and two heavy artillery groups, therefore it was necessary to add artillery capacity from outside the Canadian Corps. This was accomplished with the addition of four heavy artillery groups, nine artillery field brigades, and three divisional artillery groups of the British 5th Division. All together, British support made available to the Canadian Corps, numbered twenty-four brigade artillery groups. There were four hundred and eighty eighteen-pounder field guns, one hundred and thirty-eight 4.5 inch howitzers, ninety-six two-inch trench mortars and twenty-four 9.45 inch mortars. These guns were also supported by 245 siege guns and heavy mortars. The firepower available to General Julian Byng represented one heavy gun for every twenty yards and one field gun for every ten yards of Canadian Corps frontage. Heavy guns were three times greater in number than those used in the Battle of the Somme.

During the final days leading up to the Vimy battle, General Ludwig von Falkenhausen, commander of the German Sixth Army, ordered 40,000 troops of the 16th Bavarian Infantry Division, which were entrenched opposite the town of Souchez, to defend to the death the northern section of Vimy Ridge. On April 3, von Falkenhausen, who commanded twenty infantry divisions, also ordered his reserve units to prepare themselves for the eventuality of relieving the front line divisions, should the battle drag on for an extended period of time. There was a problem with that strategy. The reserve divisions had been sequestered fifteen miles from the battlefield, in order to protect them from Canadian artillery shells, and hence they were too far removed from the front line to react in a timely fashion, if called upon. At the same time, Reserve Division 79, under the command of General of the Infantry, Ernst August Marx von Bachmeister was instructed to defend a large central section of the Vimy escarpment including its highest elevation, Hill 145. On the southern slope of the ridge, soldiers from the 1st Bavarian Reserve Division, under General der Infanterie Karl von Fasbender, were taking shelter from the incessant Canadian artillery fire in their elaborate tunnel system. Officers and other ranks slept, worked and ate in relative comfort and safety, removed from the threat of Canadian guns. The front line defence, along the northern portion of the ridge, was the responsibility of VIII Reserve Corps, under the command of General Georg Karl Wichura. The Germans had undertaken a plan that would allow the infantry to maintain a front line with sufficient strength to successfully defend against the first wave of 20,000 Canadian Corps troops. The German infantry generals were willing to risk the defence of their territory, on the assumption that their heavy artillery guns; the Maschinengewehr 08 machine guns and Mauser infantry rifles, would be sufficient to stonewall the Canadian assault and thereby protect 1,100 yards of front-line, including the in-depth rear sector. As a result, each company of 150 Imperial German Army soldiers (a German rifle company at full-strength was 264 men) would face at least two Canadian battalions, having a potential strength of 2,000 men.

A spring offensive against Vimy Ridge had been expected since the end of the Battle of the Somme, on November 13, 1916. Since February, it had become clear a spring offensive was rapidly progressing from planning to implementation stage. This fact was borne out by German intelligence gathering on troop concentrations west of Arras and the number of large-scale trench raids being conducted by Allied soldiers. Confirmation of British and Canadian intentions came with the desertion of a German-born Canadian soldier in February 1917, who provided German officers with a great amount of useful and important information. It wasn't until March, however, that General von Bachmeister, of Reserve Division 79, actually published a report, stating that the Canadian infantry divisions had been observed moving into an echelon formation, in what he predicted would culminate in a major assault against Vimy. The German High Command debated launching a strategic pre-emptive strike to capture the northern section of the Zouave Valley, along with a portion of the Canadian front. Although the idea received unanimous approval, it never came to fruition. The reason for not launching an offensive strike against the Canadian Corps was the on-going artillery bombardments since March 20, which had German generals thinking defence rather than offence.

The Vimy battle would be conducted in four defined stages, each dictated by the German defences at the time of assault. It was determined that fresh troops from each of the attacking Canadian Corps divisions would take over the advance on Vimy Ridge at predetermined intervals. The attack on the Pimple, the enemy stronghold situated on the northern tip of the escarpment, was to begin twenty-four hours after the assault had started. Canadian troops would engage the enemy along a 3.6 mile section, to the north between the Arras-Lens Road and Givenchy. The 1st Canadian Infantry Division, under the command of Major-General Arthur William Currie, would deploy six battalions to that particular action. The six battalions included the 16th Infantry Battalion (Canadian Scottish), 7th Infantry Battalion (British Columbia), 5th Infantry Battalion (Saskatchewan), 10th Infantry Battalion (Alberta), 15th Infantry Battalion (48th Highlanders of Toronto), and the 14th Infantry Battalion (Royal Montreal). All six battalions would attack on a 1,760 yard (one mile) front. The main objective was to capture the German trenches located along a front on the outskirts of the village of Thélus.

Canadian Corps General Sir Julian Byng would command four attacking divisions with the support of the 24th British Division of I Corps to the north of the Souchez River, and XVII Corps to the south. General Currie's 1st Canadian Infantry Division would be joined by the 2nd Canadian Infantry Division, under the command of Major-General Henry Edward Burstall, whose troops would attack the German lines opposite Thélus. While engaging the enemy, Burstall would then order a number of troops to gain control of the main trench, known as the Zwischen-Stellung line. The remaining members of the 2nd Division would resume a frontal assault on Thélus. Two of those battalions, the 27th Canadian Infantry Battalion (City of Winnipeg) and 29th Canadian Infantry Battalion (Vancouver), would fight their way into the village of Farbus. They would ultimately rendezvous with the 1st Canadian Infantry Division.

The April 9 assault would see the 3rd Canadian Infantry Division, under the command of Major-General Louis Lipsett, utilizing only half of his twelve battalions along a front of 1,320 yards, opposite La Folie Wood, a forested area immediately south of Hill 145. The six battalions were chosen from the 7th and 8th Infantry Brigades. They would attack in a south to north direction, advancing along 600 yards of ground strewn with craters, rubble, demolished trenches, and the remains of soldiers, killed in fierce fighting on the eastern slope of Vimy Ridge, two years earlier. The determination and stubbornness of the Germans, to retain control of the ridge was soon to be demonstrated by their display of firepower, which would slow, and in some cases even halt, a Canadian advance on enemy lines with machine gun and rifle fire, shrapnel shells and chemical gas.

The 4th Canadian Infantry Division under Major-General David Watson was to focus its attack on a section of German lines situated between Broadmarsh Crater and Givenchy. The primary objective of the 4th Division was to capture Hill 145 and secure the eastern slope of the Vimy escarpment. All divisional commanders had been fully apprised of the situation, noting especially that Hill 145 was the most heavily defended section on the ridge. This would mean troops of the 4th Division would be facing a line of enemy fire from the infamous Pimple. The topography of the Vimy battlefield presented unique challenges, not only to the Canadian soldiers, but to the German infantry as well. One area of enemy concern was the width of the ridge. At its narrowest point, it measured only 2,300 feet before dropping off sharply on its eastern side. That physical aspect all but eliminated any chance of the Germans launching counterattacks, in the event Canadian and British troops captured the ridge. German generals were cognizant of the landscape issues, having expressed heightened concern many times for the overall dependability of their Vimy defence positions. German strategy was dedicated to employing a front line defence, of sufficient strength, to defend against an initial assault. Following the initial attack the German generals would quickly move their operational reserves forward, before their adversary had a chance to consolidate its strength and overrun the remaining enemy positions. As a result, the defence of Vimy Ridge would rely almost exclusively, on a myriad of machine guns. Aerial reconnaissance showed the battlefield to be nothing less than a wasteland, which would expose attacking troops of the 54th, 102nd, 38th, and the 73rd Infantry Battalions to conditions that were predicted to result in hundreds, if not thousands of casualties. The Kaiser and his army were determined to defend Hill 145 at all cost, but General Byng was even more determined Vimy Ridge would be one of Canada's greatest triumphs of World War I.

Easter Sunday, April 8, 1917. 11:00 a.m.

Lieutenant-Colonel William Grassie, forty-five-year-old former real estate agent from Winnipeg, led a procession of officers and ordinary regulars to morning service, in Lamotte Camp, on the eve of the Battle of Vimy Ridge. At its conclusion, Captain G. Pringle, 43rd Battalion Chaplain wished the troops, "God's Speed," as S.E. Shortliffe and his fellow Highlanders returned to their tents to await orders concerning their departure from Lamotte. Meanwhile, throughout the evening and early morning hours of April 9, the Canadian Corps attacking forces moved to their assembly areas in the front lines. Some advanced overland to the front, guided by luminous painted, wooden stakes, while others made their way along narrow passageways in underground tunnels. Canadian and British bombardments continued throughout the night. The Germans were kept holed up in their caves, dugouts, trenches, and tunnel systems. This action would cease minutes before the main attack, in order to allow the artillery to recalibrate their big guns. The cessation of bombing activity was a prelude to what was soon to occur, beginning with the onslaught of creeping barrages.

What had begun as a beautiful moon and starlit night, suddenly became stormy with strong north-westerly winds and plunging temperatures. Within a short period of time, sleet and blinding snow had decreased visibility considerably, but despite the miserable weather conditions, Canadian soldiers were able to cut innumerable belts of heavy, barbed wire strung throughout No-Man's Land. Those troops, of the first and support waves going over the top, joined their comrades in the front-line at 4:00 a.m., ninety minutes before the assault was to commence.

Monday, April 9, 1917. Zero Hour-5:30 a.m.

The first wave of Canadian shock troops clamoured from their tunnels and trenches charging across the Douai Plain, intent on capturing Vimy Ridge. At the moment the order was given to attack, every piece of heavy artillery, within the Canadian-British arsenal, commenced a thunderous and deadly bombardment of Vimy Ridge. Thirty seconds later, the 3rd Canadian Division Engineers, under the command of Lieutenant-Colonel T.V. Anderson, detonated three gigantic mine charges beneath the German trench lines and No-Man's Land, obliterating several enemy strong points. This was quickly followed by the light field batteries shelling the Germans' 100 yards every three minutes, while heavy and medium mortar artillery pounded enemy defence systems. The result was that sixty-seven of sixty-nine enemy heavy artillery guns were knocked out of commission. As the Canadian Corps advanced, they overran a large number of enemy artillery guns. The Germans had no way to move them to the rear, as most of their horses had died during the initial gas attack. Canadian troops fought tenaciously. They swarmed German positions and captured 1,200 yards of ground, while coming under tremendous pressure from deadly machine gun fire emanating from concrete fortifications 200 to 476 feet above the Douai Plain, on the Vimy escarpment.

(source: Library and Archives Canada)
A heavy-artillery weapon, known as a naval gun,
fires from behind Canadian lines.

(source: Library and Archives Canada)
A Canadian gun crew prepares to fire-off a round of
heavy artillery, at German-occupied Vimy Ridge.

Fifty-five minutes after the spring offensive had commenced, the 1st, 2nd, and 3rd Canadian Infantry Divisions had successfully captured their first objective, referred to as The Black Line. Thirty-five minutes later, the 1st Canadian Infantry Division captured the left half of the second objective, known as The Red Line. At the same time, the 2nd Canadian Infantry Division reached The Red Line and took the town of Les Tilleuls. Meanwhile, the 3rd Canadian Infantry Division continued their assault. A mine had exploded, killing several troops of the Reserve Infantry Regiment 262, thereby allowing the 3rd Division to reach the Red Line objective, on the western edge of Bois de la Folie, at 7:30 a.m. Ninety minutes later, having secured The Red Line, General Lipsett of the 3rd Division was alerted that the infantry's left flank had become dangerously exposed to German artillery fire. The 4th Canadian Infantry Division had not yet captured Hill 145. This was only one of a number of setbacks to plague General David Watson and his beleaguered 4th Canadian Infantry Division on April 9.

The initial advance of the 4th Canadian Infantry Division disintegrated tragically, almost immediately after the troops left their trenches. They were savagely mowed down and slaughtered by German machine guns, which killed and wounded most of the 4th Division's right flank. In a further unsettling situation, the 87th Canadian Infantry Battalion (Grenadier Guards of Montreal) suffered a tremendous loss of men. In a sector where German front-lines were still intact, having received very little damage from the Canadian Field Artillery pre-assault bombardment, 155 soldiers were killed.

An official German Army report described the engagement:

...the outposts...can discern dense Canadian Columns seeking assiduously step by step to cross the pappy waste between their trenches and the German lines...hand grenades crash into the massed attackers as they advance shoulder to shoulder...the Canadian attack against the centre... peters out in the remains of the entanglements covering the German line, where corpses lie piled in khaki heaps.

All subsequent progress became excruciatingly slow and often fatal; the men of the 4th Canadian Infantry Division found themselves under constant harassment from enemy rifle and machine gun bullets, pouring down like rain from The Pimple. In addition, the soldiers had to endure deadly explosions, resulting from Canadian bombs landing short of their targets. To make matters worse, the Canadian Corps had to contend with creeping barrages exploding too far ahead of the attacking troops, thereby allowing the Germans to seek cover, regroup, and await the helpless Canucks as they charged into the enemy gun-sights.

Forced by circumstances, Major-General Watson ordered the 4th Infantry Division to "go to ground," consequently foregoing a suicidal frontal assault in the afternoon against the Imperial German Army. Instead, Watson ordered up a battalion from Divisional Reserve. That battalion, held in reserve, happened to be the 85th Canadian Infantry Battalion (Nova Scotia Highlanders). The battalion was handed the job of capturing Hill 145, the tallest and most heavily fortified section on Vimy Ridge.

At 6:00 o'clock, on the afternoon of April 9, the confident but inexperienced battalion, including S.E. Shortliffe's cousin, Private Wilbur H. Shortliffe, advanced against the enemy with rifles and fixed bayonets, stumbling through clouds of smoke, gas, and exploding shells. Fierce fighting ensued, culminating with hand-to-hand combat and the successful conquering of Hill 145 by the 85th Battalion.

While the Nova Scotia Highlanders were focused on capturing Hill 145, the German Reserve Division 79 was in the process of consolidating for a massive counter attack, aimed at purging Canadian troops from the village of Vimy. Although the counterattack did drive the Canadians from the ruins of Vimy, the Germans failed to recapture the third line, south of the village.

(source: Library and Archives Canada)
Canadian troops consolidate their positions on Vimy Ridge. April 1917.

(source: Library and Archives Canada)
A plume of earth is sent high into the air by an exploding mine near Vimy Ridge.

As daylight faded from the battlefield on that first day of the Battle of Vimy Ridge, German generals and their infantry units were still, for the most part, entrenched on the Vimy escarpment, having withstood a major assault by the Canadian Corps. It had become critical now to quickly reinforce their positions, if they hoped to defend against the Canadian Infantry. By late evening, German reinforcements were arriving with a few units from the 111th Infantry Division, deployed to the third line, near the villages of Arleux and Acheville. The remaining soldiers would arrive on Tuesday, April 10.

(source: Library and Archives Canada)
Canadians tend to a wounded German soldier on the Vimy battlefield.

Although the German generals and their officers expected a tough battle, they were astonished nonetheless, by the intensity, tenacity, and fighting prowess of the Canadian soldiers. On the other hand, a large portion of German infantrymen found themselves prisoners in their own bunkers, trapped by a logistical miscalculation. They had moved too many men to the forward trenches; a grave mistake that almost cost the Germans half of their soldiers while defending the ridge on the first day of the assault. That error in judgement allowed the

Canadian Corps to take control of a large portion of Vimy Ridge and thereby force the enemy into retreating four miles east to the Oppy-Méricourt line. The persistent Canadian Corps attacks on the southwestern section of Hill 145 ultimately bled the German infantry of ammunition, grenades and mortar rounds, thereby forcing the enemy to reluctantly withdraw.

One day after the initial assault on Vimy, the British Army moved three brigades to the Red Line at 9:30 a.m., in support of an advance to reach the Blue Line being made by the 1st and 2nd Canadian Infantry Divisions. By 11:00 a.m., The Blue Line, including Hill 135 and the town of Thélus, had fallen to the Canadian Corps. It was at this point that the advance paused for a period of ninety minutes while Lewis machine guns were brought forward. At 2:00 p.m., both General Currie's 1st Canadian Infantry Division and General Burstall's 2nd Division had now reached and secured their final objective, The Brown Line. During the mid-afternoon, around 3:15, the 4th Division, under General Watson, was attempting to take the northern half of Hill 145, but after capturing the highest peak briefly, they were pushed back by a German counterattack. Even though the Germans had been able to hold their own for a period of time in certain sectors, most other sections of the ridge were coming under heavy attack from Canadian Corps troops, to the point where the enemy was completely outflanked. With no hope of relief from reinforcements, enemy soldiers were forced to pull back; a retreat that precipitated the evacuation of German artillery units from the ridge, to an area west of the Vimy-Bailleul railway line and the Oppy-Méricourt Line. By the time night fell across the Douai Plain, on April 10, the only Canadian objective that remained unclaimed was the infamous Pimple.

The Canadian assault on The Pimple did not materialize until April 12. The initial defenders of The Pimple, the 16th Bavarian Infantry Division, had been badly mauled by Canadian artillery bombardments leading up to the April 9 assault; therefore on April 11, the German 16th Division was relieved by the 4th Guards Infantry Division. Later that evening, Canadian Corps artillery batteries pounded enemy positions again, with many of the 1.6 million shells allotted Canadian gunners for the Battle of Vimy Ridge. Besides the No. 83 – Mark 1 British T & P Fuse (Time and Percussion Fuse), Canadian gun crews were also provided with the instantaneous No. 106 Fuse. This artillery fuse greatly improved the effectiveness of shellfire against enemy targets, because it exploded on the slightest contact, thus reducing the number of dud shells. In addition to the on-going bombardments from the Canadian Field Artillery, Royal Engineers, using Livens Projectors, hurled more than forty drums of toxic chemical gas into the town of Givenchy-en-Gohelle, causing confusion and panic amongst its German defenders. (Livens Projectors were mortar-like weapons commonly used to deliver gas attacks in WWI.)

(source: Library and Archives Canada)
Canadian machine-gunners set up their weapons in shell holes.

German troops defending Givenchy-en-Gohelle were able to drive back the first Canadian attacks at 4:00 a.m. with small-arms fire. That success would be short-lived. At 5:00 a.m.; the 10th Canadian Infantry Brigade attacked, with the support of substantial artillery fire, as well as having the 24th British Division of I Corps assisting to the north. German defences eventually succumbed to the Canadian assault; the Canucks had exploited wide gaps in the enemy defensive positions. The 10th Canadian Infantry Brigade continued to fight snow, wind, and whatever resistance the German holdouts could muster, until 6:00 p.m., when The Pimple was finally captured.

(Ross war photo collection)
A Canadian officer and another soldier inspect a machine gun used during the Battle of Vimy Ridge alongside its deceased gunner.

Three difficult days had now passed since the battle first began on Easter Monday. Canadian troops had succeeded in securing a firm foothold on the Vimy escarpment by the end of April 12, but it came with a huge price in casualties. It was reported that 3,598 soldiers had been killed and 7,004 wounded, for a total of 10,602 Canadian Corps casualties. Although this number was large, it was significantly lower than what was incurred by French and British forces during attempts to capture Vimy Ridge between May and September 1915. At Vimy Ridge, four Canadian soldiers were honoured with Victoria Crosses. They were: Major Thain Wendell MacDowell of the 38th Canadian Infantry Battalion (Eastern Ontario) CEF, Private William Johnstone Milne, 16th Canadian Infantry Battalion (Canadian Scottish) CEF, Private John George Pattison, 50th Canadian Infantry Battalion (Alberta) CEF, and Lance-Sergeant Ellis Wellwood Sifton of the 18th Canadian Infantry Battalion (Western Ontario) CEF.

With an effective range greater than 2,200 yards, the air-cooled German Maschinengewehr MG08/16 was greatly feared by almost all WWI Allied soldiers.

(source: Library and Archives Canada)
Two soldiers inspect a German 77mm field gun, known to fire shells that could travel faster than the speed of sound. These artillery shells were nicknamed whiz-bangs because troops could hear a whizzing noise before the discharge sound of the gun itself.

Without a doubt, many Cameron Highlanders felt pangs of disappointment, as well as a degree of relief, when told they would be spectators rather than full participants in the Battle of Vimy Ridge, happening only a short distance away. Assigned to Divisional Reserve at Lamotte Camp, the 43rd Battalion welcomed two brigade trench mortar teams, on a snowy morning, April 10, just before the battalion was ordered to an Observation Post, in a sector controlled by the 7th Canadian Infantry Brigade. One coy of Highlanders settled into P-Line, with two platoons of riflemen moving into position in Machine Gun Fort trench, and two platoons occupying the La Salle and Quarries Line. The three other battalion coys moved to Empire Redoubt and Pylones, where the 43rd Battalion established its headquarters in Grange Tunnel, a short distance from Hill 145. Guides attached to the 7th Brigade, met the Cameron Highlanders at Empire Redoubt and escorted them to their assigned positions within the brigade command-area. Their stay in the 7th Infantry Brigade sector was short-lived; at 3:30 p.m., on April 11, 43rd Battalion Headquarters received orders from 9th Infantry Brigade Headquarters, to immediately move the Cameron Highlanders of Canada to La Follie, in relief of the 85th Canadian Infantry Battalion (Nova Scotia Highlanders).

Although not directly participating in the April 9 assault on Vimy Ridge, the 43rd Canadian Infantry Battalion was still involved in a number of "hit and run" raids directed at enemy positions situated on the outskirts and within the village of Vimy. It was in Vimy that German snipers, rifle sections, machine-gun crews, and trench-mortar batteries were solidly entrenched in cellars and bombed-out buildings. As a result, it was necessary for advancing platoons to overcome a multitude of obstacles, such as belts of barbed wire, monstrous shell craters, and chlorine gas. Overcoming the challenges, the 43rd Battalion engaged the enemy in close combat, fighting house to house, street to street, throughout Vimy village before finally subduing the German defenders and taking numerous prisoners. One Cameron Highlander, twenty-one-year-old Private John Edward Sinclair was killed on this day, April 11.

On April 14, the 43rd Infantry Battalion (Cameron Highlanders of Canada) received orders to make their way up Vimy Ridge and onto the escarpment, which had been under Canadian control for the past two days. Despite Vimy having been captured by the Canadian Corps, the 43rd Battalion's job was to mop up pockets of persistent enemy resistance. Stubborn German troops remained entrenched, determined to fight to the bitter end. That fanatical loyalty to the Kaiser would claim the lives of five Cameron Highlanders in that operation, while another eight would be wounded, and two reported missing-in-action. Private S.E. Shortliffe spent six days on Vimy Ridge, exterminating the last of the Imperial German Army troops, before leaving on April 20 for Reserve Line billets in Gouy-Servins. The men enjoyed a little R&R there, then moved into the tunnels at La Folie on April 26, where they would remain until May 5. After spending nine days squirreled away below ground at La Folie, the 43rd Battalion relocated to Villers-au-Bois, in relief of the 5th Canadian Mounted Rifle Battalion at Winnipeg Camp.

(source: Library and Archives Canada)
Canadian heavy-artillery bombardments drive German soldiers
from their trenches, happy to have survived death in order
to surrender to advancing Canadian assault troops.

(Ross war photo collection)
Two German soldiers lay dead after having failed to defend their Vimy Ridge position from the Canadian Corps attack on April 9, 1917.

Once Vimy Ridge had been taken from the Germans, it wasn't long until a court of enquiry was ordered by Field Marshall Paul von Hindenburg, to investigate the reason for the defensive collapse of the Arras sector. The inquiry concluded that General Ludwig von Falkenhausen had failed to apply the German defensive doctrine and instead adopted a series of unmoving strong points and static lines of resistance, which the Canadians isolated and eventually destroyed. In the end, Falkenhausen was removed from his command, followed by a reassessment of the German defence strategy. As a result, the Imperial German Army reverted to a "scorched-earth policy" immediately before withdrawing to the Oppy-Méricourt line.

The Canadian Corps success, which resulted in the capture of Vimy Ridge, was a mixture of micro-planning, tactical innovation, massive artillery support, and intensive training, along with the failure of the German Sixth Army to apply the policies and strategies set out in their new Defensive Doctrine. Vimy Ridge had been the very first time, during the war that all four infantry divisions fought together as one Canadian Expeditionary Force. Vimy Ridge became a symbol of pride, achievement, and human sacrifice; an event that some said, defined Canada as a nation.

These are the names of the other eighteen members of the 43rd Canadian Infantry Battalion, who perished in Vimy during the period April 13 to 30, 1917:

Sergeant Alexander Buchan,(killed 1 mile west of Vimy), Sergeant Arthur W. Hempshall, Private Graham Marshall (body not recovered), Private George Adams,(body not recovered), Private Paule Puletich, (body not recovered), Private William Ferrier Smith, Private Duncan T. Mactavish, Private William Victor Coo, Private Andrew Bremner, Private Richard Simpson, (body not recovered),Private James Joseph Cantlon, Private Alfred R. Hoare, (body not recovered), Private Roderick W. Macdougall, (body not recovered), Private Wilson Moore, Private James Beaton, Private George Bremner, Private William Leslie Robinson, and Private Robert William Willson.

(Ross photo)
A must when paying a visit to the battlefields of the Western Front is to spend time at the Vimy Ridge Memorial, situated atop what was once called Hill 145.

(source: Library and Archives Canada)
A view of the village of Vimy as seen from the crest of Vimy Ridge, after it had been captured and secured by the Canadian Corps.

(source: Library and Archives Canada)
Jubilant and victorious Canadian soldiers celebrate as they make their way to a rest area behind the lines, after successfully capturing Vimy Ridge.

Chapter Thirteen
MAY/JUNE 1917

> "The art of war is simple enough. Find out where the enemy is. Get him as soon as you can. Strike him as hard as you can, and keep moving."
>
> Ulysses S. Grant

The month of May was described by some as a "brief lull before the big storm." It would soon become evident that the big storm was to be Passchendaele, and Passchendaele would be defined as a "wholesale massacre." Before that battle was to take place, the 43rd Canadian Infantry Battalion (Cameron Highlanders of Canada) would engage the Imperial German Army in the Avion Sector in June, followed by Lens in August. Now that Vimy Ridge was under British control (and would remain so for the balance of the war), Allied forces could, again, focus their attention elsewhere on the Western Front. General Douglas Haig and his generals were of the opinion that it was highly unlikely Kaiser Wilhelm II would sacrifice his countrymen in a suicidal counterattack, predicated on an assumption they could recapture Vimy Ridge.

The perception that May was a month of peaceful co-existence between the Germans and Canadian forces appears misleading when one examines the 43rd Battalion casualty list. In May, a total of seventeen Cameron Highlanders lost their lives, during the second deadliest month of 1917. The first fatality in May occurred on the second day of the month, when twenty-two-year-old Private William J. Fear was killed. Two days later, enemy fire claimed the lives of Private Robert Taylor and Private Benjamin Kuryk, age nineteen. On May 5, Private Abraham Harris was killed when the Cameron Highlanders were moving to quarters in Goodman Tunnel on the eastern slope of Vimy Ridge. Enemy machine gun fire peppered the front and support lines, causing several Canadian Corps casualties. The following day, May 6, the 43rd Battalion relocated its four coys from Goodman Tunnel to Villers-au-Bois. During that particular operation, Private Frederick Moran and Private Alexander Beaton were mortally wounded. The Cameron Highlanders of Canada remained in Villers-au-Bois, until ordered to relieve the 42nd Canadian Battalion, on May 19-20, in the second line of the Bailleul-Raiumont-Loos Line.

Other Cameron Highlanders who became deceased in May were: Private Samuel Whiteside (May 7), Lance-Corporal James A.S. Hill (May 21), Private James McKenzie Morton (May 24), Private Harry V. Dexter (May 24), Private George L. Anderson (May 24), Private Edwin James Pannell (May 25), Private George Barrons (May 26), Private Arthur Baker (May 26), Private John Richardson (May 27), Private William Lewis Wisenden (died from wounds, May 28), and Private George C. Dickie (died from wounds, May 29).

As mentioned in the previous chapter, the result of the German infantry failure to subsequently defend Vimy against the Canadian assault, precipitated an in-depth reassessment of all strategies, including those associated with planning, logistics, and defence issues. The most major change was the immediate resumption of a strategy, last implemented during the Battle of the Somme, known as the "Scorched Earth Policy." The implementation of such a policy meant that the enemy would destroy anything and everything deemed potentially useful to their opponents. The list included such things as: communication and transportation systems, fortifications, and on some occasions the complete obliteration of towns and villages.

In the wake of Julian Byng's promotion to the rank of full general and commander of the British Third Army in June of 1917, Major-General Arthur William Currie became Canadian Corps Commander.

The general, who changed the spelling of his surname from Curry to Currie sometime within the years 1894 to 1899, was born in Napperton, Ontario near Strathroy on December 5, 1875. Arthur W. Currie's claim-to-fame was an illustrious military career, in which he became the first Canadian-born soldier to command all four of Canada's infantry divisions during the latter part of the Great War. Currie worked his way up through the ranks, beginning as a pre-war gunner, then commander of the 2nd Canadian Infantry Brigade in 1914. A year later, he was promoted to commander of the 1st Canadian Infantry Division, a post he held until June 1917 when he was made Canadian Corps Commander. General Currie was a graduate of the University of Toronto. In 1894, he moved from Ontario to Vancouver Island, where he taught school for five years before accepting a position in 1899 as a provincial manager with the National Life Insurance Company.

For much of June, the 43rd Battalion was entrenched along the eastern slope of Vimy Ridge. There they fought off boredom by participating in work parties until June 25. It was on that date that all four 9th Brigade battalions were ordered to relieve the 8th Canadian Infantry Brigade in the Avion Sector, situated between the Lens-Arras railway and Lens-Arras road. The directive, issued by the 9th Brigade commander, Brigadier-General Frederick William Hill, was simply to "capture the Avion Trench from the Germans." On the night of June 25, a torrential rainstorm swept across the battlefield, driven by strong, gusting winds. Canadian infantrymen were forced to slog through ankle-deep, glue-like mud that sucked the boots and putties off their feet and legs. Those horrendous conditions eventually forced a halt to the 43rd Battalion's relief operation of the 5th Canadian Mounted Rifles Battalion (Quebec), until shortly after daybreak, on June 26. After the relief mission had been completed, the 38th Infantry Battalion (Eastern Ontario) was positioned on the left side of the 43rd Battalion while the 58th Infantry Battalion (Central Ontario) was situated on the right. One hour after the 5th Canadian Mounted Rifle Battalion had been relieved, the 4th Infantry Division commenced an attack on the German front, extending to Avion Trench. Private S.E. Shortliffe and the Cameron Highlanders were ordered to engage the enemy in an aggressive fire-fight. They hoped to eliminate as much German resistance as possible, and thereby capture and defend all trenches and outposts against any future enemy counterattacks. Troops of the 43rd Battalion climbed up their ladders and quickly scrambled over the trench parapets, making their way across the open fields, towards enemy lines. The assault proved successful. They captured and consolidated the German front line trench, paused, then rushed and overwhelmed the enemy repeatedly, ultimately capturing the German support line.

After a brief rest, two platoons of Highlanders were dispatched at 10:30 p.m., on the evening of June 26, to penetrate and capture the next German line, named Avion, near Lens. Later that night, at 1:00 a.m. on the 27th, enemy flares suddenly illuminated the sky, revealing the silhouetted forms of Canadian soldiers approaching the Avion lines. German trenches came alive with a barrage of heavy rifle and machine-gun fire, creating a perilous situation for Canadian troops, as thousands of rounds of bullets exacted a heavy toll on the men. One of the casualties was a 43rd Battalion Platoon Commander, Lieutenant Anderson. Quickly, it became obvious the Avion Line was far too heavily defended for the Cameron Highlanders to capture alone, without incurring heavy losses. It was decided that the Highlanders would return to the line position, captured the previous night.

Two Cameron Highlanders of Canada were killed in the Avion action on June 26. They were: Sergeant Alexander McLeod[4] and Private John A. Anderson.

Throughout the day on June 27, plans were made to involve heavy gun support, coordinated with another 43rd Battalion ground assault on the Avion trench, scheduled for 2:30 a.m. At the designated time, a number of 84mm Mark II field guns began a series of bombardments stretching along the Avion Line, some three miles away. Artillery gun crews, of six men per heavy weapon, were able to load and fire thirty rounds of shells every minute. The massive number of shells being shot, on occasion, created so much heat that the huge seven-foot- long

---

4   In 2003, Sergeant McLeod's name was discovered carved on a wall in Goodman Tunnel, which is situated beneath the Vimy Ridge Memorial.

cannons overheated and warped, causing artillery bombs to completely miss their targets.

As weapons boomed and shells whistled, Private S.E. Shortliffe and his battalion, made their way in the dark, slowly and cautiously, along a sunken road toward Avion. Suddenly, within minutes of starting their advance, they encountered several shells exploding in front of them as the Cameron Highlanders prepared to cross near, the Old Mill. Soldiers hurled themselves to the ground. They sought protection from bullets and artillery shells bursting all around them. Company officers ordered their men to drag the wounded off the roadway and move them to a protected part of the terrain. Runners were dispatched to request immediate, medical evacuation of the wounded and artillery support for the troops. Sergeant Charles Robert Dayton and Private Lindsay H. W. Cairns died on this day in June 1917. Sergeant Dayton's body was not recovered.

Once the injured had been taken care of, the Cameron Highlanders formed platoons, and with the assistance of artillery support, continued on to their objective where they joined the 38th and 58th Canadian Infantry Battalions. In a combined combat operation, the three battalions were able to force the German Infantry from Avion Trench. In the process, the 43rd Battalion suffered twenty-three casualties on the night of June 28. Included in that total were nine soldiers who died as a result of enemy bullets and bombs. Among those killed were: Lance-Sergeant Hendry Keith, Private Arthur Lyle, forty-four-year-old, Private Charles Thomas Jennings (body not recovered), forty-three-year-old, Private William Phillips (body not recovered), Private Thomas Rushton (body not recovered), Private Alfred Saxton, Private Robert Smart (body not recovered), eighteen-year-old Private Alex Ross Wright, and Private Peter Oag.

In addition to those Cameron Highlanders already mentioned, six other members of the 43rd Canadian Infantry Battalion died in June 1917. They were: Private Robert Service (June 15), Private John George Lightfoot (June 18), Private Jack Favel (June 22), Private Jasper Y. Paterson (June 29), Private George P. Sussams (June 29), and Military Medal recipient, Sergeant Alexander Drysdale (June 29).

Chapter Fourteen
JULY 1917

"We make war that we may live in peace."

Aristotle

Far from the noise and horror of war, the sound of church bells and horns were heard from coast to coast in joyous celebration, on July 1, 1917. It was Canada's 50th Birthday. In villages, towns, and cities, families and friends lined streets to cheer long parades of volunteers preparing to leave for England. The eventual destination would be the Western Front. The day ended with patriotic songs, speeches, and to the delight of all — fireworks.

Private Stephen Ernest Shortliffe celebrated Dominion Day with his fellow Highlanders in a sweltering, foul-smelling Avion Trench, occasionally scanning No-Man's Land for any sign of enemy activity. The most effective and safest way to observe German troop movement was by using a device called a periscope. Invented 467 years earlier by Johann Gutenberg, and later perfected by Sir Howard Grubb, this particular instrument allowed troops to watch the enemy from the safety of their trench, without having to raise their heads above the parapet wall and risk a fatal bullet. Within range of the 43rd Battalion's periscope, a group of German officers discussed the pros and cons of launching a counter-attack against the battalion, in the hope of recapturing the Avion Line. Although thoroughly discussed, debated, and thoughtfully considered, the plan was never implemented. Except for the occasional rat-a-tat-tat of machine- gun fire, Dominion Day spent in Avion Trench was quiet and somewhat boring. Even the intermittent sound of gun fire appeared more like gunnery crews interested in killing time, rather than engaging the Canadian enemy.

German machine-gunners were well aware the majority of British Expeditionary Force troops feared and loathed the MG-08. This water-cooled Maschinengewehr 08 was a very accurate, deadly, tri-pod mounted, light artillery weapon. The Germans also were cognisant of the fact the MG-08 had two major disadvantages: weight and versatility. Canadian Corps gunners mainly used a much lighter, twenty-six pound Lewis machine gun, and the British used the Vickers. The German sixty-six pound MG-08 was a beast of a machine to lug around; it often required three or four men to transport, assemble, and fire the lethal weapon. It did, however, have the ability to fire fifty-calibre bullets, at a rate equivalent to eighty infantry rapid-fire rifles.

During the late evening and early morning, German raiding parties, equipped with rifles, bayonets, stick grenades, flame throwers, and supportive machine-gun fire, inflicted considerable damage and casualties on the Avion line. The appearance of raiding parties had been expected by battalion officers, since the Highlanders first captured Avion on June 28th. Therefore it was not a complete surprise to learn that the Germans had successfully breached a section of line during a late-night raid. The Cameron Highlanders quickly responded by shooting and bayoneting several of the invaders, and the survivors made a hasty retreat to their lines, leaving many dead and wounded comrades behind. The counter-raid, made on the Avion Trench, was responsible for the deaths of two Cameron Highlanders and injuries to six other soldiers. After the enemy had evaporated into the blackness of the night, a quiet fell over the front line. The battalion assessed the extent of damage inflicted on the Avion trenches by the Germans. After the assessment report had been drafted and submitted, the 43rd Infantry Battalion was ordered to withdraw from the Avion sector as they were being replaced by the 116th Canadian Infantry Battalion.

At 4:35 a.m. on July 2, the Cameron Highlanders of Canada relocated to Brigade Reserve, three miles from the village of Vimy. Later that day, the battalion left for Winnipeg Sector, also referred to as the "Tunnel Area," where they were joined by Lieutenant R.H. Young and Lieutenant W.H. McNally. From the Winnipeg Sector, the battalion moved to Niagara Camp, where they relieved the 44th Canadian Infantry Battalion (Manitoba) at 4:00 p.m. on July 3. The Cameron Highlanders spent the next five days at Niagara Camp, in Chateau de la Haie, training and performing road construction as part of a 150-man work party.

On July 6, reinforcements, numbering twenty-five men, were taken on strength by the 43rd Battalion, at Chateau de la Haie. At 2:00 o'clock in the afternoon on July 8, Major William K. Chandler, the acting battalion commander, left for an important meeting at 9th Brigade Headquarters, to discuss plans for a battlefield visit by King George V. The visit was cancelled twenty-four hours later. Four days after Major Chandler's meeting at 9th Brigade Headquarters, Brigadier-General Frederick W. Hill arrived in the afternoon of July 10, to personally congratulate and praise the men of the 43rd Battalion for their role in the Avion-sector combat operation. At the conclusion of Brigadier-General Hill's visit, the Cameron Highlanders departed for Bluebull Tunnel where they relieved the 1st Canadian Mounted Rifle Battalion (Saskatchewan) at 6:00 p.m. The site of this relief operation was along a flat plain, extending southward from the village of Souchez to the western side of Vimy Ridge, in the Zouave Valley.

It had been a long and stressful ten days since the 43rd Battalion last received a respite from the front-line trenches, and there was no indication relief would be on its way anytime soon. This realization hit home when the battalion found itself back in Avion, in the same left sub-section and facing an attack on July 20 at 11:45 p.m. A raiding party of fifteen German soldiers was spotted by battalion snipers from their observation post, as the enemy approached the Canadian barbed wire. Two of the soldiers cautiously crept forward, peered nervously over the wire, paused for a brief moment, and returned to their main group. Suddenly, a few minutes later, the entire raiding party appeared, rushing the Cameron Highlander observation post, firing their rifles, and lobbing grenades. Immediately, Corporal Stewart took charge of the situation and with the help of his fellow soldiers, successfully drove off the enemy attackers. At the conclusion of the raid, one enemy soldier had been mortally wounded.

Cries of "Bitte hilfen Sie mich!" ("Please help me!") were heard coming from the area where the activity had just taken place. The Highlanders assumed a number of Germans had been wounded and left behind by their comrades. Shortly after the raid, a patrol was sent out, however, inexplicably none of the enemy soldiers were found. During the early morning hours of July 21, a second patrol of Cameron Highlanders discovered ten German beret-like caps and ten rifles with fixed bayonets, but still no trace of wounded soldiers. It was determined that the soldiers, who were heard pleading for help, had been evacuated so hastily back to their lines, that they neglected to retrieve their rifles and headgear. The raid resulted in ten wounded Highlanders, including one officer, Lieutenant C.E. Otton.

The following evening, at 11:00 o'clock, a further defensive patrol was deployed from the left sub-section of Avion, to intercept an anticipated, large enemy raiding party. To the surprise of everyone, the Highlanders encountered only four Germans, who opened fire with semi-automatic Luger pistols and Mauser rifles. Two Cameron Highlanders were wounded before the Germans disappeared into the night. Two hours later, at 1:00 a.m., on July 24, the Germans launched an asphyxiating gas attack against the 43rd Battalion front-lines. The attack left a number of soldiers gasping for air as they struggled to place gas masks over their faces. An eerie cloud of yellowish gas swept over the battlefield and slithered into the trenches, making it difficult for the men to observe enemy troop movement beyond the battalion observation post. The night ended with five members of the 43rd Battalion wounded; four had been severely overcome by chlorine and phosgene gas.

The 9th Canadian Infantry Brigade's Field Artillery began their bombardment at 5:00 a.m. on July 25, featuring eighteen minutes of constant, heavy barrages, aimed at German positions immediately in front of the 43rd Battalion's Avion front line. When it was finished, there was the usual expectation of some sort of retaliation, however, the response was quite limited and caused only a small amount of damage and no casualties. Until now, July had been a hot, dry month, but during the night it rained; monsoon-type downpours produced flooding, erosion, and treacherous muddy conditions. These conditions continued, during a relief operation at 9:15 p.m., on the evening of the 25th, when the 72nd Canadian Infantry Battalion (Seaforth Highlanders of Vancouver) took over from the Cameron Highlanders of Canada, in the Avion front line.

After spending the last five days at the front, Private S.E. Shortliffe and his comrades were relieved to finally be moved to the rear section, away from the threat of death by bullet, bomb, or bayonet. The remainder of the month was fairly quiet. This allowed commanders time to discuss, review, and expedite plans for the next major mission. One had originally been scheduled for the last week of July, but because of inclement weather was now planned for mid-August.

Five ordinary regulars with the 43rd Battalion died in the month of July. The first was Scottish-born, twenty-one-year-old Private Andrew McCrindle on July 17. His death was followed two days later with the passing of Private George Hay Mitchell. On July 21, Private John Ellis Caverly died from wounds at a military hospital in Surrey, England. Private William Mitchell was killed in action on July 25 and Private Gordon Livingston on July 26. Private Livingston was the eighty-eighth soldier from the 43rd Canadian Infantry Battalion (Cameron Highlanders of Canada) to die on the Western Front in the first six months of 1917.

Chapter Fifteen
AUGUST 1917

"No one goes into battle thinking God is on the other side."

Terry Goodkind

Canadian troops were engaged in yet another battle during August, somewhat similar to the one fought four months earlier, at Vimy Ridge. In July, British First Army Commander General Henry Horne asked the newly promoted commander of the Canadian Corps, General Sir Arthur W. Currie, to develop and execute a strategy that would culminate in the capture of the city of Lens. After giving the subject a great deal of thought, Currie presented his plan to General Horne. Currie affirmed that the Canadian Corps would engage as many German Infantry Divisions as possible. That would leave a limited number of enemy infantry divisions free to fight the British Expeditionary Force, in the Third Battle of Ypres, which had recently commenced on July 31. He opposed the idea of using all his men and resources to capture Lens while the Kaiser's army maintained a significant advantage from atop Hill 70. General Currie was of the opinion that in order to capture and defend Lens against German counterattacks, it was imperative that the Canadian Corps first take Hill 70; also known as Sallaumines Hill.

In order to achieve the desired objective, Currie submitted a plan designed around three stages. It would concentrate an attack along a 3,900 yard (2.2 mile) German front, using troops from the 1st and

2nd Canadian Infantry Divisions. During the first stage, troops of the Canadian Corps were to capture the top of Hill 70, before moving east to the numerous enemy trenches placed along the downward slope of the hill. The second stage called for the capture of the German second position on the crest of Hill 70, while the final stage would involve the lower part of the eastern side of the slope, where the enemy's third line was located — almost one mile from where the Canadians would start their attack.

They were to establish defensive positions, utilizing concentrated artillery fire to push back all counterattacks, and inflict as many casualties as possible on the German infantry. Currie persuasively and effectively articulated his case to General Horne, to have Hill 70 recognized as a limited offensive priority.

Hill 70 was an absolutely horrific place; it was incredibly polluted, devastated beyond description, and reeking of rotting corpses and chemical residue. The assault, scheduled to commence on the outskirts of Lens, at 4:25 a.m. on August 15, involved three Canadian attacking divisions, as well as one division of reserves. The primary objective was to capture the main German defensive positions situated on the eastern slope of Hill 70.

General Currie employed ten battalions in the attack; the 3rd Canadian Infantry Division, including the men of the 43rd Battalion (Cameron Highlanders of Canada), was held in reserve. The main assault force included the 1st Canadian Infantry Division, which attacked the north side of Hill 70. The 2nd Canadian Infantry Division attacked the summit. Two brigades from the 2nd Division were in combat south of Hill 70, in Cité Edouard, St. Émile and St. Laurent. The 4th Canadian Infantry Division operated in a diversionary capacity.

Defending Hill 70 were the German 7th Infantry Division, 4th Guards Infantry Division, 185th Infantry Division, 11th Reserve Division, and the 220th Infantry Division, under the command of Otto von Below, General der Infanterie of the German Sixth Army.

The week prior to the Battle of Hill 70, Private S.E. Shortliffe and the 43rd Battalion were billeted in Camblain L'Abbe, 14 miles south-west of Lens. Most of the battalion's time was spent practicing musketry, hoping to qualify for an upcoming Divisional Rifle Elimination Competition.

On the morning of August 10, Major William K. Chandler accompanied his seventy qualifying team members and five alternates to Divisional School, in Ferfay. The men competed against soldiers from several other battalions, the winners advancing to the Canadian Corps Rifle Meet in September. The remainder of the 43rd Battalion rifle team continued with daily training sessions until evening, when they gathered in the chaplain's service hut and were entertained by sixteen soldiers calling themselves, "The Dumbbells."

The troupe's name was associated with the dumbbell arm patch, worn on the uniform of the men of the 3rd Canadian Infantry Division, signifying "strength." The Dumbbells travelled from Bruay, at the invitation of Lieutenant-Colonel Grassie, of the 43rd Infantry Battalion, to raise the spirits of his soldiers and take their minds off the war. The evening consisted of song, comedy sketches, and jokes. The comedy group had been founded around the time of the Vimy battle by Merton Plunkett, a soldier from Orillia, Ontario. Plunkett's group of entertainers would do anything to bring joy and laughter to war-weary trench soldiers. As fighting raged all around them, the troupe transported props, costumes, and an upright piano to the front lines. The Dumbbells' musical repertoire included original songs, as well as several songs sung by soldiers as they marched overland, one of those being the popular, "It's a Long Way to Tipperary."

Soldiers of WWI loved to sing, and so they did, for hours into the late evening, in the service huts. The favourites were: "Keep the Home Fires Burning," "These Wild, Wild, Women are Making, a Wild Man of Me," and "I Know Where the Flies Go."

In a torrential rainstorm at 8.15, on the morning of August 11, the 43rd Battalion left Camblain L'Abbe for two days of brigade manoeuvres, near Carenoy. The inclement weather forced the cancellation of the afternoon session. Based on weather predictions over the next two days, it was decided to reschedule the second day of manoeuvres to Monday, August 13 at 10:00 a.m. Ernie Shortliffe and his B Coy comrades had no sooner arrived back at their billets in Camblain L'Abbe at 4:30, when the sun came out and a gentle breeze began to blow.

After dinner, another evening of entertainment commenced at 8:00 p.m. The musical concert featured the Pipe and Drum Corps of the 43rd Infantry Battalion. These concerts were always well attended because Highland Regiments passionately enjoyed the music of the pipes and drums. It was the bagpipers who led them into battle and generated terror in the hearts of the enemy with their pipes' unusual, haunting sound.

Sunday, August 12, originally planned for manoeuvres, was rescheduled as a day of rest, the only activity being a church service at 10:00 a.m. Later in the afternoon, two officer reinforcements, Lieutenant A. McEwan and Lieutenant J.H. Horn, reported for duty with the 43rd Battalion. Two days later, Lieutenant-Colonel Grassie received a message from 9th Brigade Headquarters; the battalion was to relocate to Auchel, at 8:10 a.m., on the 15th of the month.

Shortly before dawn, on August 15 at 4:25 a.m., the combat operation against Hill 70 got under way and within twenty minutes, two of the attacking Canadian infantry divisions had already succeeded in their first objective. By 6:00 a.m., the 2nd Canadian Infantry Brigade, of the 1st Canadian Infantry Division, had reached their next objective. The speed at which the Canadians were reaching attaining their goals was astonishing when considering the relentless machine-gun fire they encountered.

Three days into the operation, the Germans had fired between 15,000 and 20,000 shells of sulphur mustard, a blistering agent named Yellow Cross gas. Exposure to this particular toxic agent resulted in horrific skin blisters, inflamed, swollen eyes, internal haemorrhaging, and vomiting blood. A victim of mustard gas suffered excruciating discomfort, sometimes lasting five weeks, before the soldier died a horrible, painful death. One's demise by mustard gas was so inhumane and frightening, that it prompted Nurse Vera Brittain to write:

I wish those people who talk about going on with this war whatever it costs could see the soldiers suffering from mustard-gas poisoning. Great mustard-coloured blisters, blind eyes, all sticky and stuck together, always fighting for breath, with voices a mere whisper, saying that their throats are closing and they know they will choke.

The battle to conquer Hill 70 took only three days, ending on August 18, 1917. A major reason for the Canadian success at Hill 70 was its firepower. In addition to over 200 artillery pieces, the Canadian Corps also had thousands of riflemen and over 190 machine guns, which spit out 20,000 bullets every minute. Machine-gun crews, using both the heavier Vickers and lighter Lewis guns, cut down counterattacking German soldiers like a hot knife slicing through butter. Bodies covered the battlefield. Artillery fire also played a dominant part in the battle; thousands of shrapnel shells blanketed Hill 70, killing many of the enemy in their shallow trenches. The 1st Canadian Infantry Brigade alone, fired over 11,000 shells from their twenty-four guns, at the German lines.

Once Hill 70 had been secured by Canadian Corps, General Currie shifted his attention to the second and most important objective, the industrial coal city of Lens. Lens had been under the control of the Imperial German Army since October 1914. They had captured the city during the "Race to the Sea." Three years later, the Canadians occupied Hill 70, overlooking the German-held city. Despite a massive saturation of bombs directed at Lens, the Germans tenaciously held on. The operation relating to Hill 70 and Lens lasted ten days, from August 15 to August 25. Within the same time frame, two ordinary regulars from the 43rd Battalion suffered fatal injuries. They were: Private George E. Mathesius (body not recovered) and Private William Smith. In total, 9,198 Canadian troops were killed, wounded, and missing in combat operations against Lens and Hill 70. German casualties were estimated to be approximately 25,000, with 1,369 taken prisoner by Canadian troops during the ten days.

While the opening salvo was fired at Hill 70, the 43rd Canadian Infantry Battalion left Camblain l'Abbe at 8:10 a.m. on August 15. They headed northwest, through Estrée, Cauchie, and Ranchicourt, with meals and a rest in Houdain, before continuing to Divion,

Camblain Chatelain, and finally Auchel. It was a fifteen-mile march, completed in a little over seven hours.

On August 18, three divisions of the Canadian Corps captured Hill 70, and the Cameron Highlanders prepared for the 3rd Infantry Division Dumbbell Competition. After morning assembly, the four platoons of B Coy joined the other 43rd Battalion platoons at the rifle range and training grounds in Auchel. They competed against each other for ten hours. The platoon competition consisted of events such as: musketry, bayonet, and grenade attack. The winners from A Coy accumulated the most points, the No. 1 Platoon, under the command of Major Taylor. Members of the Major's victorious team received a red Dumbbell badge from 3rd Divisional Headquarters, which were sewn on their combat uniforms and proudly worn.

The day before the Canadian Corps launched its assault on Lens on August 21, the Cameron Highlanders of Canada gave up their billets in Auchel at 6:45 a.m., and began a thirteen-mile trek southwest to Petit Servins. This trip was practically identical to the one made six days earlier, with a route passing through Camblain Chatelain, Divion, Houdain, and now Fresnicourt, where the men stopped to eat and rest before finally moving forward to Petit Servins. After an overnight rest, the Highlanders were back on the road the next morning at 7:30; this time a five-mile march ending in Bully Grenay, eight miles east of Lens. From their billets in Bully Grenay, the men of the 43rd Battalion observed large clouds of black smoke billowing into the morning sky, caused by what the soldiers jokingly called "coal boxes," shells that created thick, black smoke.

Hill 70 had been an exhausting and costly battle, but it paled in comparison to the attack on Lens. At Lens, the Canadians faced an enemy well entrenched, dug in amongst the ruins of the city, defending heavily fortified and vitally important positions. Thirty minutes before the start of the Canadian Corps attack, German field guns started an intense bombardment of Canadian positions. At precisely 4:25 a.m., the 6th Canadian Infantry Brigade launched an organized frontal assault with a number of infantry brigades, against a ferocious bayonet charge by soldiers of the German 4th Guard Infantry Division.

Strong enemy resistance resulted in the 6th Canadian Infantry Brigade's attack practically dissolving into chaos. A large number of soldiers were killed and wounded, creating a situation that severely impacted the overall effectiveness of the Canadian attack. Consequently, several combat units did not achieve their objectives, although three small parties, of less than twenty men, did manage to attain them. Two brigade attacking-units completed their mission, but that success did not come until the late evening of August 21.

The attack on Lens was, in the opinion of some, a dismal failure. Canadian Corps infantry divisions incurred heavy losses of both men and weapons, whereas Hill 70 was considered a victory. The failure of Canadian Corps commanders and troops to ultimately capture Lens allowed the Imperial German Army to continue its occupation and defence of the city until shortly before the end of World War I.

On the morning of August 22, the Battle of Lens was a disturbingly sad topic of conversation in the 43rd Battalion mess hall, as accounts of the fighting and casualty reports were made known to the soldiers. Many of the soldiers killed in the Lens operation had been close friends of several Cameron Highlanders, especially those who served in a battalion with the 6th Infantry Brigade or in regiments mobilized in Winnipeg. Until the morning of August 22, the 43rd Battalion had been the benefactor of a short hiatus from the rigours of combat, having been in the reserve line. Their leave ended at 2:00 p.m. Orders were posted to vacate the reserve line and move to support section by 9:00 o'clock that evening. Shortly after midnight on August 23, moving in platoon formation and separated by 200 yards from each unit, the 43rd Infantry Battalion left Bully Grenay, to relieve the 28th Canadian Infantry Battalion (Saskatchewan), in the cellars of Cité St. Pierre. After settling in at 3:00 a.m., the Cameron Highlanders were roused from their sleep by incoming German artillery fire. It was in retaliation for a small raid carried out on enemy lines earlier in the evening by troops of the 4th Canadian Infantry Division.

As suddenly as it started, it ended. Quiet returned to Cité St. Pierre, but only until 5:00 a.m. Heavy bombing resumed once again, for about an hour. At the conclusion of heavy-gun artillery shelling, the medium and light guns took over for the remainder of the day. Because of its intensity, Colonel Grassie repositioned 43rd Battalion Headquarters farther from the front as a precautionary measure. In the afternoon of August 23, NCOs from each Company conducted roll calls to determine the battalion's current combat strength. Reports indicated 571 Cameron Highlanders, comprised of 547 ordinary regulars and twenty-four officers.

On August 25, two officers and one hundred troops from the 43rd Battalion were formed into two work parties and ordered to clear front-line trenches and excavate salvage dumps. After ducking sniper bullets for much of the day, the men of B Coy returned to support line to rest, eat, and spend the next several hours watching and listening to both sides shell each other. This would also be the day when one of the youngest members of the 43rd Battalion was killed. The soldier was seventeen-year-old Private Adam Kadannek of Manitoba. Bombs fell until 3:00 p.m. on the 26th, when the Cameron Highlanders were organized again into a work party of 102 men, plus two additional carrying parties of 83 ordinary regulars and two officers. By the end of the second day, all work had been completed and another Cameron Highlander had lost his life; Private Angus R.G. Moore.

The final days of August were exceptionally busy for the Cameron Highlanders of Canada as they continued to defend positions close to the city of Lens. D Coy happened to be the 43rd Battalion's closest unit to German defence installations, and therefore the most vulnerable to attack. Officers from D Coy suspected the Germans would launch a major gas attack, sometime around midnight on August 29, while the weather was still dry and clear, and the wind favourable. Fortunately for D Coy, the gas attack failed to materialize, but they did become a primary target for some extreme shelling and machine-gun fire. This activity prompted the company commander to address the situation, making an urgent appeal to Brigade Headquarters at 4:30 a.m. for retaliatory fire to take the pressure off D Coy. A response was forthcoming, however it altered the situation very little. Therefore it was necessary for D Coy to seek assistance again, at 5:10, 5:30, 7:20, 10:20, and 11:25 a.m. on the morning of August 29.

At noon, the remaining troops of the 43rd Battalion were ordered to move to the right side of the frontage, held by the 87th Canadian Infantry Battalion (Grenadier Guards of Montreal). D Coy, which had been undergoing several hours of intense shelling, was told to extend their forward posts. Company commanders were also advised of a new trench, being dug that evening, extending from the junction of Conductor and Chicory trenches to Nun's Alley. After completion, it became the responsibility of the 43rd Battalion to establish observation and sentry posts as far north as the 58th Battalion positions. On the evening of the 29th, at 10:30 p.m., Special O Coy discharged 200 drums of asphyxiating gas towards the Lens railway station, where a large number of enemy soldiers were entrenched.

Three hours after releasing the toxic gas, D Coy had succeeded in taking control of a frontage previously held by a Grenadier Guards platoon. The next morning, August 30, at 9:30 a.m., D Coy came under a severe mortar attack from German 7.58 calibre Minenwerfe (a class of German short range mortars), firing shells weighing ten pounds, at distances ranging between 2,600 and 3,900 feet. Shortly after D Coy came under fire, the 9th Canadian Infantry Brigade advised the 43rd that the 58th Battalion was about to conduct artillery shelling inside Nun's Alley, at 1:00 p.m., to rid the post of all its German occupiers.

Thirty minutes after the artillery attack ended, the enemy responded with machine gun fire, concentrating on Nun's Alley, in case Canadian soldiers attempted to capture the site. As the combat action continued on into the mid-afternoon, C Coy sent runners to Battalion Headquarters to report both Captain Angus John Gardiner and Lieutenant Fisher had been badly wounded. The company commander requested the two officers be evacuated immediately and replaced. Lieutenants Fowler and Green, chosen as replacements, arrived shortly after the request was made, however, medics arrived too late to save the life of twenty-six-year-old, Simcoe County, Ontario-born, Lieutenant John Thompson Fisher.

D Coy continued to receive the brunt of the German field artillery attack until 8:00 p.m., when the enemy guns fell silent. After seven hours of fierce shelling, the lull provided 9th Brigade officers with an opportunity to assess trench damage and troop casualties. The 58th Infantry Battalion, which initiated the attack against the German positions, reported they had killed twelve enemy soldiers and taken three prisoners — one being an officer. Besides the death of Lieutenant Fisher, twelve Cameron Highlanders were listed as wounded.

The final two combat-related fatalities for the month occurred on August 30-31. During those two days, the enemy took the lives of twenty-one-year-old Charles Edward Wheadon and twenty-nine-year-old Private Alexander McBain.

The warm days of summer were now beginning to fade, replaced by cooler temperatures, shorter days, and a significant change in the weather on the Western Front.

Chapter Sixteen
SEPTEMBER 1917

"There never was a good war or a bad peace."

Benjamin Franklin

On into the month of September, D Coy continued to persevere despite constant and heavy artillery fire being directed at their position. Again, coy officers petitioned the field artillery to assist with a substantive response in retaliation, but were told artillery gunners had over-extended their allotted number of shells, and therefore D Coy was on its own, at least for the time being. The response to their request was understandably unsettling, but they were a determined lot who were not prepared to take "No" as a final answer. Immediately following receipt of the news, a telephone call was placed to the field artillery liaison officer, resulting in D Coy being advised that their request for artillery support would be moved up the chain of command, in the hope of instituting an artillery response.

The first evening in September was crisp and clear. A brilliant, bright moon cast a bluish hue across the dark and grotesque No-Man's Land. It would have been a perfect night, except for the smell of decay, cordite, and stale chemical gas, together with the sound of machine-gun fire and exploding 7.7 calibre artillery shells. German field guns began their usual nightly assault against the 43rd Battalion and D Coy. It was another evening of hell as enemy bullets and bombs claimed seven victims, one a fatality; a thirty-two-year-old, married Scotsman from Monifieth, by the name of Private William Stark. The incoming bombs continued to pound D Coy throughout the night and into the late afternoon of the following day before subsiding.

The weather on September 2, 1917 was bright and sunny. A moderate breeze blew out of the southwest, and then switched to a westerly direction around 3:00 p.m. bringing with it a much cooler airflow. Now that the activity against D Coy was finished for the time being, the Canadian Brigade Artillery started a retaliatory response. Within a matter of a few hours, after the start of the Canadian shelling, another call went out to the 9th Infantry brigade artillery liaison officer advising him that the eighteen-pounders were falling well short of their targets again. The difference in this particular call was the fact that it came from the commander of C Coy; he was concerned about friendly fire hitting his support trenches and killing his brigade troops, such as 43rd Battalion soldier, Private Robert Abigail, who died on September 2.

In the early morning of September 3, the breeze, which had altered direction ten hours earlier, continued to blow in the direction of Lens. This provided the 43rd Battalion with another window of opportunity to release 200 canisters of chlorine and phosgene gas. The Canadian gas attack was quickly answered by the Germans dispatching their own chemical weapons. A number of enemy gas shells landed within the confines of the 43rd Battalion headquarters. In the midst of this gas attack, the enemy also fired off several rounds of medium and heavy artillery shells. Some landed in the billet area of C Coy and fatally wounded one Cameron Highlander, twenty-four-year-old Private James Taylor. Sporadic artillery fire continued throughout the night until 5:30 a.m., when a tense calm fell over the Western Front for the remainder of the day. At 10:00 p.m., in a smooth operation completed in less than eighty minutes, the 43rd Battalion relieved the Black Watch Regiment of the 13th Canadian Infantry Battalion. By 2:00 a.m. on September 4, the Cameron Highlanders had been moved to new billets at Bouvigny Huts.

After a day of rest and clean-up, the 43rd Canadian Infantry Battalion left Bouvigny Huts at 8:45 in the morning, on September 5, for Fraser Camp in Bois des Alleux. They passed through Gouy-Servins and Villers-au-Bois, arriving at 11:30 a.m. While en route to their destination, Private James Ellis was fatally wounded by enemy sniper fire. The following morning, the 43rd Battalion was on the move again. Using light railway from the level crossing at Chaussee Brunehaut, they rode to another crossing, situated on the Bethune-Arras road where they were met by army guides. Two trains were allocated to the battalion; the first departed at 8:00 a.m., the second at 9:30 a.m. Private S.E. Shortliffe and B Coy, together with men from A Coy, bagpipers, scouts, bombers, and a communication section, boarded the first train for Neuville-Saint-Vaast, arriving at 11:00 a.m. At 1:00 p.m., Major W.K. Chandler, second-in-command of the 43rd Battalion, with his Adjutant, Coy Commanders, scouts and signalling officers, departed Neuville-Saint-Vaast to conduct an inspection of a new trench line situated directly opposite Méricourt Trench. In the latter part of July, that location had been the site of intense combat action involving the 43rd Battalion, and other 9th Brigade battalions pitted against the German's 36th Reserve Division. While Major Chandler inspected the terrain and trench systems, 43rd Battalion troops rested before leaving for the front-line, on September 7, to relieve the 2nd Canadian Mounted Rifles Battalion (British Columbia).

A plan prepared by the battalion's Colonel Grassie at a breakfast meeting, on September 7, laid out a strategy that saw his troops occupying No-Man's Land. The plan was to have a number of platoons occupy the narrow wasteland and establish forward observation, sentry, and weapons posts, within a few hundred yards of the enemy. If this proved successful, the Cameron Highlanders would have the benefit of immediate, close range contact with German soldiers from the onset of an attack. Details of the strategic plan were clearly presented by the battalion commander and thoroughly discussed with his officers. Since there was no consensus as to whether to proceed with the plan or not, the meeting was adjourned until 4:00 p.m., for further discussion.

After evening meals, members of the 43rd Battalion departed minutes before 7:00 p.m. to relieve the 2nd Canadian Mounted Rifles Battalion near Méricourt Trench. They moved into support position, on the right side of the Méricourt Line, in Quebec Trench, with Coys A, B, and C. Four platoons from beleaguered D Coy were reassigned; two moved to Battalion Reserve in New Brunswick Trench and the other two platoons relocated to Canada Trench, where the men joined Battalion Headquarters. Lewis machine-gunners were ordered to a ration dump near Vancouver Road. They rendezvoused with scouts from the 2nd Canadian Mounted Rifles Battalion, who guided the gun crews to their respective units. Shortly after midnight, September 8, a telecom message was transmitted by the relieving companies to their battalion headquarters stating: "Your F.219 has been attended to," followed by the name of the coy commander. This coded message was confirmation the 2nd C.M.R. Battalion relief had been carried out successfully.

The front line of the 43rd Canadian Infantry Battalion encompassed a large section of ground. It consisted of an area from Moosejaw Road to Quarries Road; A Coy was situated near the 12th York Battalion on the right, and C Coy on the left, adjacent to the 4th Canadian Mounted Rifles Battalion (Central Ontario). Meanwhile, Coys B and D were advancing along La Folie Road to Petit Vimy, with guides from the Canadian Mounted Rifles leading the way.

September 8 was a cool day. A heavy ground mist shrouded the battlefield preventing Canadian troops from observing what was taking place in front of them, along the German lines. Using the weather as a cover from German observation, Lieutenant-Colonel Grassie scrutinized the new lines from 9:00 a.m. to 3:00 p.m., advancing as close as 600 yards from enemy positions. The close proximity of the Canadian line to the enemy was immediately brought to the attention of 9th Infantry Brigade Headquarters. A communiqué was issued, advising all troop movement east of the Arras-Lens railway to be conducted only within the trench system, especially between the hours of 6:00 a.m. and 8:00 p.m.

At 4:00 that afternoon, a cloudless, blue sky with brilliant sunshine replaced the earlier heavy fog. In his war diary, Lieutenant A.E. Grimes, the 43rd Battalion Adjutant noted the situation in the front line was unusually quiet and therefore a good opportunity for night patrols to reconnoitre the area near the German occupied Méricourt line.

September 9 was much like the afternoon of the previous day. Sunshine and warm temperatures made it ideal for watching an exciting aerial display high above the front lines. It was a spellbinding occasion for S.E. Shortliffe and his friends. They watched fighter pilots, with the Royal Flying Corps, engage equally determined and skilled adversaries in the sky over Northern France. German pilots of the Deutsche Luftstreitkräfte (Imperial German Flying Corps) showed their expertise at aerial combat, crippling five RFC planes for every German plane shot down. The average life expectancy of an Allied fighter pilot in World War I was eleven days.

Two years prior to William Avery "Billy" Bishop becoming a celebrated Canadian hero, he had served in the rat-infested trenches of the Western Front, as an infantryman. It was in one of those front line trenches, in 1915, that Bishop came to the realization that there had to be a better place to fight a war than in a foul-smelling, hole in the ground. Not long after, he watched a squadron of bi-planes return from aerial combat and land in a nearby field.

"It's clean up there! I'll bet you don't get any mud and horseshit on you up there. If you die, at least it will be a clean death."

Billy Bishop got his wish and eventually left the battlefield to become a fighter pilot. He earned the moniker, "ACE" by shooting down a total of 72 enemy planes. This notable accomplishment earned him the Victoria Cross.

Germany dominated the skies. This was due, in part, by their many skilled pilots, as well as the excellent design and development of various models of WWI aeroplanes. One plane in particular, the Fokker Dreidecker tri-plane, the darling of the German fleet, was flown by Baron Manfred von Richthofen — the Red Baron. The twenty-five-year-old Von Richthofen was flying his red Dreidecker on April 21, 1918 when he was killed trying to record his 81st victim. Speculation and debate persisted long after the war, as to who actually shot Baron Manfred von Richthofen's plane out of the sky. One name mentioned was Canadian Captain Arthur Roy Brown, Royal Air

Force 209 Squadron, who was born in Carleton Place, Ontario on December 23, 1893.

Baron Richthofen's fabric-covered, wood-frame Fokker Dreidecker was one of only 900 manufactured with twin Spandau machine guns, capable of firing 7.92mm calibre bullets, between the blades of a synchronized propeller system. On the other side, the British designed and manufactured several superb models of fighter, surveillance and reconnaissance planes, the most notable being the Sopwith Camel.

After entering combat service in June 1917, the pilots of this single-seat bi-plane shot down an incredible 1,300 enemy aircraft between then and the end of the war. The "Camel" had a potential air speed of 115 miles per hour, a flying range of 300 miles, and an altitude ceiling of 20,000 feet. The fighter plane was similar, in many respects, to German fighters — armed with two 7.7mm Vickers-type, mounted machine-guns. Besides the Sopwith Camel, the British also designed and built other models: the Dolphin, Snipe, and Sopwith Pup.

At 8:00 p.m., September 11, the 58th Battalion (Central Ontario) arrived to relieve the 43rd Battalion (Cameron Highlanders of Canada) in the front line; the 43rd moved into the support line. Confirmation was received at Battalion Headquarters at 11:30 that A Coy had taken possession of Montreal Trench and B Coy was occupying New Brunswick Trench. The other two coys were ordered to take up support positions in Canada Trench. However, before the Cameron Highlanders could do so, brigade headquarters rescinded the order for C Coy and had them provide support for two under-strength, British combat units — the 13th York Regiment and Lancaster Regiment. In the meantime, officers and soldiers with 43rd Battalion headquarters were relocated to C.P.R. Trench. A member of the 43rd Infantry battalion, who was wounded on three previous occasions, passed away from injuries received at Lens, in August. Private James Denison How, born in Shelburne, Nova Scotia, son of Reverend and Mrs. Henry How of Annapolis Royal, died on September 11, 1917.

A welcomed cessation of enemy activity, between September 12 and September 17, was used to form two battalion work parties; one of 155 soldiers and the other of 270 men. The work parties constructed new field works (trenches), in addition to rehabilitating and maintaining a number of other existing trenches. Fighting trenches in Vimy and Lens varied in size depending on the terrain. Typically, they measured between seven feet and nine feet deep, and five feet to six feet wide. Dugouts were approximately sixteen feet below surface. In comparison, German dugouts were a minimum of twelve feet deep and occasionally were as deep as a three-storey building.

Trenches were intentionally designed in a zigzag configuration to reduce straight line-of-sight to thirty feet, thereby protecting Canadian soldiers from enemy enfilade rifle fire, should the trench line be breached in a raid or frontal assault. This particular design also lessened the impact on the troops from severe concussion waves resulting from exploding artillery shells within the trench system.

When it came to developing a trench system, British and Canadian armies employed three distinctive methods. The first was known as "entrenching," the second "sapping," and the third "tunnelling." The most efficient method was entrenching. It was also considered the most dangerous. It involved large work parties excavating the full length of a trench while standing above ground, in the line of fire. Protection for soldiers was minimal. Entrenching was usually carried out during times when the workers were less likely to be observed by the enemy, such as night, or during periods of smoke screens and heavy fog. Sapping extended the length of a trench by removing the end face in either direction. Since working space was very limited, only a limited number of men were able to perform the excavation work at any given time. The last method, known as tunnelling, proved to be the most practical and successful. Trench tunnelling used a process similar to sapping, except a roof of soil was left undisturbed until the trench was completed. On numerous occasions many of these "roofs" collapsed and buried soldiers working below. Engineering manuals of the British Army suggested a 450-man workforce required six hours to complete 275 yards of trench work.

New Brunswick Trench was determined to require substantial rehabilitation as a result of recent heavy mortar shelling. Restoration work was needed to repair a large portion of the trench; several areas of the walls, parados, and parapets had completely collapsed. Even rehabilitating a trench had its dangers on the Western Front. Live artillery shells lay buried in the ground. There were many times when unexploded bombs remained hidden beneath the subsoil. As a result, it was not uncommon for a soldier's shovel or pickaxe to strike and detonate a bomb, while he was digging a trench or repairing a damaged one.

As an example, on September 13, a work party from B Coy discovered two un-detonated bombs when their shovels penetrated an area of soft soil. The terrifying sound of metal striking metal was the last thing heard before two deafening explosions erupted, sending soldiers and dirt flying into the air. After landing on the ground, members of B Coy, without regard for their own safety, rushed to drag the four soldiers out of range of sniper and machine-gun fire. Not a single bullet was fired from the other side of No-Man's Land. All four soldiers suffered severe injuries; imbedded shell fragments, deep lacerations, dismemberment, broken bones, concussions, and perforated ear drums. All four privates were evacuated by light rail to a casualty clearing station in Neuville-Saint-Vaast. The fact that enemy snipers and machine-gunners did not take advantage of the situation was surprising, but not unheard of. On occasion both Allied and German infantrymen acquiesced and allowed a very brief amount of time for the wounded to be removed from No-Man's Land, without fear of being shot. It was a humanitarian act, in an inhumane war. Company commanders on both sides, however, seldom gave their "official" approval to withhold fire and, in most cases, specifically disallowed stretcher-bearers from retrieving wounded comrades. Sometimes those orders were ignored, despite the possible consequences associated with acts of insubordination.

September 17, four days before the end of summer, was the final day for rehab work on the front-line trench system, employing 155 ordinary regulars and two officers from the 43rd Battalion. Once the work was completed, the support line was transferred to the Princess Patricia's Canadian Light Infantry, at 12:20 a.m., September 18. The Cameron Highlanders of Canada moved on to Vancouver Camp, in Neuville-Saint-Vaast; the last Coy arrived at 3:30 in the morning.

Twelve hours after entering Vancouver Camp, the battalion was on the move again. This time, they travelled 3.6 miles on a narrow gauge, light railway line to Ottawa Camp, five miles northwest of Arras, near the historic Abbey of Mont-Saint-Eloi. (Extensive narrow-gauge railway systems served the front-line trenches of both sides in World War I.) In close formation the Cameron Highlanders marched from the support line, with 500 yards between each coy, until they finally reached the rail yard. There, at Territorial Dump, they boarded trains at 3:30 p.m. A Coy and B Coy were transported on Number 1 train with Lieutenant Smart. Number 2 train carried C Coy and D Coy, under command of Lieutenant McNally. The last train, with Major Whitaker, transported the 43rd Battalion Headquarters staff and all additional infantry personnel to Ottawa Camp.

When they arrived, the troops once again saw the familiar sight of the abbey, perched high on a hill overlooking the Douai Plain, in full view of Vimy Ridge. The Abbey of Mont-Saint-Eloi, which was constructed in the 7th Century, was destroyed (except for two towers) in 1793, at the beginning of the French Revolution. In 1836 French authorities restored it, but during the war of 1914-18, the five upper levels were demolished by German artillery fire.

At Ottawa Camp, Private Shortliffe and the Cameron Highlanders relaxed for two days, in between preparing their combat kits, in anticipation of a forthcoming combat operation rumoured to take place in the Ypres Salient. Accounts had been circulating; the Third Battle of Ypres had not developed as expected. This was evident by the high rate of casualties suffered by both British and ANZAC Forces, with only a small territorial gain to show for their sacrifice. Therefore, after the Canadian Corps success at Vimy Ridge, speculation was building that Passchendaele would be the next major test for General Currie's Canadian Corps.

Another big event was occupying the minds of the men of the 3rd Canadian Infantry Division. It was a full day devoted to track and field, marksmanship, and grenade-throwing competitions. This divisional event preceded the competition between all four infantry divisions, scheduled to be held September 29.

On Monday, September 24, at 7:45 a.m., B Coy assembled on the training grounds of Ottawa Camp to begin combat drills. These drills ran until the noon hour. Afterwards, Private S.E. Shortliffe and his comrades proceeded to Divisional Gas School, where they renewed their small-box respirators and replaced their Hypo Helmet gas masks. The Hypo Helmet gas mask was introduced in July 1915, but only provided real protection against chlorine gas. A similarly designed gas mask, called the P-Helmet, featuring two mica eye goggles in place of a single visor, followed the Hypo Helmet and was made available to the infantry in November 1915. The most recent gas mask was, the PH Helmet. It too, was identical to the P-Helmet, except it was treated with a mixture of hexamethylene tetramine, to neutralize the deadly phosgene gas. This particular protective gas mask gear was used from January 1916 until February 1918.

After returning with a new, small-box respirator and a PH-Helmet, Private S.E. Shortliffe joined his coy at 3:00 o'clock for thirty minutes of target practice, then attended an afternoon lecture in the YMCA tent, presented by Lieutenant-Colonel Carthew, commander of RFC No. 16 Squadron. This would be the first of two sessions; a second was scheduled for the following day. The lectures explained the battlefield role of the various planes, aerial firepower support available to ground forces, types of shells and calibres of bombs carried by the planes, and finally, an overview of aerial surveillance and photography reconnaissance capabilities. Soldiers found the lecture sessions interesting, informative, and helpful, especially the explanation concerning ground assault troops and pilots working together during a combat operation to ensure success of the mission.

Those who had attended the previous day's lectures were dispatched to the taped trenches on September 25, at 7:45 a.m. They began attack practice and special bomb and machine gun training. At 2:45 p.m., Lieutenant-Colonel Grassie, Major Chandler, and four company commanders travelled by horseback to No. 16 Squadron in Chamblain l'Abbe, near Arras. While the 43rd Battalion Commander and his party had reached the aerodrome, eight additional officers, six NCOs and four ordinary regulars, were arriving by army bus. The men began by inspecting several Sopwith fighter planes, learning about the newly developed high-impact bombs, and other special weaponry, used by the Royal Flying Corps and the Royal Naval Air Service. At the conclusion of the information session, Colonel Grassie accepted an invitation from the commander of No. 16 Squadron, to take a short flight in a two-seater Sopwith bi-plane. The same invitation was also extended to the Battalion Adjutant, Lieutenant A.E. Grimes, three other officers, and one ordinary regular. Meanwhile at Ottawa Camp, near Mont-Saint-Eloi, troops of the 43rd Battalion were enjoying a two-hour brass band concert, in an open field adjacent to their billets.

The next two mornings, September 26 and 27, were set aside for attack practice in the taped trench areas, followed by mandatory clean-up of huts and grounds in the camp area. In the meantime, Colonel Grassie, Majors Chandler and Charlton, Captain Galt, Lieutenants Smart, Fowler, Shankland, and McNally and fifty other ranks left at 8:00 a.m. for the small French hamlet of Wailly, situated approximately ten miles from Mont-Saint-Eloi and four miles southwest of Arras. While there, the officers and infantrymen observed an interesting presentation and demonstration by the British Tank Corps, on the utilization of the armoured tank in ground-combat operations. This concept was being aggressively promoted within the Canadian Corps, as a potentially important component in fighting a ground war, with its motorized weapon support, on the battlefield. The idea, although considered by some as having merit, was not universally praised by most Canadian Corps officers. Those officers were somewhat sceptical of the benefit an armoured tank might bring to a ground attack when conditions like marshlands, deep mud, and wide craters, would be serious challenges for a tank. This concern was clearly demonstrated; some officers were obviously reluctant to endorse the idea of armoured tanks, especially after they were aware of their reputation for being unreliable.

The first tank arrived in Europe on August 30, 1916, and within two weeks had made its debut in the Battle of the Somme. Its initial appearance was not an auspicious occasion; only thirty-six out of fifty tanks saw combat. Two things were mainly responsible for their ineffectiveness in the theatre of war: mechanical malfunctions and becoming mired in mud.

Despite its short-comings, though, the tank managed to reduce the cavalry to a state of redundancy. Up until the Battle of the Somme, many of the calvary's combat engagements saw a tremendous number of troops and horses lose their lives, at the hands of enemy machine-gunners, during horseback frontal attacks or while hopelessly stuck in deep mud. The visionary behind the large, moving mass of steel weaponry was Lieutenant-Colonel Ernest Dunlop Swinton. It was Colonel Swinton's personal achievement when he drove the first tank he had painstakingly designed. Swinton's armoured vehicle reached a top speed of four miles per hour on level ground, and turned sharply while climbing parapets and traversing eight-foot-wide shell craters, all within a twenty-mile radius. The fighting tanks, on display for the 43rd Battalion to inspect, were described in detail, emphasizing advantages and soft-pedaling disadvantages, in an assault operation. Members of the 43rd Battalion inspected two tank models. The first was a thirty-ton monster. Most of the officers and other ranks felt it was appropriately named, "Big Willie." A second and smaller version was known as "Little Willie." At the end of the day, it appeared coy officers were still divided over whether the armoured tank was a great idea or just a flash-in-the-pan. Some found it to be an excellent mobile attack machine. It fired massive amounts of rifle and machine gun bullets and increased the battalion's ground advantage by its firepower supporting the assault troops. The more cautious officers were concerned about certain limitations in the construction and design of the tank, in particular its vulnerability to becoming immobilized after receiving a direct hit by a powerful enemy artillery shell. But all were in agreement that the steel plating was extremely effective in repelling small arms fire.

Most troubling to the ordinary regulars, was the interior working environment of the tank. Being confined inside an armoured tank was as deadly as being exposed to chemical weapons in the trenches. The interior air was incredibly contaminated, much of it deadly carbon-monoxide. In addition to the real threat of carbon-monoxide poisoning, tank crews had to contend with fumes emitted from gasoline and oil, and the smell of cordite. Excruciating heat, generated by the tank's guns and engine, produced a hot and uncomfortable interior. Tank drivers and gunners had to also wear steel helmets and chain mail gas masks; all standard issue for a Willie tank. At the end of the demonstration and lecture, the infantrymen and officers of the 43rd Battalion returned to Ottawa Camp. Most of those in attendance were not convinced of the tank's usefulness and reliability, however, they were resigned to the fact they would, in all probability, be fighting next to a Willie tank sometime in the very near future.

September 28 was a day of considerable activity in Ottawa Camp. An assembly at 9:00 a.m. was followed by bayonet and target practice. Later in the day, the battalion was given a choice of attending either a band concert in the YMCA Hut or being entertained by the Dumbbells at 3:00 p.m. and again at 8:00 p.m. That evening, the troops were informed all training sessions scheduled for the 29th had been cancelled. Troops would be attending the Canadian Corps Athletic Meet in Villers-au-Bois. This competition involved all those who had qualified earlier, at battalion and divisional levels. Soldiers competed in track and field and strength and endurance events, as well as in the highlight of the meet, the Canadian Corps Rifle Competition. Winners of the rifle competition were eight members of the Canadian Light Horse Regiment. Those marksmen were: Lieutenant Ernest Wadge, Sergeant Edward Alexander Faulkner, Lance-Corporal Oscar Drakeley, and Privates Roy E. Jackson, Athol Dudgeon, H. Scott, J. Tyller, and J.L. Clarke. The winning team was presented with the Canadian Corps Rifle Shield by Major-General David Watson, commander of the 4th Canadian Infantry Division.

Sunday, September 30, 1917, was a day in which members of the 43rd Canadian Infantry Battalion and the 116th Canadian Infantry Battalion attended Divine services at 10:00 a.m., led by Captain G.C.F. Pringle, battalion chaplain. Immediately following church services, a ceremonial parade and presentation of medals and decorations took place. Canadian Corps Commander, General Sir Arthur W. Currie, K.C.M.G; C.B., presented Military Crosses and Military Medals to eleven soldiers of the 43rd Infantry Battalion Cameron Highlanders of Canada. Recipients of commendation were: Major T.W. Taylor (Military Cross), Lieutenant F.S. Fowler (Military Cross), Lieutenant H.W.R. Gemmel (Military Cross), Sergeant F. Wigston (Distinguished Conduct Medal and Military Medal), Sergeant G. Wood (Military Medal), Corporal H.E. Baker (Military Medal), Private J.E. Sanders (Military Medal), Private J. Leitch (Military Medal), Private A.W. Staniland (Military Medal), Private G.A. Brown (Military Medal) and Lieutenant J.D. Verner (Military Cross).

At the conclusion of the ceremony, a list of names granted leave from combat duty was posted. The granting of leaves at this particular time reaffirmed the rumours; the 43rd Battalion would soon be going into combat, in the Third Battle of Ypres. One of the jubilant soldiers selected in the first furlough grouping was Private S. E. Shortliffe.

Chapter Seventeen
OCTOBER 1917

"Older men declare war, but it is the youth who must fight and die."

Herbert Hoover

The month of October began as it would end — wet, cold and miserable. Despite the disgusting weather, Ernie Shortliffe was happy to be leaving to enjoy a small degree of normality, even if only for a short time. On the recommendation of friends and his coy commander, Ernie chose the town of Doullens, France, approximately twenty-five miles from Camp Ottawa, as the place to spend his leave. As Ernie was departing, three officers arrived to assist the 43rd Battalion in an operation against the German-held Méricourt line, planned for the night of October 5, however, due to the persistent inclement weather, the mission was cancelled. The following day, October 6, Private John McKay was killed, possibly by a shrapnel shell as his body was never found.

During the time Ernie was on leave, the 43rd Infantry Battalion continued to train and rehearse for a major battle. On October 11, at 9:00 a.m., the Cameron Highlanders of Canada bid farewell to Ottawa Camp and Mont-Saint-Eloi. They had spent the last twenty-three days at Ottawa Camp; the next camp, in Frevillers, was twelve miles away. After reaching Frevillers, the Cameron Highlanders joined the other battalions from the 9th Infantry Brigade, in preparing to host a special visit by General Sir Henry Sinclair Horne, commander of the British

First Army. Although everything and everyone was ready to welcome General Horne, word was received at the last minute, cancelling his visit. It was learned later that General Horne was called back to his headquarters in advance of an assault about to take place, against Passchendaele Ridge. The British were determined to secure a victory in the Ypres Salient, especially one as significant as Passchendaele, but in order to achieve this goal, it would eventually require the leadership and sacrifice of the officers and men of the Canadian Corps.

As Private S.E. Shortliffe's comrades in Frevillers continued their long hours of physical conditioning, combat drill, and rapid fire rifle practice, Ernie was relaxing on the banks of the Authie River with a loaf of French bread, red wine, and a pretty mademoiselle. Ever since he landed in France, on November 14, 1916, Private S.E. Shortliffe had counted his blessings, giving thanks each and every day for not having fallen victim to the bullets, bombs, and bayonets at Vimy Ridge, Lens, Méricourt, and Avion. Now, after ten months of duty on the Western Front, Stephen Ernest Shortliffe found himself speculating how long his luck would last before the "Sands of time run out."

Chapter Eighteen
OCTOBER 14, 1917

"Battles are above all else struggles of morale. Defeat is inevitable as soon as the hope of victory ceases."

Excerpt from French Army Field Regulations

It was Sunday morning, October 14, 1917; a simply glorious day was about to begin in the French countryside of Nord-Pas-de Calais, in a town named Doullens, in the Region of Picardie. The citizenry of Doullens were sometimes referred to, as "Doullennais" or "Doullennaises," and were extremely proud and patriotic. It was not uncommon to find people born in Doullens being able to trace their heritage as far back as 1595, a period when the town had been besieged and occupied, and many of its inhabitants massacred by the Spaniards. Doullens had been a part of France since the year 1225. In about the same era, both the Church of Notre Dame, with its Gothic architecture, and the Church of St. Pierre were built. In 1917, both of these structures still dominated the town's skyline, however, only the Church of Notre Dame was still being used as a house of worship. The Church of St. Pierre had been damaged many years before and never restored, being used as a barn for poultry and livestock during much of the 19th Century.

Narrow cobblestone streets wound their way through the town, past rows of small cottage-style homes, stores, cafes, and attractive inns. One inn in particular stood out among all the others. It was a two-storey, red-brick building, with a small, rectangular sign hanging about two feet above the entranceway, with the name: L'Auberge de Doullens. Situated only a five- minute walk from the town's market square, L'Auberge de Doullens, with its unique oval windows, custom crafted gables, and attractive clay-tile roof, had been probably built between 1643-1715, during the reign of Louis XV, King of France. The original exterior architecture had been meticulously preserved through careful restoration, while modernization had been made to the interior in order to enhance its functionality.

L'Auberge de Doullens had for many years been a popular bed and breakfast establishment — a favourite with visitors and locals alike. It was admired by guests for its relaxing decor, exquisite meals, extensive selection of Bordeaux wines, and the large varieties of decadent pastries and delectable French breads. Until the outbreak of war in 1914, tourists of wealth and influence travelled from various parts of continental Europe to the Picardie Region to explore and enjoy the beauty of the countryside and the warmth of its people. World War I dramatically altered the landscape of France, but it did not change the people. During the four years of war, the inn was patronized by men in uniform from Great Britain, Australia, New Zealand, and Canada. These guests were not interested in spending their precious furlough and combat pay in the bars and brothels of Paris, London, or Dublin. Those staying at L'Auberge de Doullens were content with peace and quiet, and safety from the bullets, bombs, and bayonets on the Western Front. To a certain extent, Doullens was an anomaly. Unlike similar-size towns in Northern France, it had escaped the massive devastation of the Great War, even though situated only hours from the front-lines. Doullens, however, would not entirely escape the ravages of war. It became the scene of combat action during the Amiens offensive, in August 1918.

The tick-tock emanating from an old grandfather clock in a downstairs hallway could distinctly be heard counting the minutes before the pendulum announced a new hour. Dawn ushered in a brilliant, sunny morning. White, wispy clouds drifted lazily across a vibrant, blue sky. Rays of sunshine penetrated a small bedroom through an east window where a young man, with dark, short-cropped hair and a thin moustache, was beginning to awake. Outside, the serenity of the morning was abruptly interrupted by the raspy sound of a bird, perched on a tall oak tree near the window. This particular bird, was called an "ortolan" or "gros oiseau," and was considered, by the French, to be a special delicacy, especially when roasted in Armagnac, a French brandy. At dinner, the ortolan was served as part of a medieval ritual, which included the guests wearing linen napkins on their heads.

A small automobile, affectionately nicknamed the "Baby Peugeot," rumbled down the street. On the sidewalk, a cyclist rang the handlebar bell on his bicycle to alert a family of Sunday strollers. Four elderly gentlemen, dressed in blue cotton trousers and white linen shirts, sat around a wrought-iron table in the courtyard of L'Auberge de Doullens sipping their morning coffee from demi-tasses. As the men smoked their pipes and discussed the war, they could clearly hear the all too familiar sound of machine gun fire and exploding shells somewhere off in the distance. Curious, one of the white-haired gentlemen raised a pair of binoculars to his eyes and focused on a formation of German black Gothas dropping bombs on targets a few miles away. "Mon Dieu," he exclaimed as he described what was happening.

What the elderly gentleman was witnessing was the final attempt by the Germans to harass the Allies before consolidating their forces in the Ypres Salient, in the defense of Passchendaele.

Meanwhile, the aromatic smell of pipe tobacco drifted from the courtyard below to the slightly open bedroom window where a soldier was stirring from a night's sleep. Squinting at the sight of the intrusive daylight, he rolled over and reached for a gold pocket watch lying on a night table near his bed. After checking the time, he pulled aside the warm, woollen blankets and quickly lifted his five-foot, nine-inch frame from the bed. He then gathered a large towel and facecloth from inside a closet and hurried down the hall for a morning hot bath.

On the main floor of the inn, there were the familiar sounds of pots and pans being placed on a kitchen stove amid the clatter of dishes being set on the dining room table. There was also the faint murmur of familiar voices, intermingled with a soft female voice singing in French. That melodious sound belonged to Madame Suzanne Antoinette Bonnet, co-owner of L'Auberge de Doullens with her husband Michel. Madame Bonnet was an attractive lady, who possessed a youthful exuberance and a sincere, warm smile. Unlike Monsieur Bonnet, a chef d'escadron (unit commander) in the French Army, Madame Bonnet was remarkably proficient in English. This was a particular quality that served her well with the mostly unilingual army clientele.

The Bonnets were a comparatively small family by French-Catholic standards, having only one child, a dark-haired daughter named Monique-Estelle. This nineteen-year-old mademoiselle possessed her mother's charm and her father's sense of responsibility. Most days she could be found at the Hôtel de Ville (Doullens city hall), where she was employed as an administrative clerk. At the end of each workday and on weekends, Monique-Estelle helped with chores around the inn, especially with the preparation of meals for the guests.

As the young soldier slowly made his way from the bedroom to the dining room, he paused momentarily on the stairs to view a portrait of Michel Bonnet. In the photograph, Monsieur Bonnet, dressed in a French officer's uniform, was posed sitting stiffly in a high-back chair, both hands placed on top of each other on what appeared to be a carved-ivory sword handle. His expression was unsmiling and serious, with piercing, dark eyes that seemed to follow the soldier as he proceeded to walk down the stairs. Another striking feature of the man in the oval picture frame, was his full-face beard. A beard was commonly grown by both officers and other ranks of the French infantry; a fact that did not go unnoticed by the men of the British Expeditionary Force, who often referred to them as "Poilu," meaning hairy one.

As the soldier, dressed in his regimental kilt, stepped into the hallway and past the grandfather clock, he was greeted by a scene of eggs, bacon, porridge, French bread, honey, tea, wine, and a variety of French pastries, all laid out in abundance on the dining room table. After bidding the other guests a good morning, he took his seat at the table.

The only Canadian soldier spending his leave at L'Auberge de Doullens was me, Private Stephen Ernest Shortliffe, a member of the 43rd Infantry Battalion, Cameron Highlanders of Canada. After a delicious breakfast and a final glass of wine, I excused myself and returned to my room where I packed my belongings in a haversack. It was time to take leave of the inn and re-join my battalion now encamped at Frevillers, 22 miles north of Doullens. Our battalion has been there since 11 of October.

Furloughs were something every foot-soldier lived for, but sadly, in too many cases, didn't survive long enough to receive. There was a definite inequality in the granting of time away from combat duty. An officer was given as many as four furloughs a year, while ordinary regulars had to serve with the Canadian Expeditionary Force (CEF) for twelve months before being eligible for a one-time, fourteen-day pass. There were, however, exceptions to the rule. Occasionally, a compassionate company commander would give his troops a leave from active duty, especially after they had spent an unusually long period of time on the front-line where they were subjected to intense hostile fire. Battalion commanders also scheduled leaves for soldiers prior to, or immediately after, a major combat operation, depending on the circumstances at the time.

Canadian infantrymen continually vented their frustration concerning the inequality of the furlough system. In their opinion, it was a blatant, discriminatory practice against non-commissioned officers (NCOs) and privates. The "grunts," as they often called themselves, were the men who were called upon to do the heavy lifting, without regard for life or limb. These trench warriors prayed they would survive Jerry's bombs and machine-gun fire, in order to move up the list. It was not uncommon for soldiers totally exhausted from a disproportionate number of days in the trenches, to volunteer for extremely dangerous field assignments. The motivation to place one's life on the line, was the promise of a leave from combat duty at the end of the assignment. It was a risk many soldiers were willing to accept, in order to secure a short reprieve from the battlefield. The issuance of furloughs continued to be a contentious issue with the ordinary regular for most of the war.

Upon returning to my room, I quickly finished packing. In front of a full-length mirror, I double-checked my uniform to ensure boots, belt buckle, cap badge, and the nine tunic buttons were perfectly polished. Satisfied, I slowly walked to the door, taking one last look to make sure I hadn't forgotten anything, before turning and heading downstairs.

Bidding "au revoir" to Madame Bonnet and her daughter Monique-Estelle, Private S.E. Shortliffe left on his journey to join his comrades in Frevillers. Shortly after leaving the inn, he crossed the Authie River and joined a long procession of troops, vehicles, and weapons heading north to the Belgium frontier. The main road from Doullens to Frevillers was typical of most throughout much of French Flanders — narrow, rutted, muddy, and sometimes extremely dusty. From time to time, convoys had to detour around large areas of shell craters, in order to keep the supply of soldiers, weapons, and ammunition moving northward. Private S.E. Shortliffe's journey on Sunday, October 14, would cross the Nord-Pas-de-Calais countryside where several significant battles had been fought, and where Allied forces still frequently engaged the enemy.

The seemingly endless line of soldiers marched alongside transports of all sizes; some motorized, and others horse-drawn. The scene was reminiscent of caravans of nomadic tribes crossing Africa's Sahara Desert. Instead of an idyllic scene of sand dunes and palm trees, though, the British Expeditionary Force caravan encountered shell craters, rusted barbed wire, immobilized war machinery, and air filled with the stench of death. The poor condition of the main road was often responsible for bringing the procession to an abrupt halt, in order to change a flat tire on one of the many canvas-covered trucks carrying supplies. Army transports, field ambulances, ammunition wagons, and contingents of reinforcements were all moving in a singular direction, towards the Western Front. Moving in the opposite direction were field ambulances, containing the severely wounded on their way to a military hospital in either France or England.

After walking a considerable distance, Private S.E. Shortliffe stopped for a short rest and to eat the lunch prepared for him by Monique-Estelle at the inn. Removing his haversack, Ernie sat down to eat lunch next to a tall tree, only one of a small number untouched by the ravages of war. At the end of his meal, Ernie pulled out a Craven "A," lit it up and carefully exhaled a smoke ring into the October air. Watching nearby was a young soldier, a red-haired Irishman, who said he was all out of cigarettes and wondered if Ernie could spare a "fag." Before the Irishman finished his sentence, a flat metal case was tossed his way. The soldier, a member of the 36th (Ulster) Division, said he was part of a four-man Vickers machine-gun crew attached to General Hubert Gough's British Fifth Army. He said in June his unit had fought in the Battle of Messines and it was during that battle that the 36th Division was declared one of the best combat divisions in the British Expeditionary Force. In July, after the Battle of Messines had ended, the 36th (Ulster) Division joined other infantry divisions from Great Britain, Australia, and New Zealand for the Third Battle of Ypres (Battle of Passchendaele). During the first month of the battle, his combat division had endured thirteen straight days of heavy artillery fire while moving weapons and supplies through the mud in the Ypres Salient.

The young man continued to tell Private S.E. Shortliffe that despite exhaustion and diminishing morale, General Gough had ordered the 36th (Ulster) Division to advance against a number of extremely well-fortified and heavily-defended German positions, which had been untouched by the British Field Artillery. Flicking his cigarette butt into the air, the Irishman concluded by telling Shortliffe his division had suffered 3,600 casualties by mid-August, which represented fifty percent of their total strength. It was clear the Irishman needed a break from war. As the two rose to depart, a group of shell-shocked British infantrymen silently shuffled, zombie-like, along the roadway. Others could be heard coughing, wheezing and vomiting — a definite sign of chemical gas exposure.

After finishing our smokes, we stood up and shook hands. Wishing each other God-speed, we went our separate ways. As I joined a procession of comrades heading north, I also observed a number of Bosche POWs, being escorted by an Aussie platoon. They were on their way to internment camps, somewhere near Doullens or perhaps Amiens. For them the war is over. Lucky bastards!

As Private S.E. Shortliffe resumed his march to Frevillers, he heard a voice calling his name. Glancing over his shoulder, he recognized the familiar face of a fellow Cameron Highlander. Somehow, this young man had managed to finagle a ride on a wooden supply wagon on its way to the 43rd Battalion Quarter-Master store. The soldier, a Scotsman from Aberdeen, had emigrated to Canada in 1910 and enlisted in Winnipeg on May 9, 1916, on the same day as Private S.E. Shortliffe.

Scotty and I had been part of a group of about a dozen men from our coy to have completed a year of duty and therefore, qualified for a fourteen-day furlough. Scotty had spent his time in Paris and had many stories, most of which were significantly more exciting than mine. I'd relaxed and rested, ate wonderful home-cooked meals, and enjoyed the companionship of a young mademoiselle. My friend, on the other hand, had partied along the River Seine and in most of the cafes on the Champs–Elysees.

The Scotsman paused for a moment in his storytelling to retrieve a bottle of 1907 Bordeaux. The wine was a gift from the proprietor of a small Parisian café on Boulevard de Grenelle, a ten-minute walk from the famous Eiffel Tower. The soldier, accompanied by a bevy of femme fatales, had routinely frequented the café during his two-week stay in Paris. There was little doubt that his patronage contributed substantially to the overall income of the establishment. To demonstrate his appreciation, the owner had presented the Canadian soldier, during his last evening in the City of Lights, with the bottle of wine, which he now offered Ernie. Several long swigs quickly produced an empty bottle.

As the two friends raucously sang the last chorus of "Mademoiselle from Armentieres," an aircraft engine could be heard approaching the convoy. It was the unmistakable sound of a German Fokker. Everyone and everything came to a halt. Soldiers and prisoners scrambled for cover. Private S.E. Shortliffe automatically did what he had been trained to do; leap off the wagon to avoid enemy fire and roll into a nearby ditch for cover. Within a split second, machine gun bullets spewed forth from the Fokker bi-plane. Lead projectiles pierced transport vehicles, causing petrol tanks to erupt in an explosion of orange and red fireballs. Heroic efforts were made to disable the plane, however, without success. There was only one strafing run made before the enemy pilot banked his fighter and disappeared off into the horizon.

In the aftermath of the attack, Private S.E. Shortliffe stood up and surveyed the chaotic scene around him. Officers shouted orders. Prisoners were rounded up and secured. Medics and stretcher-bearers rushed to the wounded. Disabled vehicles were pushed off the road. The wooden limber that Private S.E. Shortliffe and his fellow Highlander had been riding on had been riddled with bullets. Both driver and horses lay in pools of blood. Ernie shouted for his friend but heard no response. On the opposite side of the wagon, a medic yelled that he had found a wounded soldier — but it was too late. The young man from Aberdeen, Scotland had died instantly, struck in the head by a bullet, which entered above his right ear.

After burying the dead in shallow graves in a nearby field, the convoy regrouped and continued on its way. Private S.E. Shortliffe finally arrived in Frevillers, in the late afternoon. After locating his billet, he reported for duty. A sergeant handed Ernie a list of items to be obtained from the quartermaster to be carried with him when the battalion relocated later that evening. The list included: two days of rations with mess cans, five Mills bombs, shovel, gas mask, small-box respirator (SBR), 150 rounds of .303 ammunition, steel helmet, Lee Enfield rifle, bayonet, leather jerkin, wool blanket, ground sheet, extra woollen socks, packsack, and the old reliable greatcoat.

Within an hour of finishing supper, the weather had changed from pleasant to simply bad. The weather, on the Western Front is enemy number-two, in this war. It can and usually does, deliver everything, at any time of day. Monstrous rainstorms, dense fog, and cold mist, sweltering heat, gale force winds, thunderstorms, and ice and snow. That is what I have to look forward to every day I live in this Godforsaken hell. The worst weather for me is a cold north wind and a heavy rain. That is especially true during morning parade and battalion inspections. Today, after inspection, we left Frevillers and marched four miles south to the village of Tincques. There, we boarded a train for an overnight ride to Godewaersvelde, which is situated along the frontier between France and Belgium.

Chapter Nineteen
OCTOBER 15, 1917

"The nation must be taught to bear losses. No amount of skill on the part of the higher commanders, no training, however good, on the part of the officers and men, no superiority of arms and ammunition, however great, will enable victories to be won without the sacrifice of men's lives. The nation must be prepared to see heavy casualty lists."

General Sir Douglas Haig Chief of Staff of the
British Expeditionary Force (BEF)

The train, carrying four battalions of the 9th Canadian Infantry Brigade, (including the 43rd Battalion) arrived in Godewaersvelde at 11:25 a.m. on October 15, during a severe wind and rainstorm. After detraining, the Cameron Highlanders were piped into their next camp on the outskirts of a 450-year-old French village named Caëstre, situated three miles south of Godewaersvelde. Two weeks prior to the arrival of the 43rd Battalion, Caëstre had suffered a devastating German artillery attack on September 30. Eighteen-pounders had caused extensive damage as well as killing several of its 1,517 citizens.

Over the next two days, immediately following parade inspection at 9:45 a.m., the 43rd Battalion Coys were divided into platoons, each unit consisting of twenty-nine privates, a platoon captain, one sergeant, two corporals and two lance-corporals. Once this had been completed, all platoons attended a series of lectures and demonstrations concerning modern combat warfare. Special attention was given to the salient mud and water in Flanders and how it would impact on the success of raids, night patrols, reconnaissance intelligence gathering and trench warfare. These were only a part of the many components making up a combat program designed specifically to ensure victory on the Western Front. Since the beginning of WWI, all combatants had embraced a plan to fight in and from an excavation in the ground, called a "trench." That strategy may have been a serious miscalculation on the part of both the Triple Entente and Triple Alliance. Trench warfare, in the opinion of historians, may have prevented the Great War from ending months, or even years earlier, thus saving many lives. However, military strategists were convinced that the war would be either won, or lost, in the trenches. That mindset continued to prevail until the final shot was fired, on November 11, 1918.

Troop training at Caëstre Camp also revisited the subject of chemical gas deployment and personal protection. Syllabuses, the army training manuals, repeatedly stressed the importance of gas masks and SBRs. Part of the chemical-warfare training was to educate the soldiers on recognizing and preparing for an attack of chlorine, phosgene, and mustard gasses. It was in the spring of 1915, when troops of the 1st Canadian Infantry Division, under Lieutenant-General Edwin Alderson, experienced their first gas attack during a combat operation, near the village of Neuve Chapelle. Regularly scheduled training sessions and improved gas protection equipment reduced the fatality rate throughout the remainder of the war. It may be surprising to many to learn that only four percent of all war casualties were the result of exposure to chemical weapons.

On October 17, Private John McLaughlin, a twenty-five-year-old former Scottish farmer and member of the Cameron Highlanders of Canada, passed away from severe injuries inflicted upon him weeks earlier by the enemy. Private Mclaughlin was buried in St. Sever Cemetery, Rouen, France.

Chapter Twenty
OCTOBER 18, 1917

"The power to wage war is the power to wage war successfully."

Charles Evans Hughes

On October 18, Canadian Corps regiments gradually arrived in the Ypres Salient. It was the job of the Canadian Infantry to relieve II ANZAC Corps who were entrenched in Flanders plain, in close proximity to 's Graventafel Ridge and Passchendaele Ridge. It was the first time all four of Canada's infantry divisions were under the single command of a Canadian military officer. Lieutenant-General, Sir Arthur William Currie, an intelligent, pragmatic individual with impeccable integrity, was considered by many as the most capable commanding officer ever produced by Canada.

Arthur W. Currie was one of the first Canadians to answer the call-to-arms, on August 5, 1914, one day after England declared war on Germany, Austria-Hungary, and Italy (The Triple Alliance). Within eight months of having enlisted, Currie had risen to the rank of lieutenant-colonel and commander of the 2nd Canadian Brigade, during the Second Battle of Ypres, in April 1915. Less than half a year later, Currie was promoted to the rank of lieutenant-general with the 1st Canadian Infantry Division. In his new role as division commander, General Currie led the 1st Division into battle at Mount Sorrel, in the spring of 1916, followed by the Battle of the Somme in September, and the Battle of Vimy Ridge in April, 1917. In June 1917, he became

Sir Arthur William Currie when knighted by His Majesty, King George V of England. It was shortly thereafter that Currie was given command of the four Canadian infantry divisions, replacing General Sir Julian Byng.

(source: Library and Archives Canada)
Canadian Corps Commander, General Sir Arthur William Currie (seated in the middle), poses with his officers. The Battle of Passchendaele, October 26 – November 10, 1917.

Prior to deployment of Canadian troops to the Ypres Salient, General Currie issued an order for the selection of a number of experienced officers to reconnoitre the salient. The officers were told to pay special attention to the condition of the battlefield and report to General Currie their impressions and opinions. The battlefield's condition would certainly impact the success or failure of the forthcoming Passchendaele operation. Many of the chosen officers, who had experienced the salient in 1915, were astounded and overwhelmed by what they saw. No one recognized the battlefield, as they had known it. They even had great difficulty identifying typical, recognizable landmarks, such as farms, homes, forestation, and many of the once-familiar streams. Much of what they remembered had been completely obliterated, wiped off the face of the earth, and now transformed into a rugged, barren lunarscape. One particular stream, Ravebeek, had become a pond of stagnant water, joining the swamplands and marshes scattered about the salient. The only distinguishable reference point remaining was a muddy road leading to Zonnebeke and 's Graventafel, where Flemish towns and villages once existed.

A damaged and abandoned trench situated in the Zonnebeke battle zone, ten km from Ypres.

Once the officers had completed their battlefield inspection, they returned to Canadian Corps Headquarters. Their route took them through Ypres, a 700-year-old, medieval city. Situated in the heart of Belgian West-Flanders, Ypres had, at one time, been the hub of a flourishing and lucrative textile trade, however, after Louis XIV of France conquered the city in 1678, it transitioned into a produce and dairy farming economy.

Over the centuries, Ypres had experienced countless conflicts and bloodshed from foreign aggressors, mainly the French and Spanish. Each time the Belgians came under attack, they defended Ypres from the ramparts encircling a large part of the city. Once again, Ypres and its 18,000 citizens were coming under siege, in the twentieth century, with incessant bombing reducing the city to rubble. Eventually, it was left to the British to defend, while its citizens sought security, comfort, and solace, miles from Ypres, in France and Great Britain.

The enormity of the devastation, the number of enemy fortifications, the placement of barbed wire, trenches, troops, and the mud were all described in great detail by the officers to General Currie. After reading the report and listening to their comments, Currie was curious to see for himself what his troops were going to be faced with, in order to capture Passchendaele. General Currie set off into the salient to personally observe what awaited the Canadian Corps on the plains of Flanders. At a meeting upon his return, Currie told the Canadian Corps commanders that Passchendaele was an attainable objective, but at a very high cost. That cost, he predicted, would be 16,000 Canadian soldiers killed, wounded, missing, or captured. The actual number of casualties was 15,654.

At the same time General Currie was crawling through the salient mud, at 8:00 o'clock in the morning, Lieutenant Douglas Smith, of the 43rd Canadian Infantry Battalion, had joined three coy scouts heading to the forward lines, from their camp in Caëstre. The purpose of the lieutenant's trip was to observe enemy activity in the area, and then report his findings to 9th Infantry Brigade GHQ (General Headquarters). After reaching a forward observation post, Smith was also joined by a Lieutenant Ward and Lieutenant Robert Shankland, fellow officers from the 43rd Infantry Battalion. Lieutenants Smith, Ward, and Shankland, together with their scouts, then proceeded to conduct an intensive, daytime reconnaissance mission of the front, including No-Man's Land.

At the Caëstre camp, the 43rd Battalion Adjutants and Company Commanders were busy studying scale-models of enemy trench systems, defense installations, machine gun placements, barbed wire locations, streams, and ponds on an elevated section of land called Bellevue Spur. Later on, they were joined by officers of the 52nd, 58th, and 116th Infantry Battalions for a meeting at 9th Brigade Headquarters. There, they discussed troop strengths, field reconnaissance, and intelligence reports, and reviewed assault plans for each of the battalions. On the agenda was an urgent matter concerning the promotion of a number of soldiers from the rank of private to non-commissioned officer. Each coy commander was told to submit a list for consideration. Private S. E. Shortliffe was among those to be considered.

Chapter Twenty-One
OCTOBER 19, 1917

"War is a series of catastrophes which result in victory."

Albert Pike

One week before the Battle of Passchendaele was scheduled to begin, Lieutenant-Colonel William Grassie, commanding officer of the 43rd Battalion, made a trip to the forward lines on October 19, at 8:30 in the morning. Accompanied by two coy officers, the colonel needed to know what would be required to ensure a seamless, casualty-free transfer of his troops to the positions held by the New Zealanders. At the conclusion of the fact-finding mission, the colonel instructed both officers to remain with the New Zealand battalion until the 43rd arrived in the line. In the meantime, at Caëstre Camp, B Coy and Private S.E. Shortliffe were being kept busy with more gas-warfare training, conducted by instructors from the 9th Infantry Brigade. Following the training session and a route march at 3:30 p.m., all the soldiers were ordered to assemble outside battalion headquarters. The purpose of the assembly was to hear an announcement by Colonel Grassie. The commanding officer explained that, on the previous night in Caëstre, several Cameron Highlanders and ANZAC soldiers had been involved in a fight that resulted in the 9th Brigade Military Police arriving on the scene to break it up. The colonel ended his rebuke by announcing that the entire battalion would be confined to camp until further notice.

Colonel Grassie's reprimand was intended to demonstrate to the troops that there were consequences for certain actions, regardless of whether it was a brawl in a bar or refusal to carry out an order on the battlefield. The colonel pointedly reminded the men they were held accountable under military law, mentioning as he often did, a statement attributed to Major Victor Wentworth Odlum. Major Odlum, commander of the 7th Infantry Battalion (British Columbia), told his troops in 1915, during the Second Battle of Ypres:

Any NCO or soldier who absents himself without leave from the trenches, from a parade, to proceeding to the trenches, or from a working party, which is to work in area exposed to fire, will be tried for Desertion and the penalty for Desertion is death.

During the Great War, punishment handed out by a court martial did not always reflect the crime committed. The degree of severity ranged from minor to excessive — from a loss of pay to execution. It was generally a no-win situation for those brought before a court martial. In many cases, ninety percent of all British troops, found guilty as charged, could expect to receive two other types of punishment, rather than execution. These could be either several hours of extreme, difficult exercise dressed in full battle gear, or field punishment. During field punishment, soldiers were bound and spread-eagled on an erect, large wagon wheel and remained there, in an open field, for hours, regardless of weather.

When soldiers discarded their weapons and fled from the battlefield during a combat operation, they were considered cowards and deserters. After being apprehended, their fate was a quick court martial, followed by a death sentence carried out by a firing squad at sunrise. The death penalty was supposedly intended to discourage cowardice, dereliction of duty, extreme bad behaviour, insubordination by failing to comply with an order, or the deliberate homicide of officers. Today, the majority of people would consider the punishment of death by a firing squad for those offences to be draconian, to say the least. Once a sentence was handed down, the condemned soldier was escorted to an area near the place of his detention, bound to a pole or ordered to stand in front of a wall, then blindfolded and shot by a twelve-man firing squad, under the command of a sergeant and one officer. It was the responsibility of the officer to ensure the condemned soldier did not survive the hail of bullets. Although Great Britain and her Dominions did enforce the death penalty for desertion, Australia exempted her troops from such punishment.

During WWI, a total of 216 Canadian servicemen were condemned to die by a firing squad. Twenty-five of those sentences were carried out. These are the names of those soldiers who were tried, found guilty and executed.

(1) Sergeant William Alexander, thirty-seven years of age, 10th Infantry Battalion (Desertion) — (2) Lance-Bombardier Frederick S. Arnold, twenty-six years of age, 1st Infantry Brigade (Desertion) — (3) Private Fortunat Auger, twenty-five years of age, 14th Infantry Battalion (Desertion) — (4) Trooper Alexander Butler, twenty-eight years of age, Royal Canadian Dragoons (Murder) — (5) Private Harold George Carter, twenty-three years of age, 73rd Infantry Battalion (Desertion) — (6) Private Gustave Comté, twenty-two years of age, 22nd Infantry Battalion (Desertion) — (7) Private Arthur Dagesse, thirty-three years of age, 22nd Infantry Battalion (Desertion) — (8) Driver Benjamin DeFehr, twenty-eight years of age, 1st Reserve Park (Murder) — (9) Private Leopold Delisle, twenty-six years of age, 22nd Infantry Battalion (Desertion) — (10) Private Edward Fairburn, twenty-two years of age, 18th Infantry Battalion (Desertion) — (11) Private Stephen McDermott Fowles, twenty-one years of age, 44th Infantry Battalion (Desertion) — (12) Private John Maurice Higgins, twenty-five years of age, 1st Infantry Battalion (Desertion) — (13) Private Henry Hesey Kerr, twenty-five years of age, 7th Infantry Battalion (Desertion) — (14) Private Joseph LaLancette, twenty-one years of age, 22nd Infantry Battalion (Desertion) — (15) Private Côme LaLiberté, twenty-three years of age, 3rd Infantry Battalion (Desertion) — (16) Private Wilson Norman Ling, twenty-two years of age, 2nd Infantry Battalion (Desertion) — (17) Private Harold Edward James Lodge, twenty years of age, 19th Infantry Battalion (Desertion) — (18) Private Thomas Lionel Moles, twenty-six years of age, 54th Infantry Battalion (Desertion) — (19) Private Eugene Perry, twenty-one years of age, 22nd Infantry Battalion (Desertion) — (20)

Private Edward James Reynolds, twenty years of age, 3rd Infantry Battalion (Desertion) — (21) Private John William Roberts, twenty-one years of age, 2nd Regiment Canadian Mounted Rifles (Desertion) — (22) Private Charles Welsh, twenty-eight years of age, 8th Infantry Battalion (Desertion) — (23) Private James H. Wilson, thirty-seven years of age, 4th Infantry Battalion (Desertion) — (24) Private Elsworth Young, twenty-one years of age, 25th Infantry Battalion (Desertion) — (25) Private Dimitro Sinizki, twenty-two years of age, 52nd Infantry Battalion (Cowardice).

On December 11, 2001, Ron Duhamel, Minister of Veterans Affairs, stood in the House of Commons and offered an apology on behalf of the Government of Canada, to the families and descendents, of those soldiers executed during WWI.

(An intriguing question arises from the execution of these twenty-five young Canadian soldiers — Were the families made aware of the circumstances surrounding their death?

In my opinion the answer would be, yes. The army would have no alternative but to disclose the charge(s) brought forth, the decision of the Court Martial, and the result that soon followed. To do otherwise, would have misrepresented how these family members had perished. It is within the realm of possibility that the families may have received the two war medals, but definitely not the scroll commemorating their sacrifice in the line of duty, nor the Memorial Plaque (Deadman's Penny), which states — "He Died For Freedom And Honour."

In order to not disgrace the family name and be subjected to public ridicule, it is assumed that each of the twenty-five families would have said that their son "was killed-in-action." This reasoning is borne out by the fact that an obituary notice, which appeared in a Toronto newspaper on September 9, 1916, said that the family of Private Edward James Reynolds had received official notice that their son "had been killed in action." In addition, a Reynolds memorial marker in St. John's (Norway) Cemetery in Toronto reads — "Edward James 1896 – 1916. Killed In Action — Interred in France."

Private Reynolds was executed by a firing squad on August 23, 1916, and is buried in Longuenesse Souvenir Cemetery, Pas-de-Calais, France.

Chapter Twenty-Two
OCTOBER 20, 1917

"In peace, sons bury their fathers.
In war, fathers bury their sons."

Herodotus

A greatly anticipated event for most Canadian soldiers, was the day when parcels and letters arrived from family and loved ones. Mail from Canada connected soldiers on the Western Front to their homeland, which they dearly loved and missed. Ernie collected his bundle of letters and moved to a quieter spot where he could sit and read his mail. On this day his package included several letters from his parents, one each from brothers Melbourne and Delbert, and an early birthday card from his sister, Mabel, a United States Army nurse. In her card, she made mention of the fact that she was awaiting deployment to France, to care for wounded Americans who had been fighting the Germans since June 26. An envelope from Ernie's mother, Sophia, contained a number of newspaper clippings from the *Digby Courier*, relating to volunteers from the local area serving overseas. One article in particular mentioned Private Wilbur Harris Shortliffe, a former employee of the *newspaper*, who enlisted in the spring of 1916. A total of four Shortliffe family members volunteered to serve in the war effort on the Western Front. Three failed to return.

The war in Europe, contrary to popular belief was no, nonstop combat. The army often provided its infantrymen with periods of rest and relaxation. In Reserve, men could enjoy the time away from the front-line to read, take a hot bath, or see and listen to the nightly entertainment in the YMCA hut. In addition to these relaxed moments, it was still necessary to check and maintain one's combat kit. Sergeants and corporals made sure every weapon and piece of equipment was combat-ready. This meant laying out all combat items on the ground and conducting an inventory, replacing any items that were missing or damaged. Troops carried a minimum of twenty items into battle, not including their ammunition. Each soldier lugged a heavy rifle, bayonet, and as many as four grenades, in addition to a bedroll, rations, water, mess cans, greatcoat, underclothes, bandages, and even his pay book. Combined equipment, uniform, and body weight, added considerable difficulty to a soldier's fighting ability under some extreme battlefield conditions.

The army combat-uniform, worn by the men of the 43rd Battalion, was of British design. The tunic featured nine brass buttons; seven on the jacket panels and two on the upper pockets. Instead of trousers, highland battalion regiments wore Scottish kilts, however, in battle a brown leather apron was worn over the kilt to offer some camouflage protection. Other uniform items included cloth puttees and a pair of British-made ammunition boots. On the head, a Glengarry cloth cap with a regimental badge was worn except when it was replaced by a steel combat helmet, called the "Brodie."

The Brodie was the brainchild of John Leopold Brodie of Great Britain, who designed and patented it in 1915. Although the helmet was considered by most troops who wore it as reasonable protection from fatal head injuries, it was an extremely heavy and uncomfortable piece of battle gear. As a result of feedback from those who had to endure the discomfort of wearing the helmet, it was modified in 1917 by the simple insertion of a rubber cushion headband. This effective modification, provided soldiers with comfort, but unfortunately, no less weight. The Brodie still weighed just a few ounces under two pounds. Over the course of the war, the Allied steel helmet took on several nicknames: "Tin Hat, Trench Helmet, Shrapnel Helmet, Tommy Helmet, and Doughboy Helmet." The Germans, in 1917, wore a steel helmet named the "Stahlhelm." This headgear, which went by the moniker "Salaatsschussel" or "salad bowl," replaced earlier soft headgear and the Prussian-style spiked helmets, called "Pickelhauben." The purpose for issuing steel helmets to their respective infantry soldiers was to provide protection from steel fragments such as airburst shrapnel. Regrettably, both the Brodie and the Stahlhelm were not bulletproof.

One of the most important items issued to a soldier, next to his gas mask and small-box respirator, was the British Lee Enfield rifle. The Enfield .303, however, was not always part of the Canadian arsenal of weapons. From the beginning of the war until the early part of 1917, Canadian troops were supplied with a pull-action, light-artillery rifle, developed by Scottish inventor, Sir Charles Ross. "The Ross" as it was often called, had friends in high places, one of whom was named Sir Sam Hughes. As minister of Militia and Defence, Sam Hughes unabashedly promoted the rifle's use by the Canadian Expeditionary Force, therefore, it didn't come as a surprise to anyone within the military when the Ross rifle became the official assault rifle. The Ross, although acknowledged as an excellent target practice rifle, with accuracy up to 500 yards, also had an even greater reputation for its unreliability. Two of the most serious shortcomings of the Ross rifle, were: (1) the firing mechanism often jammed and (2) the bayonet often failed to remain attached to the rifle. In combat situations, Canadian troops found that instead of being able to rapidly fire-off between twelve and fifteen rounds per minute, they were limited to a few shots before the rifle jammed. To correct this malfunction, soldiers were compelled to use the heel of their boots to pry open the bolt.

Eventually, a decision was made to retire the Ross rifle and replace it with a very popular gun designed by American, James Lee. This combat rifle had been in use by the British Army since 1914, but Canadian soldiers could only hope and pray that one day they too would carry this particular gun into battle. The Lee Enfield was produced for the first time in 1907, at the Royal Small Arms Factory, in Enfield England. Named for both inventor as well as where it was manufactured, the Lee Enfield .303 was a single-shot, five-round,

mine was produced (in USA?) in 1900 and used in the "boer war": heavier and more accurate

short magazine, or SMLE (Short Magazine Lee Enfield). The Enfield was crafted from solid maple and weighed approximately twenty pounds. A unique feature of the rifle was a small compartment located in the butt of the gun, where soldiers kept a small container of gun oil or cigarettes and matches. There was almost unanimous agreement among the soldiers that the Lee Enfield was an extremely accurate weapon, and in many respects, similar to the German Gewehr 98 (G98). This was a bolt-action Mauser rifle, featuring a five-round, internal clip-loaded magazine. Three of the many items that played an indispensable role in a soldier's success and survival were his rifle, steel helmet, and bayonet.

On October 20, at 8:00 p.m., Lieutenant-Colonel W. Grassie, D.S.O. issued Operation Order No. 135; a directive advising his officers to have their units join the other battalions of the 9th Canadian Infantry Brigade at "X" Camp, near the village of St. Jean, two miles north of Ypres. Once the Cameron Highlanders of Canada had arrived at their new camp, the colonel and company officers began to formulate a specific plan for the relief of the 3rd Canterbury Battalion, of the 4th New Zealand Brigade. The operation was scheduled to take place Sunday, October 21, at Pommern Redoubt, near Frezenberg, in the Ypres Salient.

The relocation of the 3rd Canadian Infantry Division from Caëstre to St. Jean was under the direct supervision of fifty-one-year-old Brigadier-General Frederick William Hill, commander of the 9th Canadian Infantry Brigade. Combat units under his command included: the 43rd Battalion (Cameron Highlanders of Canada), the 52nd Battalion (New Ontario), the 58th Battalion (Central Ontario) and the 116th Battalion (Ontario County). In addition, Brigadier-General Hill also commanded the 31st, 33rd and 45th Field Batteries, the 36th Howitzer Battery, 9th Trench Mortar Company and the 9th Canadian Machine Gun Company. Brigadier-General Hill was one of only six Canadian officers in WWI to be presented with the Distinguished Service Order (DSO), The Companion of the Order of Bath (CB), and the Companion of the Order of St. Michael and St. George (CMG). The 3rd Canadian Infantry Division, under the command of forty-three-year-old Major-General Louis Lipsett, was comprised of three brigades, twelve battalions, eleven field-artillery batteries, seven trench-mortar groups, three machine-gun units, six companies of engineers, numerous field ambulances and casualty clearing stations, medical staff, and a mobile veterinarian section. Potential combat strength was 20,000 officers and other ranks.

Chapter Twenty-Three
OCTOBER 21, 1917

"In my dreams I hear again the crash of guns, the rattle of musketry, and the strange, mournful mutter of the battlefield."

General Douglas MacArthur

A relaxed sleep has become a rare thing these last few nights. Nightmares on the other hand, are more frequent and much more disturbing. Tonight, I was about to fall asleep at 2:00 a.m., when I received news that all battalions of the 9th Brigade would be breaking camp within a few hours. No sleep again tonight. Lack of sleep is adding to the stress. Many of us have developed inexplicable headaches. The medics tell us to drink plenty of water and eat our meals. Except for water consumption, most of the men are experiencing a reduced appetite for beef mulligan, which is not uncommon before a major battle. I think it is the miserable weather these past few days that is causing my headache. Even at this moment, a severe storm out of the east is lashing our camp with wind and rain. A typical stormy day, on the Western Front!

During a strong wind and heavy rain, officers and foot soldiers assembled in the morning darkness, in full battle dress, for a parade inspection. At the conclusion, an order to "quick march" was shouted by a sergeant-major. The troops turned, faced the bitter wind and pelting rain and silently marched to the Caëstre railway siding. Arriving thirty-five minutes later, the men quickly boarded the waiting train. Their ride on this stormy morning took them north, where they crossed the frontier into Belgium, proceeding to St. Jean via Ypres on foot. Once aboard, Private S.E. Shortliffe could hear the asthmatic wheezing sound of the locomotive as it slowly huffed and puffed its way up the track. Black coal dust covered each stoker as they hurriedly shovelled the coal into a firebox, building up steam, in order to drive the locomotive's large wheels and keep the train speeding to Ypres. The only passengers were soldiers of the 9th Brigade, travelling ahead of their supply vehicles. A convoy of army transports left at 5:30 a.m., carrying ammunition, artillery equipment, medical supplies, food, and other essential goods. Upon the convoy reaching the outskirts of St. Jean, a group of eight guides met them and escorted cargo and drivers to "X"-Camp.

Within minutes of the train's departure from the railroad siding, the night sky suddenly burst forth in a brilliant display of light from flares, followed by thunderous roars of heavy artillery guns. A short while later, the sky returned to inky black and the guns fell silent. All one heard was the sound of clickety-clack as the train's wheels sped along the tracks. Military train- travel across the countryside of northwestern France was far from first class, especially for ordinary regulars and NCOs. Accommodations for these Canadian infantry-men were boxcars. They were intensely cold in the winter, inferno-hot in the summer, noisy, and most times reeking of animal excrement. Horses, donkeys, and pack mules were frequently loaded into boxcars and transported to the Western Front by rail, therefore, it was not unusual for soldiers to share sleeping spaces with a menagerie of four-leggedpassengers. Officers and their batmen (assistants/valets), on the other hand, rode in the warmth and comfort of modern coaches at the tail-end of the train. They were, for the most part, removed from the smoke and smell of burning coal, and the noise up ahead.

In order to reach the safety of Ypres, the only other alternative to rail was overland by road. The latter was, by far, the more dangerous of the two options. Road travel to Ypres encompassed two infamous routes — Shrapnel Corner and Hellfire Corner. Both locations saw scores of troops mowed down by German machine-gun fire, or blown to smithereens by artillery shells.

(Ross photo)
This large building in Vlamertinghe, near Ypres (Ieper) was once a casualty clearing station where as many as 1,000 casualties could be accommodated at any given time. Surgical procedures were conducted here, including amputations.

As daylight filtered through the wooden slats of the boxcar door, Private S.E. Shortliffe checked his gold pocket watch — it was 8:00 a.m. Four hours had passed since he and his comrades left Caëstre. An NCO yelled to the men to prepare to arrive in the village of Vlamertinghe, three miles west of Ypres. Upon sliding open the heavy door, the Cameron Highlanders could see cemetery upon cemetery, with the all-too-familiar white crosses marking the graves of thousands of fallen soldiers, from the British Commonwealth. As Shortliffe and his comrades scanned the Belgium landscape, the train slowed as it passed the Vlamertinghe New Military Cemetery. Located approximately one mile south of the town of Vlamertinghe, this cemetery was the final resting place for 1,813 soldiers, 155 of them Canadian. Many buried there had died while being treated for their wounds at a local field hospital or casualty clearing station in Vlamertinghe. Most were recent casualties of the Third Battle of Ypres.

As the military troop-transport train slowly pulled into the railway siding on the outskirts of Ypres, the locomotive dispensed a loud sigh and a hiss, and vented a cloud of vapour that enveloped all those standing on the station platform. Private S.E. Shortliffe and the Cameron Highlanders of Canada had reached the end of the pre-war Poperinghe-Ypres-Courtrai rail line; the closest terminal to the City of Ypres. As the men detrained, they came face to face with the bombed-out remains of what had been a very large, red-brick building, a short distance east of the railway station. A soldier from the 43rd Battalion, who had fought with the 2nd Canadian Infantry Brigade in the Second Battle of Ypres in 1915, explained to Private Shortliffe and his fellow Highlanders that they were looking at the Hospice du Sacre Coeur, also called the "Ypres Mental Asylum."

Every soldier who arrived in Ypres had a special story to tell, relating to what he witnessed after stepping off the train and marching into the demolished city. Corporal R.G. Pinneo, of the 10th Canadian Infantry Brigade (4th Canadian Infantry Division), was one of those soldiers:

Our arrival at Passchendaele was on a train that took us up through Vlamertinghe to the outskirts of Ypres. There we got off. The first things I saw as I got out of the train and looked to the east towards the German line were five German observation balloons in the sky. I said to myself, "It won't be long now." And it wasn't. While we were still unloading our equipment the Germans started to shell the train. The confusion was murderous. We were dodging here and there, trying to shelter and unload at the same time. We were lucky. We only came in for the first of it and we managed to form up and start off through Ypres. The company behind us got it hard — they had sixteen men killed and forty wounded. We were shelled all the way as we marched through Ypres to the Menin Gate and out the Gravenstafel Road. We called it the Grab-and-Stumble Road.

We stopped at this cemetery and we thought at first they were pulling our legs when they said this was our billet. It was a terrible place; there was no cover, no place to go, no dug-outs or anything. The graves and tombstones had all been knocked to hell by gunfire, and even the crypts

Bullets, Bombs and Bayonets | 219

and coffins had been blasted open. You could see the sheeted dead. We bivouacked as best we could. All night long a British battery of 15-inch howitzers just at the back of us was blasting away and the Germans were answering. There was a direct hit on the runner's bivouac of the 44th Canadian Infantry Battalion (Manitoba) and that was the end of them. Ypres was a terrible place. I was there three times and I never heard the name without a shiver of apprehension.

Within a couple of hours, the 43rd Canadian Infantry Battalion, together with the three other battalions from the 9th Canadian Infantry Brigade, had arrived in Ypres — a city virtually in ruins from daily shelling that had occurred since October 19, 1914. The Cameron Highlanders of Canada, wearing their kilts and heavy Brodie helmets, entered the ancient city from Poperingseweg. This particular route was frequently used by the British Expeditionary Force when making their way to the salient via Menenpoort (Menin Gate). Led by pipes and drums of the 43rd Battalion, the regiment marched down the cobblestone streets, amid the devastation and debris that once was the home of 18,000 Belgians. The soldiers were shocked by what they saw, and saddened by the damage, especially to the many historical structures. St. Martin's Cathedral, a 335-foot high, 547-year-old church, which once towered over Ypres, had been reduced to a huge pile of rubble comprised of broken concrete, bricks, stained glass and wood.

Directly adjacent to St. Martin's Cathedral was Lakenhalle, or Cloth Hall, a three-storey building that was hit by artillery shells for the first time in the early part of November 1914. Incendiary bombs followed on November 22, and it was these bombs that were responsible for most of the horrible damage to its structure. Despite being shelled and fire-bombed, the medieval building still stood three months later — but without a roof. Walls that had stubbornly withstood the onslaught of enemy artillery fire continued to provide a sanctuary for 1,500 British troops. By April 1915, German field-artillery batteries had increased the frequency and shell size of the bombs falling on Ypres. This created even greater damage to Cloth Hall, which ultimately forced the British to evacuate and relocate their troops.

The famous Lakenhalle or Cloth Hall, as it appeared before the First World War.

Cloth Hall was the target of enemy incendiary and heavy artillery bombardments commencing on November 22, 1914 and lasting for most of the war. By the end of the Great War, the once majestic medieval building was mainly a pile of rubble.

Two years after the British abandoned Cloth Hall as a refuge for their men, the 43rd Canadian Infantry Battalion marched past what was left of the 700-year-old former textile building, on October 21, 1917. All that still existed of the 400-foot long structure was a belfry, a clock and four turrets. A century later, Cloth Hall is once again a signature attraction in the city of Ypres (Ieper), having been completely rebuilt to its original size and architectural design.

Even though Ypres came under siege for much of the war, German boots only touched its soil once. The date was October 7, 1914. On that day, 8,000 troops arrived on foot and horseback from the southeast part of the city, along Meensestraat to Grote Markt. It was in the city square where horses, carts, carriages, motorized vehicles, field kitchens, artillery weapons, and soldiers all converged. Shortly after their arrival, German officers demanded that they and their troops be provided with food and lodging, as well as provisions for their horses. By 9:00 o'clock that evening, the Germans had been fed and billeted at Cloth Hall, as well as in army barracks, schools, the railway station, and in private homes.

With the occupation of the city by 8,000 enemy soldiers, local businesses anticipated a bonanza in business. To their great disappointment, a significant increase in revenue did not materialize. A major part of the problem was, instead of using Flemish francs to pay for goods and services, the Germans expected Belgian shopkeepers to enthusiastically accept the German Reichsmark or a host of pre-printed coupons. Refusal by the people of Ypres to accept German currency and coupons was of no concern to the enemy, because they were the occupiers. The city and its citizens were at the mercy of the Germans.

After having spent the night in Ypres, the German cavalry and infantrymen left the city at 8:30 a.m., taking with them 8,000 loaves of unpaid-for fresh bread and moving to higher ground, not far from the city. The cavalry rode off in a southwest direction towards Vlamertinghe and the Channel ports on the coast, while the German infantry headed overland to Dickebusch. On October 12, 1914, the cavalry had moved to positions at Catsberg, in the nearby village of Meteren.

On that same day, the British 2nd Calvary Division, under the command of General Herbert Gough, engaged the German 4th Calvary Corps. This battle was followed by another attack on October 13, by the 1st Battalion Warwickshire. As a result of that operation, the German commander, General von Hollen withdrew the 4th Calvary Corps and retreated to the elevated areas around Ypres and the Leie stream, south of Lille, France. Rather than return to Ypres, von Hollen concentrated his force along the French-Belgian border.

Six days after the Germans moved out of Ypres, British IV Corps Commander, General Henry Rawlinson led his 7th Division and 3rd Cavalry Division into the city. Rawlinson's primary job was to establish a defense system on the east side of the city, in order to prohibit the Germans from using Ypres as part of a route to the seaports on the English Channel and North Sea. Although severely outnumbered, British troops were able to hold their own against the enemy, including a successful counterattack at Gheluveld, on October 31, 1914.

In defiance of massive German bombardments, a large segment of the Ypres population continued to live and work in the city, in the spring of 1915, as well as within the surrounding municipality. There were a number of reasons why the people did not want to leave Ypres, besides their love and loyalty to the community. For many, it was simply the money. Retail stores, bakeries, and cafes, for example, did a thriving business, thanks mainly to the thousands of troops who continually passed through Ypres, billeted in the immediate area, on their way to the salient.

Night-time usually brought on another bout of enemy shelling, forcing families to seek refuge in cellars and within the confines of the ramparts along the canal. Upwards of as many as twenty heavy-artillery shells pounded the city every hour. Besides the collateral damage in human life, many of the larger artillery shells were responsible for the destruction of the sewer and water systems in Ypres. The loss of this infrastructure greatly impacted those who chose to remain in the city. Even though there was a heartfelt reluctance to abandon Ypres, a decision nevertheless had to be made to evacuate its citizens. The order came, on April 21, 1915, in the wake of another day of severe shelling. Young and old found themselves refugees in their own country. Many departed their beloved city for the safety of France, England, and nearby Poperinghe, eight-miles west of Ypres. Those who refused evacuation in April were eventually forced out in early May, Mayor Réne Fidèle Colaert being the last to leave the city.

(Ross photo)
Ypres (Ieper) was totally destroyed in WWI, however, the city was rebuilt incorporating the original architectural styles associated with Flemish Medieval and Renaissance designs. This is how Ypres (Ieper) appears today.

Although everyone was ultimately forced to leave Ypres in the spring of 1915, most of the population eventually returned after the war to rebuild their lives and their city. Cloth Hall, St. Martin's Cathedral, and the Ypres Town Hall were three of many historical structures rebuilt to their original design, paid for by Germany as part of a reparation settlement. The restoration of Cloth Hall took thirty-nine years to complete (1928-1967); the original Renaissance structure had required 100 years to construct, finally finishing in 1304. From the Middle Ages up until the mid-1840s, Cloth Hall had been the centre of a flourishing, textile industry. This was during a time when small boats were able to traverse the Yser Canal up the Ieperlee River, and dock at the west end of Cloth Hall to load and unload textile goods.

This was also a period in Belgium's history when hateful propaganda, originating from within the Catholic Church, was used to demonize individuals whom the church perceived as sorcerers and witches. Bishops and priests spread stories from their pulpits that witches and sorcerers could transform their physical bodies into various shapes and sizes of animals — one being a cat. After altering their physical selves into four-legged felines, they supposedly roamed at night throughout the neighborhoods of Ypres. During their nightly travels, they were said to invoke curses upon people while performing evil and perverse deeds and communicating with Satan. The frightened and paranoid citizenry soon demanded the city put to death all cats, with no exceptions. In some Belgian towns, cats were slaughtered en masse. In Ypres, Cloth Hall, being the tallest building with a 230-foot-high belfry, became the site of a ritual called, "tossing of the cats." Death upon the cobblestone street below the belfry was intended to cleanse Ypres of all evil and misfortune.

By the year 1817, these four-legged felines were no longer loathed or feared, thus the tossing of the cats ritual at Cloth Hall ultimately ended. As fate would have it, a ritual of death was replaced by a celebration of life, to honour the cat. The festival, known as "Kattenstoet," featuring a large parade, continues to be held in Ieper every third year, in May. Today, instead of tossing live cats as they once did, now soft, plush, cuddly toy cats are thrown from the floats to the many spectators who line the streets, directly below the belfry of Cloth Hall.

As mentioned previously, Ypres was a Flemish-speaking city, as were the villages and towns within the province of West-Vlaanderen (West-Flanders). British and Commonwealth soldiers were therefore presented with an interesting linguistic challenge when it came to pronouncing the names of towns and battlefields. A good example was Ypres. British soldiers continually struggled with the proper way to pronounce the name. It wouldn't take long before an enterprising, young British Tommy came up with a unique vocabulary to replace certain names, which soldiers found difficult, or impossible to wrap their tongues around. The creativity of the British soldier was almost instantaneously accepted and utilized by most United Kingdom troops. During WWI, Ypres would be called "Wipers," Ploegsteert became "Plug Street," Wytschaete was "White Sheet," and Poperinge was simply abbreviated to a three-letter word, "Pop."

The name Wipers was so popular, that it was used as the name of a wartime newspaper called, the *Wiper Times*. It came to fruition one day during the winter of 1916. The Sherwood Foresters, a British regiment, discovered a printing press and materials while patrolling an area near Cloth Hall in Grote Markt. Their discovery sparked an idea; produce their own newspaper, written especially for Allied soldiers serving at the front. One hundred copies of the first edition rolled off the press on February 12, 1916, containing a variety of poems, jokes, and human-interest stories, including both serious and satirical articles on infantry life at the Western Front. The second issue, unfortunately, was the last to be printed near Cloth Hall. A German artillery shell blew up both building and printing press, forcing the Sherwood Foresters to start all over. With a new location and equipment, ten more editions were published, read and enjoyed by servicemen at the Western Front. Publication of the *Wiper Times* continued until the end of the war.

The 43rd Canadian Infantry Battalion marched through the bombed-out city of Ypres, on their way to St. Jean and "X" Camp. As Private S.E. Shortliffe and the Cameron Highlanders passed Grote Markt they came upon the ruins of Menin Gate. This was one of two famous landmark entrances over the canal leading into Ypres. The other faced southward towards Lille, France and was named Lille Gate, although most Flemish-speaking Belgians referred to it as "Rijsel." Unlike Menin Gate, Lille Gate survived the massive bombings of the war.

Approaching Menin Gate, an order could be heard, "Eyes front." Each Highlander focused his attention on the soldier in front, marching four abreast in unison, arms swinging in perfect synchronization, rifles resting on shoulders. The sound of hobnail boots echoed on the cobblestones of Meensestraat, distinctly evident above the sound of bagpipes and the 110 beats per minute rhythm of the drums. At the head of the battalion column, a sergeant-major shouted, "Close the door!" Those three words were repeated by each line of soldiers until the last four men exited Menin Gate, at which time they hollered — "Door is closed!"

This was a poignant moment for the infantrymen of the 43rd Canadian Infantry Battalion. Many of the officers and ordinary regulars who passed through Menin Gate, on October 21, 1917, perished in the Ypres Salient. Private S.E. Shortliffe was one of 161 Cameron Highlanders of Canada who did not survive.

The 43rd Battalion was part of a total of forty-eight Canadian Corps battalions involved in moving troops, weapons, ammunition, tents, kitchens, food, animals, and field ambulances to campsites in St. Jean, St. Julien, and Poelkapelle. While the closest camp in proximity to Passchendaele, was Poelkapelle (four miles), the 43rd Battalion was situated seven miles away, at St. Jean; the same distance to Passchendaele as St. Julien.

The Canadian Corps Divisions were commanded by four seasoned veterans of several very important combat operations. Division Commanders included: Major-General Archibald Cameron MacDonnell of the 1st Canadian Infantry Division, Major-General Henry Edward Burstall, 2nd Canadian Infantry Division, Major-General Louis Lipsett, 3rd Canadian Infantry Division, and the 4th Canadian Infantry Division under the command of Major-General David Watson. Plans were formulated and objectives assigned to each of the twelve Canadian Infantry Brigades and their respective battalions.

The 43rd Canadian Infantry Battalion (Cameron Highlanders of Canada) was given the task of capturing a battlefield, which had claimed thousands of casualties — Bellevue Spur. To accomplish this, the Cameron Highlanders had to cross Marsh Bottom. On the other side were enemy trenches, extremely well protected by extensive amounts of barbed wire, secured to iron rods, and corkscrewed into the ground. Unlike British rods which were rounded, (similar to the eye of a needle), enemy barbed-wire stakes were finished with a sharp, spear-like point, primed to impale an overly zealous soldier. Once the initial wire was breached, Private S.E. Shortliffe and his comrades advanced through No-Man's Land, assisted by rolling barrages. After that, they engaged machine-gun crews defending the many, strategically-placed pillboxes blanketing Bellevue Spur.

Chapter Twenty-Four
OCTOBER 22, 1917

> "Far, far from Wipers I long to be, where German snipers can't snipe at me. Damp is my dug-out, cold are my feet, waiting for the whiz bangs to send me to sleep."
>
> World War I Soldier's Song

The blaring sound of Reveille at 6:30 a.m., on Monday, October 22, heralded the beginning of another day on the Western Front. Loud calls to "Rise and shine boys" echoed in the ears of the semi-comatose infantrymen, as they awoke from another night of fitful sleep. Within two hours of being awakened, the men of the 43rd Battalion were packed and on their way from "X" Camp in St. Jean, to the Right Support sector at Pommern Redoubt, four miles north of Frezenberg. Pommern Redoubt was situated halfway between Ypres and Passchendaele. It was here that the Canadian Corps established its headquarters, in an area previously occupied by II ANZAC Corps. The Cameron Highlanders of Canada's journey from St. Jean to Frezenberg, led by Major Ferguson, took four, excruciatingly long hours to travel 2.6 miles. It was a trek made along corduroy roads and over numerous networks of wooden walkways, called "Duckboards." These boardwalks, snaking their way around shell craters, swamps, and marshlands, reminded S.E. Shortliffe of the wooden sidewalks in his home town of Freeport, Nova Scotia. Crisscrossing the muddy fields, Shortliffe and his coy cautiously worked their way along the duckboards, stopping momentarily to witness a grotesque and disturbing scene of death. Numerous bodies, both foe and comrade, were piled one upon the other, unburied, left to rot and sink beneath the mud. All had died shocking and appalling deaths. Some had been riddled by machine-gun fire. Others were dismembered, disembowelled, or shredded by the impact of shrapnel shells. Surprisingly, a number of the dead showed no sign of trauma, having met their demise by concussion, generated by enormous explosions from heavy artillery shells. Several bodies appeared to have drowned in the mud, half-submerged, arms outstretched as though pleading for someone to save them, while others floated face down in water-filled craters. All were vulnerable as fodder for the ravenous, giant rats. A member of the 43rd Infantry Battalion, Private Charles William Hill, age twenty, was killed in the line of duty on October 22, 1917.

The Cameron Highlanders continued to move steadily and carefully over the slimy duckboards, trying to pay less attention to the dead, and more to preserving their own lives. A glutinous quagmire of foul-smelling mud surrounded the boardwalk on all sides. One inattentive step, a moment of absent-minded carelessness, could be a soldier's last on earth. German snipers, with rifle telescopes mounted on their Mausers, together with machine- gunners, took great satisfaction in killing Canadian troops as they made their way across the open fields of Flanders. Bullets sprayed mud and whizzed past the ears of the men from the 43rd Infantry Battalion, forcing the brave and the fearful, to cling to the boardwalks to avoid being targets. Nearby, trench mortar shells launched plumes of foul-smelling mud, drenching each man in a salient-dung, as they lay prone on the slime-covered boards.

(source: Library and Archives Canada)
Two Canadians from the Signal Section work to acquire a communication connection.

(source: Library and Archives Canada)
Canadian Pioneers risk life and limb in order to lay wooden duckboards atop the mud in a very hostile environment in the Ypres Salient. These boardwalks help to facilitate the movement of Canadian troops and supplies in Flanders.

Upon their arrival, Major Ferguson reported to 3rd Division Headquarters, at Pommern Redoubt. Minutes later, he attended a meeting with Major-General Louis Lipsett, 3rd Canadian Infantry Division Commander, and the other battalion and brigade commanders. In attendance were: the commanding officers of the 7th, 8th, and 9th Canadian Infantry Brigades, the battalions of the Royal Canadian Regiment (RCR), Princess Patricia's Canadian Light Infantry (PPCLI), 1st, 2nd, 4th, and 5th Canadian Mounted Rifles (CMR), as well as the 42nd, 43rd, 49th, 52nd, 58th, and 116th Canadian Infantry Battalions.

The purpose of the meeting was to discuss, review, and confirm battle plans, mission objectives, and assault positions for brigades and battalions prior to Zero Hour on October 26. The moment the meeting concluded, the ground shuddered with the sound of the Canadian Field Artillery guns. They had started a ferocious, pre-battle bombardment of enemy lines, along the slopes of Passchendaele Ridge. The majority of that heavy artillery was under the command of three senior officers, Lieutenant-Colonel Andrew McNaughton, Brigadier-General Edward Morrison, and Brigadier-General Henry Massie. Over almost four days , ending on Thursday, October 25, their artillery batteries offered up massive displays of firepower directed at German positions. During the ninety-six hours of bombardments, artillery gunners zeroed in on enemy fortifications, as well as aiming at the German big guns. A significant number of these heavy guns were successfully destroyed or disabled, thanks to the accuracy of Canadian Field Artillery gunners using a weapon-target-detection system, designed and developed by Lieutenant-Colonel Andrew McNaughton. McNaughton's system employed sound-ranging and flash-spotting technology. His expertise and knowledge provided Canadian Corps gunners with the ability to accurately pinpoint the location of each German artillery weapon that was firing at Canadian positions, and therefore be able to destroy them in advance of October 26.

Today promotions were posted outside the entrance of Battalion HQ. To my surprise, I found my name on the list. I later learned that I was taking the place of fellow Highlander, Lance Corporal Clifford Hadfield who had taken ill. As of this moment I now hold the rank of lance corporal with the 43rd Battalion. I was given a chevron and told to have the coy tailor sew it on my tunic. I am one of two members from our coy to make the list. The other is Wilfred Kendall Turner. We both expect to be assigned our responsibilities later today.

During the mid-afternoon, the 43rd Battalion assembled for a pre-battle briefing given by the Acting Battalion Commander, Major Ferguson, with the assistance of the four coy commanders. Troops were presented with information arising from an earlier discussion with 3rd Infantry Division Commander Louis Lipsett; he had elaborated on the German defense installations placed along a six-mile section of Passchendaele Ridge. It was obvious to everyone reflecting on the British and ANZAC experiences over a period of almost three months that the Canadian Corps was going to be hard-pressed to make the significant breakthrough expected of them against the Imperial German Army. The German 4th Army, under General Friedrich Bertram Sixt von Armin, was more than capable of successfully defending Passchendaele. At least fifteen highly trained infantry divisions were securely entrenched along the full expanse of Passchendaele Ridge. These included elite units from the 6th Bayerische Infanterie Division, 2nd Garde Reserve Division, 10th Ersatz Division and the 3rd Reserve Infanterie Division.

No one assumed that October 26 was going to be a walk in the park. Both combatants acknowledged it would be a day of considerable sacrifice and great suffering. There was, however, optimism within the Canadian Corps rank and file, especially among the men of the 43rd Canadian Infantry Battalion, who were convinced the Canadian Corps would succeed at Passchendaele, where others had tried, but failed.

The Ypres Salient front-line extended a distance of approximately twenty-four miles, in October, 1917. For the most part, that frontline had remained relatively static since April 1915, when Lieutenant-General Edwin A.H. Alderson's 1st Canadian Infantry Division occupied a section of the Allied line. Now, a few days before the Battle of Passchendaele, reconnaissance information, furnished by pilots from the Royal Flying Corps, reported Germany's XIV Corps was preparing for the defense of a twelve-mile front of farmland in Diksmuide, a city in West-Flanders famously known for its butter. Flight observers also noted that the six-mile-long height of land at Wytschaete was occupied by IX Reserve and Gruppe Staden, while four Eingriff Divisions were positioned on Passchendaele Ridge. Inexplicably, a number of the Eingriff Divisions had been relocated from Passchendaele and repositioned approximately seven miles further north of the village. This questionable change in strategy placed German infantry troops at a severe disadvantage. Should a situation arise during battle urgently requiring these troops to provide support, they would be too far removed from the front to quickly respond to the defense of Passchendaele. This could leave Passchendaele vulnerable to a massive Canadian assault on the German lines, resulting in the loss of one of the most strategically advantageous piece of real estate.

Since July 31, 1917, more than fifty British and ANZAC divisions had attempted to capture Passchendaele Ridge from the enemy, while during the same period, eighty-three German infantry divisions had successfully defended the ridge. These German divisions had been commanded by: Crown Prince Rupprecht of Bavaria, Major-General Von Stumpf, Field Marshall General Erich Ludendorff, and General Friedrich Sixt von Armin. Three weeks before the Canadian Corps moved into the salient, General Arthur Currie ordered the commander of the 1st Canadian Divisional Engineers, which comprised the 1st, 2nd, and 3rd Canadian Field Companies and the 107th Canadian Pioneer Battalion, to make the necessary improvements to existing communication and transportation systems. Where no system existed, construction was to commence immediately to establish one. Roads were vital in logistical operations for the deployment of troops and supplies from rear positions to front-line. Planning, implementation and supervision were handled by the Engineers and Pioneers of the Canadian Corps. The manual labour of trenching and the construction of roads was the responsibility of ordinary regulars with axes, picks, and shovels. Besides the significant relevance associated with the building of roads, there was also considerable attention paid to the establishment and maintenance of fighting trenches.

Training manuals defined a trench as: "A long, narrow excavation in the ground, the earth from which is thrown up in front to serve as a shelter from enemy fire or attack."

In order to establish this particular subterraneous excavation, physical manpower, using picks and shovels, was required. Networks of both defensive and offensive in-ground passageways played an integral part of WWI combat strategy. Unlike the trenches of the Douai Plain at Vimy, or at the Somme, those in West Flanders in the Ypres Salient, required improvisation in order to accommodate a major problem — water. This necessitated the digging of shallow ditches, reinforced with sandbags, wooden planks, timber, and wire mesh. Fighting trenches, sometimes referred to as "field works," were not new to war. They had been part of warfare dating back to Roman times, throughout the American Civil War, and as recently as the South African Boer War.

Trenches were designed and built in a zigzag pattern, with short curves followed by straight sections of thirty feet in length before curving again. This trench pattern was repeated throughout the front and support lines. Army engineers had their reasons for not designing and constructing straight-line trenches.

1. This design greatly reduced the possibility of troops being subjected to enfilade rifle fire, should the enemy breach part of a trench during an assault or raid.
2. The design was based on the assumption that any concussion, debris and shell fragments resulting from a bomb explosion would be confined exclusively to a thirty-foot section, rather than the full length of a straight-line trench.

The trench system, in the Great War, was introduced to the battlefields of Western Europe in the fall of 1914. The trenches were basic in design; narrow, shallow, and crammed with troops, shoulder-to-shoulder. In 1915, a massive buildup of Triple Entente and Central Power troops materialized along a combat front from the Swiss border to the Belgian North Sea. The result of deploying troops along a front that extended such a great distance across Western Europe meant that fewer soldiers occupied less space in the trenches. By 1915, trenches had become deeper and much more elaborate. In the deeper trenches, soldiers were not only protected from small arms fire but also from large infantry assaults and bombardments, especially with dug-outs built to withstand medium to heavy artillery fire. As the trench system expanded, the war evolved into an exercise of attrition. In many ways it had become a stalemate.

Fire-steps and fire-bays were special features incorporated into the functionality of fighting trenches. Fire-bays bore a striking similarity to castle turrets and were usually positioned sixteen feet apart within a trench system. Observation and listening posts were situated at right angles to the front-line and were defended by huge concentrations of barbed wire. Fire-steps were significant indentations, dug into the semi-circular sections of the field works, facing No-Man's Land. A fire-step provided a place where a highly skilled sniper could apply his expertise as a marksman. One such soldier, considered by many as Canada's deadliest sniper, was Private Frances Pegahmegabow (later promoted to corporal) of the 1st Canadian Infantry Battalion (Western Ontario). Private Pegahmegabow was credited for having shot and killed 378 German soldiers. In addition to his skill at using a rifle, it was also noted that he personally took 300 prisoners. Francis Pegahmegabow, who enlisted in August 1914 and was deployed overseas in February 1915, became the highest-decorated First Nations soldier in World War One. He was awarded the Military Medal at the Second Battle of Ypres, a Military Medal Bar at the Battle of Passchendaele, and a second Military Medal Bar at the Battle of the Scarpe.

A soldier's time spent in a water-and-mud-sodden trench was insufferable at best, even without the added stress of exploding bombs. Combat-hardened troops were no different than green recruits when it came to fearing for one's life on the Western Front. Death could come at any moment from a sniper's bullet, a shrapnel shell, a machine gun bullet, a bayonet blade, or the inhalation of poison gas. In addition to the typical weapons of war, there were also the daily, non-lethal torments, for example: large rats, body lice, and fleas. If these things didn't make a soldier's skin crawl, there was always the stench of decaying bodies, combined with the foul smell of overflowing latrines and the pungent odour of chlorine gas, to make even the toughest infantryman puke his bully beef. As one can imagine, a soldier's olfactory sense was constantly being assaulted, not only by these three smells mentioned, but also by lingering odours of petrol, cordite, and smoke .

(Ross photo)
This restored trench in Boezinge, near Ypres, is a good example of how trenches were designed and constructed in WWI. During an extensive excavation and restoration program between 1998 and 2000, the remains of 155 British, French, and German soldiers were unearthed at this particular site. The majority of the remains exhumed were British who were probably killed on July 6, 1915.

A significant irritant to all trench warriors was the never-ending seepage of water into their earthen shelter. Water usually settled a few inches or higher above the duckboards, despite gasoline-powered water pumps chugging full-out to remove it. Maintaining a water-free trench in the Ypres Salient was a never-ending challenge with a no-win result. Some infantry units resorted to improvisation in order to keep their soldiers' feet dry. The 2nd East Yorkshire Regiment stationed near the village of Boesinghe, built duckboard walkways resembling elevated foot-bridges. These boardwalks were ingeniously engineered to be supported on a raised cribbing, which kept the wooden planks elevated inches above the water level on the trench floor. This clever method, although functional, was not universally accepted in the salient; it required an abundance of materials and additional manpower to construct.

(source: Library and Archives Canada)
One of many Canadian artillery guns mired in the mud and clay of Flanders plain during the Battle of Passchendaele.

On the morning of October 22, the Cameron Highlanders were told to anticipate a possible surprise enemy attack, however, after thirty minutes, the order to "Stand Down" was given and life in the trenches returned to normal.

Mornings meant breakfast and breakfast usually meant a can of cold rations. Occasionally, while stationed in the trenches, soldiers made a breakfast of oatmeal, eggs, and bacon cooked on a small primus stove. Sometimes, depending on the situation, breakfast was delivered to the front-line by the field kitchens. Even the faintest smell of food drifting across No-Man's Land was usually an invitation to be attacked, not because of the aroma of bacon in the air, but because Canadian soldiers were probably distracted, consuming their meal. During the First World War, an incredible amount of food was shipped from Britain to the men fighting in France and Belgium. Approximately 3.2 million tons of food was cooked and supplied to the soldiers on the Western Front. In order to supply an infantry division of 20,000 troops each day, it required at least 2,000 men and horses, hundreds of wagons, and nearly 120 motorized lorries. In the beginning of the war, troops were given ten ounces of meat and eight ounces of vegetables every day, however, as the war progressed and the German blockade became more effective, quantity and quality became less than ideal. By 1917, meat was available only about thirty percent of the time on the frontline, with canned corned beef (bully beef) being the main staple of a soldier's diet. As time went on, troops of the British Expeditionary Force found that their meals included pea soup with horsemeat, stews using weeds, and tea that tasted like vegetables. Fresh food was often a rarity, therefore, baked bread invariably was very stale by the time it arrived at the front-lines, as it was said to take eight days to reach the men. Despite some dietary shortcomings from time to time, for the most part Canadian soldiers ate well, getting at least the recommended 3,574 calories a day. After morning meal, the trench warriors continued with small chores, including an inventory of ammunition and water, as well as sleeping, playing cards, and writing letters to loved ones.

During the evening, both front and support lines increased their activity level substantially. Several work parties were assigned to lay barbed wire and repair trench walls damaged by erosion and bombings. In addition, sandbags were filled, raids were conducted on German lines and food, water, and ammunition were restocked. This routine was continually repeated during a soldier's stay in the trenches, not ending until a company or full battalion either went into battle, or was relieved by another unit. The length of time served in the line varied depending on the situation, although it was four days on average. That being said, it was not unheard of for a coy to spend up to fourteen days in the front-line before being relocated to either support or reserve lines.

As well as the mundane duties of trench life, soldiers were also ordered to participate in body-recovery operations. Small groups of infantrymen were assigned the gruesome task of recovering and burying the remains of fellow soldiers scattered over the battlefield, including on occasion those found in No-Man's Land. This particular job was the cause of many Canadian soldiers' terrifying nightmares. For some the nightmares continued long after the war ended.

There were other essential activities, besides combat and body retrieval. Battalion medics made concerted efforts to educate every soldier on the subject of sanitation and personal hygiene. The prevention of serious illness and communicable disease, both behind the lines and in the trenches, was pertinent to the well-being of all troops and their effectiveness in battle. As a result, a great amount of attention was paid to the construction and maintenance of sanitary facilities, in other words, battlefield toilets. Depending on where a soldier was from, a battlefield washroom could have any one of several names. Example: a lavatory, toilet, water closet, privy, restroom, and loo. An ANZAC soldier probably referred to it as a dunny. The most commonly used name was "latrine."

The task of digging a battlefield latrine always fell upon the shoulders of the ordinary regular. It was his job to excavate a series of short, open ditches, three-feet long, one-foot wide, and one-foot deep, each spaced twenty-one feet apart. The army manual, *Sanitation of Camps and Bivouacs* stated that five latrines could accommodate up to 100 men daily. Latrines were a necessity of life. They did, however, add one more obnoxious and disgusting stink to an already gigantic cesspool of salient odours.

It was extremely important for Canadian Corps troops to clearly understand the relevance of maintaining good health through proper personal hygiene. Practicing good hygiene as much as possible on the Western Front, greatly helped to prevent outbreaks of severe illness, which if not controlled, could seriously undermine the strength and well-being of troops going into battle. As part of the hygiene regimen, infantrymen were expected to diligently care for their feet. This meant daily washing, drying, and applying whale oil to prevent "trench foot." Fingernails, mouths, skin, and hair were closely scrutinized by teams of medical officers and nursing sisters. Warnings were given to anyone who failed to heed their directives. Underclothing was to be scrubbed and washed weekly, except for those front-line soldiers who were extended a reprieve until moved to reserve line at the rear. Although strict compliance to the rules was to always be observed in the camps, it was less stringent in the trenches, and for obvious reasons.

After footslogging across fields that gave us a few harrowing moments, our coy finally arrived at trenches left vacant some days ago by the New Zealanders. What everyone called trenches, were nothing more than holes, craters, and shallow ditches. It was from these positions that the New Zealand troops launched their attacks on Bellevue Spur and Goudberg Spur, on the 12 October. From what we have learned, the Kiwis lost 846 men on that day. After surveying the area, we split into smaller groups and made our way to the shallow trenches and foxholes where we settled in. In the muddy trench I shared with several of my comrades, we found empty ration cans, ground sheets, spent ammo, the usual hoard of rats, and an overpowering smell of humans decomposing. What we found were the bodies of two German soldiers in a nearby foxhole. There were also a number of shallow graves marked with steels helmets and ID tags hung on Mausers with the bayonets rammed into the mud. Our time in the former ANZAC trenches was short. A second-lieutenant arrived to tell us that B Coy and A Coy would be leaving and replaced by C and D Coy.

Arrangements for the Canadian assault on Passchendaele were rapidly falling into place. While the Canadian Corps Infantry Divisions were busy preparing for battle, General Friedrich Bertram Sixt von Armin was observing what was transpiring below Passchendaele Ridge, on the fields of Flanders. Heavy weapons, munitions, and armoured tanks were being redirected from the newly-built corduroy roads onto the muddy fields of the Ypres Salient. There to greet the Canadians were the German field-artillery batteries. As soon as they were spotted by enemy reconnaissance aircraft, the Germans opened fire with a massive bombardment, using humongous artillery guns. Many of the German guns weighed 2,825 pounds or more, with seven-foot, eight-inch barrels that could direct an artillery shell at a target five miles away.

The barrage of enemy bombs met instant retaliation. An equally strong response came from the Canadian Field Artillery, with a series of rapid fire (four rounds every sixty seconds), sustained shelling from Ordnance QF 18-Pounders.

Over the next four days, German and Canadian artillery batteries exchanged intense shelling, resulting in 1,500 Canadian casualties and an unknown number of enemy dead and wounded. Many of the Canadian casualties were the result of a powerful German weapon nicknamed "Big Bertha." This 420 cm mobile howitzer, called "Dicke Berta" by the Germans, was named in honour of Bertha Krupp von Bohlen und Halbach. Bertha Krupp was the sole heir to her father's (Friedrich Krupp) industrial and weapons manufacturing empire, upon his death in 1902. The Krupp Company manufactured the largest and most powerful mortar weapons in Kaiser Wilhelm's arsenal in World War I. Big Bertha weighed an incredible forty-three tons, with shells weighing a mind boggling 1,800 pounds. These mortar shells were so huge they could be seen with the naked eye zooming through the air, while at the same time, sounding like a steam locomotive roaring down the tracks.

General Arthur Currie's battle plan was formulated on the assumption he and his troops could pull off a surprise attack on the Germans. In order to accomplish this, he planned to delay announcing Zero Hour until just a few hours before the assault was to commence. Currie's assumption that a surprise attack was plausible had both its adherents, and its sceptics. Those who were sceptical were of the opinion that catching General von Armin and the entire Germany Fourth Army off-guard, unprepared, and surprised was overly optimistic, perhaps even as some suggested, naive. General Erich Ludendorff and the German High Command had reviewed pages of intelligence reports obtained from ground and air reconnaissance. Analysis of the information concluded a major battle was in the offing, and it was imminent. If there was any doubt, a young Canadian prisoner-of-war confirmed to interrogators what the Germans had for some time suspected — October 26 would see the start of the Battle of Passchendaele. The most important information, however, Zero Hour, remained sealed in envelopes at Canadian Corps Headquarters.

Chapter Twenty-Five
OCTOBER 23, 1917

"Never interrupt your enemy while he is making a mistake."

Napoleon Bonaparte

After a very short leave, Lance Corporal Stephen Ernest Shortliffe returned to the front on the morning of Tuesday, October 23. The previous day, Ernie and B Coy had travelled by army trucks from Pommern Redoubt to Poperinge, a distance of twelve miles. It was there, a short distance from Ypres, that the men took the opportunity to have their lice-infected uniforms fumigated, while enjoying a brief period of rest and relaxation away from the mud and stench of the battlefield. Privates and NCOs were assigned billets in former Belgian army barracks, while officers were accommodated in upscale hotels or private rest houses.

Poperinge was a beehive of activity; its streets were jammed with soldiers and locals, some of whom were former residents of Ypres evacuated in the spring of 1915. Shops, restaurants, and especially sidewalk cafes, did a bustling business serving thousands of soldiers, as well as the many nursing sisters stationed at nearby casualty clearing stations.

One of the main reasons casualty clearing stations were situated in Poperinge was the fact it was a major railway hub. Casualty clearing stations were generally placed near railway lines, thereby allowing for the movement of casualties by rail to larger and better-equipped hospitals elsewhere, far from the Western Front. It was this activity that captured the attention of the Germans who made the train station a designated target for almost daily attacks. The regularity of these bombings, specifically aimed at the Poperinge train station, began to cast suspicion on the station master, who many believed to be a German spy. A short time later, the station master simply vanished from the city of Poperinge. His sudden disappearance fuelled speculation he may have met the same fate as fifty British and twenty French soldiers who were executed for desertion and other serious wartime crimes, in a courtyard on the grounds of Poperinge Stadhuis (Poperinge Town Hall).

Poperinge's popularity with troops from Great Britain and the Commonwealth was because of its ambiance, where war-weary soldiers could unwind and enjoy themselves after spending time at the front. While ordinary regulars were provided with good, but basic amenities, officers enjoyed a number of private clubs that catered exclusively to them. Skindles Hotel was a place where officers, from captain to lieutenant-colonel, could relax, read, or enjoy a bottle of wine, a beer, or a glass of Scotch. Best of all, it was a place to sleep in a clean, warm, comfortable bed.

Talbot House, situated at 43 Gasthuisstraat in the centre of Poperinge was also a very popular rest house, catering to soldiers of all ranks. Talbot House (also referred to by its signal code TOC-H) was an attractive, three-storey building that had served as a home-away-from-home for many British soldiers, since 1915. One of the most notable features of Talbot House was the beautiful, tranquil garden in a rear courtyard. It was there that soldiers found contemplative solitude from the bombs, bullets, and bayonets of West Flanders.

On the morning of October 23, as the men of B Coy were returning to Pommern Redoubt, shelling broke out near the Canadian positions. The pattern of the bombing prompted Canadian Corps officers to suspect a raid might be about to take place, using German artillery fire as a cover. What was thought to have been a precursor to an impending enemy attack was actually nothing more than intimidation, known as "the morning hate message." While the shelling continued unabated, officers of the 43rd Infantry Battalion held a special meeting to review plans for the relief of the entire 1st Wellington Battalion of New Zealand.

Later on in the afternoon, a "Stand To" order was issued at 4:00 p.m. by battalion officers in reaction to the abrupt cessation of trench mortar shells, which had been continually falling for the past number of hours. The officers believed this was a signal for a chemical-weapon assault. Although a thick cloud of asphyxiating gas failed to materialize, shells from several German 4.5 inch howitzers did. After a short period of bombardment, the attack ended. Each Cameron Highlander of Canada Coy then ordered a roll call to ascertain if the battalion had suffered any casualties. Lance Corporal S.E. Shortliffe's Coy had gone unscathed, but the other three coys were not so fortunate. In total, four soldiers were killed and six wounded. One of the men killed by shellfire near Pommern Redoubt, was a twenty-four-year-old lieutenant named Oscar Harold Hollis. Lieutenant Hollis was fatally wounded while acting as an advance officer for B Coy. The other Cameron Highlanders to perish on October 23, 1917 were: Private John Cachtley, who died while being treated at No. 44 Casualty Clearing Station for severe bullet wounds to his arms and legs, Private Gordon Walker Hartley, and Private James Emmett Wallace.

The next troop relocation saw the 9th Canadian Infantry Brigade's twelve battalions move to within striking distance of German-occupied territory, but first each battalion compiled a list of soldiers confirmed to be combat ready for Friday, October 26. A number of 43rd Battalion troops at that moment, were being treated at a regimental aid station, suffering from a variety of ailments. Included on the list were: bronchial congestion, typhus, trench foot, dysentery, and six infantrymen suffering combat wounds. It was the responsibility of the medical officers to ensure everyone on sick parade would be fit enough to carry a rifle on the day of battle and that included the walking wounded. One of those happened to be Private Robert John Kerr, who after being treated for forty-eight hours was discharged and placed back on active duty. Three days later he was killed in action — his body never recovered. After roll call and sick parade was completed, it was determined that as of October 23, the 43rd Infantry Battalion could field a combat strength of 550 officers and other ranks.

When a soldier in WWI was faced with the overwhelming odds of being killed in battle, rather than surviving, it was only reasonable for him to consider any available alternative to actually fighting and ultimately dying. There were those who would feign illness or injury rather than face a bomb, a bullet, or a bayonet. Medics had seen many examples of this since the Canadian Expeditionary Force first arrived in Europe and were thrust into battle. Leading up to the Passchendaele mission, doctors generally expected to be told a number of creative stories to explain a variety of ailments afflicting a soldier. These stories were added to a litany of reasons for exempting some soldiers from the Battle of Passchendaele.

Soldiers reporting to sick parade were carefully screened by medical officers, paying strict attention to those suspected to be malingerers, (soldiers hoping to avoid combat). In the case of injuries, many were found to be self-inflicted. A serious injury almost certainly ensured an infantryman a one-way ticket out of Battlefield Hell and into a hospital with rehabilitation somewhere in France or Britain. The severity of one's injury depended largely on the particular instrument and method used to cause a self-inflicted wound or SIW. Desperation was the primary motivation. It was this desperate action to deceive by producing a significant wound, which was said to have been caused by a freak accident or in the line of duty. Accidents were contrived with the assistance of a large gulp of dark rum; an anesthesia against the excruciating pain that would follow the accidental discharge of an Enfield rifle pointed at a soldier's boot, blowing away part of the foot. The reasoning for this audacious decision, to use a bullet or bayonet blade to create pain, disfigurement, and humiliation, was in some cases, to avoid participating in a war they had grown to despise for its killing and maiming. On the other hand, in the majority of these cases, men were simply too fearful of dying, having seen so much of it since being deployed to the Western Front.

Contrary to those who attempted to mislead medical staff, there were many, many others who were truly sick. Illness came in various forms and severity. One that few understood or knew how to treat was the impairment of a soldier's mental state, due to stress. The awe and shock of bombs exploding and of machine guns serving up daily doses of mutilation and death created an emotional condition within the minds of soldiers called, "shell shock." Many years and several wars later, shell shock, the condition that plagued WWI soldiers, is known today as PTSD (Post-Traumatic Stress Disorder).

As time went by during the course of WWI, medics and officers regularly heard soldiers complain about being extremely tired, irritable, having a lack of concentration, and suffering from constant, head-throbbing migraine headaches. After much discussion and examination of the ailment, shell shock was finally recognized as a debilitating, mental condition. At the onset of symptoms, army doctors and nurses observed the progression of abnormal behaviours in those afflicted with shell shock, and the many, drastic personality changes in the men. Changes that were most evident included: a lack of verbal communication, staring for extended periods at nothing in particular, and being non-responsive to questions or direct orders from an officer. Numerous trench warriors ended their European wartime adventure sitting in muted silence, or hysterical laughter interspersed with bouts of screaming and mumbling. Eventually, most of the emotionally wounded were evacuated to hospitals in England before being repatriated to Canada. Men who had suffered shell shock would seldom, if ever, serve in uniform again.

In the early afternoon of October 23, thirty-four-year-old, Lieutenant-Colonel William Kellman Chandler arrived on horseback at the 43rd Battalion camp, in Pommern Redoubt, near Frezenberg, to assume command of the Cameron Highlanders of Canada Regiment. Immediately upon his arrival, Colonel Chandler issued Operation Order No. 136, in which he instructed all company commanders

"to proceed from Pommern Redoubt to Waterloo Farm in platoon formation, separated from each unit by a distance of 600 feet."

Once the battalion had arrived at Waterloo Farm it was to make contact with the 1st Battalion Wellington Regiment and then proceed to finalize the takeover of the New Zealand trench positions which were situated on the 3rd Canadian Infantry Division's right Front Sector, the location from which the 43rd Battalion would launch the attack on Friday, October 26 against the enemy on Bellevue Spur.

With fewer than two hours of daylight remaining, I joined my platoon and prepared to take leave of Pommern Redoubt at exactly 5:00 p.m. for Waterloo Farm. Even though we left at the scheduled time, we were ordered to halt our advance and wait until it was completely dark before crossing Abraham Heights. Attached to our platoon, were two ANZAC guides who were given the responsibility to make sure we all reached the other side of the height of land, hopefully without casualties. All the other platoons were provided with two guides from the 1st Battalion Wellington Regiment as well. The Kiwis did an excellent job of guiding us to the other side of Abraham Heights, despite heavy enemy fire and badly damaged slippery duckboards. As we continued on, shells exploded everywhere. It took a great amount of concentration not to lose one's balance and fall into a water-filled crater, especially in the dark. A few of the lads at the front slipped off the planks and into the mud shortly after leaving Pommern Redoubt and it took a great effort to pull them from their frightening predicament to safety. One's own body weight, combined with a heavy combat kit made the rescue difficult. Although our trek was slow and often dangerous, after several hours, we finally arrived at our destination — Waterloo Farm.

By 8:30 p.m., the majority of companies from the 43rd Battalion had taken possession of the New Zealand positions, with the exception of one company. B Coy did not reach its final destination until the early hours of Wednesday morning, October 24. The men of B Coy had encountered heavy enemy artillery-shelling and machine-gun fire culminating in a number of casualties, which slowed the troops' advance to a snail's pace.

We were a sorry-looking bunch of Cameron Highlanders by the time we reached Waterloo Farm, early Wednesday morning. Everyone was totally drenched to the skin. My kilt was caked in foul-smelling mud and both knees had the skin peeled away, exposing raw flesh. I was able to wrap bandages around both bloody areas to control the pain of the kilt chafing my legs, as well as hopefully preventing infection. I wish we could discard the kilt for a pair of trousers, if only for this one battle.

Chapter Twenty-Six
OCTOBER 24, 1917

"There was not a sign of life of any sort. Not a tree, save for a few dead stumps which looked strange in the moonlight. Not a bird, not even a rat or a blade of grass. Nature was as dead as those Canadians whose bodies remained where they had fallen the previous autumn. Death was written large everywhere."

Private R.A. Colwell, Passchendaele, January 1918

Over a period of several hours between the previous evening and early morning of Wednesday, October 24, the 43rd Battalion, together with sister battalions from the 9th Brigade, 3rd Canadian Infantry Division, had moved into position at Waterloo Farm. Occupying the right front-line was A Coy, with B Coy situated to their left. The other two companies from the 43rd Battalion, C Coy and D Coy, were ordered into right and left support areas, respectively. Once the Cameron Highlanders of Canada had concluded the relief operation, with the 1st Battalion Wellington Regiment, the Highlanders took over control of field maps, intelligence reports, and all supplies, including food and ammunition. A complete inventory was compiled and verified by officers of the 43rd Canadian Infantry Battalion and the 1st Battalion Wellington Regiment. Once completed and signed, a copy was sent by runner to 43rd Battalion Headquarters. As mentioned earlier, the relief operation was not entirely without incident, having cost the lives of Lieutenant Oscar H. Hollis and two officers from the 1st Battalion

Wellington Regiment, killed by mortar and machine gun fire. Also, on October 24 two ordinary regulars with the 43rd Battalion were killed. The infantrymen were: Private George Richard Elliot and Private James Patterson. The bodies of both soldiers were not recovered.

Peering through an opening in the sandbag parapet of our trench, I am able to have my first look at Bellevue Spur, a height of land, rising gradually above Flanders plain. This is to be our objective when we launch our assault in the coming days. Both Bellevue Spur and Passchendaele Ridge, we have been told, will be heavily defended by barbed wire, pillboxes, and several highly trained and experienced divisions of the German 4th Army. Looking to my right, I can see a small, forested area, shown on our field maps as "Berlin Wood." To the south-east of Berlin Wood is Abraham Heights, an elevated section of terrain which we crossed last night in order to reach Waterloo Farm. Not far from Waterloo Farm is a stream called Ravebeek and south of this stream is Waterfields Farm, situated behind the German lines. To the north, is No-Man's Land and beyond, that is where my comrades and I will confront the enemy and hopefully prevail in taking our objective.

Waterloo Farm is no longer the magnificent Flemish farm it once was before the war. Now, it's a sad picture of rubble, shell craters, trenches and knee-deep mud. It is also where my fellow comrades and I will nervously wait for the order to move to the jumping-off positions in No-Man's Land.

During the morning hours, Lance Corporal S.E. Shortliffe and B Coy excavated several communication trenches. When completed, the trenches connected battalion, brigade and divisional headquarters with the front-line, by telephone. As the soldiers went about their work, they occasionally came under sniper fire or the sudden blast of machine guns. When all the work had finished, two officers and two privates had been wounded. All four Highlanders were removed from the area by stretcher bearers and driven by army ambulance to an advanced dressing station in Vlamertinge, three miles west of Ypres.

Within close proximity of where the Cameron Highlanders were digging communication ditches was a 300-foot wide stretch of No-Man's Land, located in the Passchendaele Ridge sector. Passchendaele was estimated to contain as many as fifteen German infantry divisions, ready to defend the ridge and village from the pending assault by the Canadian Corps. The most highly experienced division among the fifteen was the 11.Bayerische Infanterie-Division (11th Bavarian Infantry Division). This was an elite unit of the German Fourth Army. Many of its 12,500 infantrymen had fought on several different battlefronts, since the unit was first formed and mobilized on March 24, 1915. Two of their most notable combat engagements were the Serbian Campaign and the Battle of Verdun in 1916.

After completing the communication trenches to the satisfaction of corps engineers, the Cameron Highlanders returned to Waterloo Farm just as a light rain began to fall. Rain, as forecasted, fell for the next number of days. In the trenches, soldiers peered across the expanse of the Ravebeek Valley towards Bellevue Spur and Passchendaele Ridge and saw fields awash in desolation. The landscape was only broken by the sight of heavily camouflaged pillboxes and blockhouses, protected by miles of barbed wire. The Passchendaele operation was considered, by some military theorists, as similar to the one fought by the Canadian Corps at Vimy Ridge only a few months earlier. Both elevations had been occupied by the Imperial German Army since the early days of the war. Vimy Ridge fell into the hands of the Germans just before the end of 1914, and Passchendaele Ridge in fall of the same year. Despite similarities, there was one substantial difference — battleground condition. Unlike Vimy and the Douai Plain, troops advancing on Passchendaele by foot and armoured tank would be fighting two substantial enemies — the Germans and the mud.

Within two days, the 3rd Canadian Infantry Division, numbering approximately 20,000 combat-ready troops, would find itself in a major operation. One of the lead battalions, the 43rd Canadian Infantry Battalion (Cameron Highlanders of Canada) CEF saw 101 of its brave, young men die on that first day. They would shoot, bomb, and bayonet their way up Bellevue Spur, in what has been called by many, "a slaughter in the mud." Heroic Canadian soldiers would be killed by the vicious impact of machine-gun fire and bursting shrapnel bombs. Others would die of asphyxiation from a cloud of Yperite, (poison gas).

The Battle of Passchendaele was to be West-Flanders' Armageddon.

Since the ANZAC offensive of October 12, the Imperial German Army had painstakingly made preparations for an expected monstrous assault on Passchendaele Ridge. Speculating on what General Currie's plan of attack might encompass, German generals instituted their own, tactical strategy. They positioned their most capable and battle-experienced forces on the slopes and crests within the Passchendaele occupied territory. The first line of defense was the elite machine-gun crews with their Maschinengewehr-08 weapons. These fearless warriors possessed an irrefutable reputation for loyalty, toughness, and commitment to fight as long and hard as humanly possible, even if that meant sacrificing their lives for the kaiser, while chained to their guns. Sitting in their bunkers and pillboxes, they anxiously awaited the 43rd Infantry Battalion and the Canadian advance up Bellevue Spur. Many of these machine-gun nests were first encountered by the Canadian Corps troops along Wolfe Copse, a heavily fortified area northwest of Waterloo Farm and 's Graventafel Road.

Canadian Corps Commander, General Arthur Currie was not unmindful of the fact Canadian troops faced a significant challenge from their German adversaries, who intended to preserve Passchendaele as German-held territory. Enemy combat units, numbering in the thousands from the 6th Bavarian Infantry Division and 10th Ersatz Division in and near the village of Passchendaele, were ready to defend against the Canadian Corps and General Plumer's Fifth Army. Both enemy divisions were part of the German Sixth Army, under the command of General Rupprecht, Crown Prince of Bavaria. In addition, Passchendaele was also defended by the 2nd Guard Reserve Division, under General Karl von Bulow of the Second Army, and the 23rd Reserve Infantry Division, led by General Max von Hausen, commander of the German Third Army. The overall defense of Passchendaele, on October 26, would fall under the command of General Friedrich von Armin of the German Fourth Army, under the tutelage of Field Marshall Erich Ludendorff.

In the hours leading up to the anticipated battle, German officers suggested perhaps General Currie might decide to delay the October

26 attack by twenty-four hours or possibly even longer. Due to the inclement weather, Currie might postpone the operation until weather conditions improved. Generals von Armin and Ludendorff discussed this and other possibilities with their generals during a meeting in Ludendorff's bomb-proof bunker. They reviewed reconnaissance and intelligence reports and pondered counterattack strategies. No one dismissed out-of-hand, the notion Currie could delay the attack, but then none of the generals knew for certain, "Wann wird es geschehen?" ("When will it happen?")

The incessant rain, creator of logistical nightmares and demoralizer of men, suddenly and surprisingly stopped at mid-morning on October 24. This brief respite from the rain gave troops a chance to clean and oil their guns, play a game of cards, and enjoy the sun. At 3:00 p.m., the adjutant from the 58th Canadian Infantry Battalion (Ontario Central), telephoned 43rd Battalion Headquarters and requested immediate relief for the battalion's A Coy and C Coy, which were entrenched with the 9th Infantry Brigade on the right side of 's Graventafel Road. B Coy took charge, made contact with the 58th Battalion, and carried out the relief operation.

It was hellishly difficult walking through the knee-deep mud and clay to our next position. Craters were so numerous and close to each other that it was almost impossible to determine where they started and ended. As we pushed forward, we encountered large quantities of mangled and rusted barbed wire. Some of the wire still held the decomposing bodies of Australian and New Zealand soldiers impaled on the steel barbs and rods. Most appeared to be victims of machine-gun fire, gunned down while attempting to breach the wire along 's-Graventafel Road.

After much time and effort, we finally arrived at our new position to the right of 's-Graventafel Road and within sight of Ravebeek. There was a foul, sickening smell permeating the air, a stench that seemed to get stronger the closer we got to Ravebeek and No-Man's Land. The Hun considers No-Man's Land to be a buffer zone and therefore neutral territory. Indeed, it does act as a buffer zone between us and them, however, we do not consider No-Man's Land as being neutral territory. This being said, it will probably be the jumping-off position for our battalion on

Friday. We (NCOs) have been informed by the officers that Jerry will be defending a heavily fortified line of approximately 3,300 yards in length. They say there will be at least one machine gun positioned every 110 yards along that line. It will require a concentrated effort by the 43rd Battalion to breach the 250 yards assigned to us before pushing on to our objective. I am confident we will succeed, but at what cost?

From atop Passchendaele Ridge, overlooking the Ypres Salient, German commanders basked in the warm glow of realization. They recognized that THEY controlled the high ground, and this was THEIR prominent and distinctive advantage over any Canadian Corps attack. Field Marshall Ludendorff and General von Armin confidently theorized that their infantry divisions and substantive defensive fortifications together would withstand any major assault directed against Passchendaele. Kaiser Wilhelm's Imperial German Army had successfully repulsed all attacks made on its territory, including an assault twelve days earlier, on Friday, October 12.

On October 12, during a morning monsoon-like rainstorm, troops from New Zealand's 2nd Brigade and 3rd Rifle Brigade came within a hair of being annihilated, on Bellevue Spur. At 5:25 a.m., the New Zealanders left their trenches in the dark and slogged their way up Bellevue through clay and mud, over debris and bodies, and around fields of craters. Bullets whizzed. Bombs exploded. ANZAC troops fought fearlessly, though out-gunned and out-manned. Ultimately, their advance faltered, cut short by massive amounts of uncut wire and walls of deadly machine-gun fire. Ribbons of bullets streamed down upon the New Zealand troops and forced them to scramble for cover. The fighting raged amid the smoke, gas, bomb explosions, and bullets. Parties of men with wire cutters crawled on their bellies to the heavy rolls of barbed wire strung between steel rods. It was imperative that this courageous act, under extremely perilous conditions, be successful if the New Zealanders were to continue advancing forward. None the less, German machine-gunners swept Bellevue Spur with fire, churning the salient mud into a sea of Kiwi blood and pinning the men to the ground for ten long and terrifying hours. At 3:00 p.m., the order came for the troops to retreat to the position they had held earlier that morning.

Upon their return to the trenches, a roll call was conducted to determine the extent of loss of lives during the ten-hour battle. The casualty numbers were colossal. Shockingly, 2,000 New Zealand troops did not answer afternoon roll call. In total, forty-five officers and 800 other ranks perished in battle on October 12. An additional 138 soldiers succumbed to their wounds days later, and the remaining 1,017 were listed as missing-in-action and presumed dead. October 12, 1917, was the largest, single-day loss of life incurred by the New Zealand Army in WWI and therefore, forever remembered, as the "bleakest day in the history of New Zealand."

Canadian Corps successes at Vimy Ridge and Hill 70 should have been of great concern to the Germans, however, they were unwavering in the assumption Passchendaele would never become another Canadian conquest. On the other hand, General von Armin, although confident in the ability of his officers and men, was also a realist. He understood a large and sustained assault, similar to Vimy Ridge, could place his troops in jeopardy of being able to stem the tide of the Canadian offensive. As a result, in anticipation of heavy artillery fire and a massive frontal attack by Canada's Shock Troops, the enemy decided to deploy the 6th Bayerische Infanterie Division in two key positions. These were designated: The Protective Line of the Forward Zone, and a Line of Resistance. The latter was situated approximately 550 yards behind the Protective Forward Zone.

The first objective of the 43rd Infantry Battalion was to neutralize a number of machine- gun nests standing in the way of advancing Canadian troops, on the battlefield of Bellevue Spur. Steel-reinforced, camouflaged, concrete pillboxes were guarded by a massive amount of barbed wire, thereby presenting a colossal challenge to the Cameron Highlanders of Canada. Four companies of Highlanders, approximately 125 men each, assembled for an in-depth briefing on the upcoming mission. Should the 3rd Canadian Infantry Division Field Artillery fail to inflict sufficient damage upon the German machine gun placements, it would be incumbent upon all platoon officers to employ the necessary tactics and manpower resources to render them non-functional. In order to accomplish this and avoid detection, small parties of soldiers, armed with wire cutters and grenades, would hug the ground, slither stealthily through the mud and water, and hopefully reach the wire protecting the pillboxes. In order to silence the guns, the Cameron Highlanders would snip and peel back the wire before moving surreptitiously to either side of the respective machine-gun forts. Tossing in a couple of Mills bombs would, in all probability, kill or at least seriously wound the occupants, and in turn silence the guns. Any enemy machine-gunners fortunate enough to escape the grenade blasts would be taken prisoner or possibly shot, depending on the situation at the time.

The hand grenade was found to be an effective weapon, therefore it was employed extensively by both combatants in the Great War. The Germans developed a hand grenade called the "Steilhandgranate" or Stg24. The German weapon resembled a short stick; it was no surprise that it was commonly said to be a "Stick Grenade." The grenade of choice for the Canadian infantry was the Mills Bomb, developed in 1915 by William Mills of Birmingham, England. The Mills featured a seven-second fuse delay, which required the soldier to pull the firing pin, hold for three seconds and then toss at the enemy. Timing was everything. Lobbing a Mills hand grenade too soon, however, could result in dire consequences for the one who originally tossed it. Prematurely getting rid of it could very likely result in an enemy soldier retrieving the bomb and returning to sender. To overcome such a possibility, the Mills bomb was redesigned and modified. The redesigned grenade added a lever that flipped up when the bomb was thrown, thereby releasing a striker, which ignited a four-second timer fuse.

I am using my time to prepare for battle this coming Friday. There is still plenty of last- minute work to keep me busy. Within the next while, I will choose a number of men to accompany me to one of the supply depots where we will gather essential supplies for B Coy. Items include: two-days rations for each soldier, water-filled canteens, large quantities of ground flares, and Mills bombs. As of this moment, there is still no word on Zero Hour. Our coy is now positioned on the left of 9th Brigade, in close proximity to 9th Machine Gun Coy and 9th Trench Mortar Coy. C Coy is on our left, while D Coy has been relegated to support. A Coy is in reserve. The sky is relatively clear at the moment, so I am hoping the present condition will be the same for Friday.

Officers who had been temporarily on assignment elsewhere, began arriving at their home battalions in advance of the October 26 combat operation. An officer with the 43rd Battalion, who returned from Transport Line, was a lieutenant by the name of Robert Shankland. Born in Ayr, Scotland on October 10, 1887, Shankland had emigrated to Canada in 1910, and was employed as an assistant cashier at the Crescent Creamery Company in Winnipeg prior to his enlistment on December 21, 1914. The lieutenant, who survived the war, received two prestigious honours for his service to king, the British Empire, and the Dominion of Canada. These awards included the Distinguished Conduct Medal (DCM), received while a sergeant at Sanctuary Wood in June 1916. The second honour bestowed upon Robert Shankland was the Victoria Cross, for his leadership and courage during the Battle of Passchendaele on October 26, 1917.

The sky has now turned pitch-black, but no rain is falling...yet. The strong wind, which we have often experienced, is at the moment a gentle, but very cool breeze. Except for occasional flares lighting the sky, mixed with the sound of bursting machine-gun fire, it is relatively quiet here on the Western Front in Flanders. This moment of quietude is extremely rare, so much so that it tends to make me feel somewhat apprehensive. I think of it as the calm before a violent storm.

Chapter Twenty-Seven
OCTOBER 25, 1917

"You will not be called upon to advance until everything has been done that can be done to clear the way for you. After that it is up to you."

General Arthur Currie to his troops

Thursday, October 25, 1917
Dear Family,

By the time you receive this letter, you will have perhaps read or heard about a major battle called Passchendaele. I am expecting that Passchendaele will be as important and as bloody as Vimy Ridge, but unlike the Battle of Vimy Ridge, this forthcoming operation will find me and my comrades on the front-line. We will be the first troops to go over the top and face the Hun on the battlefield and his awesome firepower. I am anxious, but not afraid. As of Monday, October 22 I now hold the rank of lance corporal. Therefore, I will carry out my newly acquired responsibilities to the best of my ability on behalf of my coy and regiment. Those situations for which I have no control, such as whether I live or die, I will leave in the hands of God to decide.

I hope you at home, as well as all my brothers and sisters are in good health. Mable mentioned in her card that Mother had developed some unknown illness and has been confined to bed for several weeks. I am hoping that it is not consumption. My sister expressed her concern for Mother's health but feels it may be a severe case of influenza. Mable understands this ailment has been very prevalent recently in Freeport.

I often think about the cold, wet, and windy October days growing up on Long Island and lately have been comparing it to the truly miserable weather, here on the Western Front. It rains almost daily. The few days of sun we see are a blessing but short lived. Fortunately, today is an extraordinarily nice day. So today we complain about the food and the enemy, tomorrow it will probably be the rain again!

Concerning the matter of combat pay, please know that my pay book presently contains a balance of $140.31 and is accumulated at $1.10 a day. I designated Dad as my estate beneficiary, therefore should I not survive the forthcoming battle, Father is to receive the amount as mentioned.

I received the tin of egg tarts you sent and they were delicious. I shared a few with my comrades and told them how most Freeport families have been enjoying these tarts for decades.

This is all the time I have to write at the moment. After the next battle, I will write again. Please convey my love and best wishes to all the family.

Your loving son,
Stephen Ernest

Thursday, October 25, the eve of the Battle of Passchendaele, dawned with a clear blue sky and a bright sun, unlike the typical days of dark clouds and driving rain. Suddenly, autumn felt like spring. Sadly, the euphoria of a positive change in the weather would quickly dissipate before the day came to a close. While enjoying a short respite from the usual miserable conditions, the 43rd Battalion was told by brigade headquarters that they would be moving into their forward lines within a few hours. It would be from this front-line location that the Cameron Highlanders of Canada would be told to, "close with and destroy the enemy."

During the evening, Coy commanders discussed operational plans. They continued to receive updated intelligence data relating to enemy positions, anticipated resistance, and German troop strength. As well, officers perused aerial photographs and listened to intelligence officers explain where the weakest and strongest entry points in the enemy lines were located. Briefings also reviewed the recommended artillery support to be provided, part of which dealt with the deployment of rolling barrages. The final item on the agenda was the coordination of special communication codes and signals to be used between the various headquarters and combat units, and their platoons and sections.

General Arthur Currie's Passchendaele strategy included an intermediate objective. This particular objective was assigned to Lance Corporal S.E. Shortliffe's B Coy, together with C Coy. D Coy would advance to the final objective where they were expected to consolidate a line on the left side of Bellevue Spur. There, they were to join forces with the 8th Canadian Infantry Brigade from the 3rd Canadian Infantry Division. Meanwhile, the last 43rd Battalion combat unit, A Coy, was moved into the support line, entrenched at either a forward position or possibly at the rear of the ridge on Bellevue Spur. Their exact location all depended on the situation at the time, including whether there happened to be a more favourable location. All four company commanders of Cameron Highlanders received their orders and scheduled times for moving their units after midnight, October 26, to the forward positions. Lance Corporal S.E. Shortliffe and his comrades from B Coy were told they must be in position at 3:00 a.m., along with C Coy. The scheduled time for A Coy was 3:30 a.m. and D Coy at 4:00 a.m.

(Ross photo)
In October 1917, this quiet stream known as Ravebeek had become a small, putrid lake containing the bodies of numerous British and ANZAC troops, who perished in combat during the First Battle of Passchendaele. The 43rd Battalion and their sister battalions of the 3rd Canadian Infantry Division crossed Ravebeek in advance of the assault on Bellevue Spur, October 26, 1917.

Commencing at dusk on the evening of October 25, the 9th Field Company erected narrow, wooden footbridges at four locations along the swollen Ravebeek. These walkways provided the 43rd Canadian Infantry Battalion with dry, easy access to their assembly areas over the former stream, now a large pond. The bridges eliminated the need to wade through cold, deep, filthy water. Once headquarters received word that all the walkways had been installed, parties of Cameron Highlanders inspected the area, ensuring all footbridges were in their proper locations and had not been damaged by enemy shelling.

Still unbelievable to think there is no word yet on Zero Hour. The men in my section are becoming increasingly uneasy. The complaining has started. Most of the men are more afraid of what awaits them tomorrow, especially the youngest of our group. The older ones try not to let their anxiety show, but I can read it on their faces. Those who are veterans of the Somme, Vimy, and Lens seem to be resigned to the fact that this is just one more battle. Some of my buddies, like myself, expect this battle to be much worse than what we have ever experienced. I suggest, the odds of surviving The Battle of Passchendaele will be about 50%.

In the final hours leading up to the assault, Canadian Field Artillery Batteries intensified their shelling of the Germans on the ridge. The principle reason behind the concentration of bombs was to induce stress and anxiety that would cause sleep deprivation and ultimately a weakened adversary due to a significant loss of appetite. The intention was to break the enemy; to create weakness and disorientation, which would eventually lead to the early capitulation of the Imperial German Army, at Passchendaele.

As the heavy artillery weapons repeatedly fired their shells at Passchendaele, some fell dangerously close to Canadian Corps positions. A number landed within a few yards of the 43rd Infantry Battalion, creating panic and trepidation among many of the troops. No one wished to become a casualty at the hands of his own army.

It is now 6:00 p.m., on Thursday, 25 October. All NCOs have now been advised by coy officers, that Zero Hour will be, at 5:40 a.m. We will be given our duties and responsibilities within the next hour. I suspect these will include the establishment of several forward observation and sniper posts in No-Man's Land. These posts will play an important role in preventing enemy infiltration into our forward lines. A successful intrusion by the Germans, could seriously compromise our surprise assault on Bellevue Spur.

An operation order, declaring Zero Hour to be 5:40 a.m., was officially communicated to all Canadian Corps divisional, brigade, and battalion commanders, including General Herbert Plumer of the British Fifth Army. Field maps showing artillery barrage lines and distances, including time schedules, were provided to platoon leaders and

NCOs. The plan was for the Canadian Expeditionary Force to go over the top, advancing in loose formation rather than in tight units, and to leapfrog in waves behind the creeping barrages of the heavy artillery. The speed at which troops advanced was expected to be considerably slower because of the knee-deep, salient mud. During the early evening of October 25, scouts ran 300 yards of tape along duckboards and bridges to the rear support positions. This was done to assist D Coy and A Coy in locating their respective assembly areas. While this work was being conducted, officers from the four coys met to finalize platoon objectives and establish possible chain of command, in the likelihood an officer fell victim to an enemy bullet, bomb, or bayonet, during Friday's assault.

Final roll calls were taken and lists turned over to the adjutants of each battalion, at their respective battalion headquarters. The compilation of troop totals would determine the combat strength of the Canadian Corps going forward in the morning, in its assault on Bellevue Spur.

Roll call for the 43rd Canadian Infantry Battalion (Cameron Highlanders of Canada) resulted in a list that identified a combat strength of twenty-one officers and 511 other ranks. In addition to the 532 soldiers going into battle, twenty-nine infantrymen and six officers would be attached to 43rd Battalion Headquarters for the duration of the Passchendaele mission. In retrospect, the original battalion had numbered thirty-nine officers and 1,020 other ranks when it was formed on December 18, 1914, in Winnipeg. Three years later, there were 492, or forty-six percent fewer troops than the number of Cameron Highlanders who had left for England on June 1, 1915. During the 43rd Battalion's time in the theatre-of-war in Europe, there had been numerous reinforcement drafts taken on-strength, but unfortunately, like other combat units on the Western Front, most of these troops had become casualties. It is estimated that only 100 soldiers from the original 1,059 in 1914 would see combat action in the Battle of Passchendaele, on October 26. The only Cameron Highlander of Canada soldier to be killed the day before the Battle of Passchendaele was Private Thomas Otway Thomas. The twenty-year-old infantryman, from the 43rd Battalion, was in all likelihood killed by an airburst shrapnel shell. No remains were ever found to bury.

The nerve-racking wait is almost over. In a matter of a few hours, my comrades and I will slog through the mud of Flanders in full kit to find and kill Germans. In the meantime, I listen to the haunting sound of our battalion bagpiper playing, "Piobaireachd of Donald Dhu." Its lilting sound echoes through the cool, night air as Chaplain Pringle leads us in prayer — Yea, though I walk through the valley of the shadow of death, I will fear no evil...

PART THREE
Passchendaele

Chapter Twenty-Eight

"They are hard pressed on every side, yet not crushed; they are perplexed, but not in despair, persecuted, but not forsaken, struck down but not destroyed."

2 Corinthians 4:28

Like Vimy Ridge, the Battle of Passchendaele was a defining moment in Canadian military history. By the time General Arthur Currie's Canadian Corps assembled in the Ypres Salient to relieve ANZAC troops in mid-October 1917, Passchendaele had already generated 250,000 British, Australian, and New Zealander casualties. One month later, Canadian forces at Passchendaele drove up that total by 15,654, including 5,000 killed in battle.

In 1914-15, the medieval City of Ypres and the flat landscape surrounding it in West-Flanders, was essentially all that remained of Belgium. Since August 4, 1914, the former, free and independent nation had, for the most part, been absorbed into the clutches of the Imperial German Army. In 1915, a bulge in the British occupied front-line extended well into German-held territory, known as the Ypres Salient. After the Second Battle of Ypres (April-May, 1915), the original bulge of 1914 had been reduced with the front-line situated not more than three miles from the centre of Ypres. In 1917, the Germans had compressed the size of the salient to a protrusion of 3.1 miles, resulting in enemy artillery batteries being able to fire at will on British positions, from not only the front but also on both sides of the bulge.

The salient was considered one of the most dangerous, horrible, grotesque battlefields on the Western Front. Heavy rains, beginning in August 1917, combined with prolonged artillery shelling over a three-year period, had reduced the ground to a quagmire of mud and clay, in some places as deep as three feet. Thousands of bodies littered the battlefield, many dismembered and decapitated. Ravenous, monstrous-sized rats devoured everything and anything in sight. The Ypres Salient was undeniably the worst nightmare a soldier could experience. The topography favoured the German defenders, as it was they who controlled the ridges and crests, the most important of those being Passchendaele Ridge. The infantry divisions of the Canadian Corps, on the other hand, would commence their assault from low-lying Flanders plain, navigating around craters and through mud, careening their way toward the German lines. Passchendaele Ridge was the highest land formation northeast of Ypres, and therefore a most highly sought-after piece of real estate. For months the British and ANZAC forces had tried desperately to capture the crescent-shaped ridge, but it was all for naught, as each attempt failed miserably.

Militarily, Passchendaele presented a difficult, if not unique, challenge. It was one that the Canadian Corps had to overcome in order to achieve success. While the 43rd Battalion launched their attack from ditches, slit trenches, and foxholes, the Germans defended their territory by primarily utilizing a solid system of interlocking pillboxes. This system consisted of five front-defence lines known as the Hindenburg Stellung, the Albrecht Stellung, the Wilhelm Stellung, the Flandern I Stellung, and the Flandern II Stellung. Whereas British, Canadian, Australian and New Zealand trench lines were uniform in design and exact in placement, enemy trenches were isolated and scattered. The German trenches featured defensive strong points positioned in various locations, all heavily protected by barbed wire. Their pillboxes were manned by elite machine gun and rifle crews, all handpicked for their marksmanship skills, courage, and tenacity while displaying a loyal dedication to fight until bombed, shot, or bayoneted.

(source: Library and Archives Canada PA-002162)
Men of the 16th Canadian Machine Gun Company hold the line entrenched in muddy holes and slit trenches in Flanders. Private Reginald Le Brun, the machine-gunner closest to the camera was the only soldier in this photo to survive the Second Battle of Passchendaele.

Part of a fraternity of six kilted regiments to be thrust into action in the Battle of Passchendaele, the Cameron Highlanders of Canada rose cautiously from their shallow holes and advanced, slowly and deliberately, toward enemy lines and Passchendaele village, 4,000 feet beyond their jumping-off lines. Impeded by waist-deep mud, some soldiers faltered, finding themselves losing contact with their comrades, as well as with the artillery barrages moving ahead of them. Mired in mud, many became helpless victims of the incessant machine-gun fire and exploding shrapnel shells. At the end of the first phase of General Currie's Passchendaele plan, the 43rd Infantry Battalion had advanced their assault 3,300 feet across a blood-soaked Flanders' battlefield, before being halted 300 feet short of the objective. In retrospect, the Cameron Highlanders of Canada paid a horrendous price in lives lost and wounded for a little more than half of mile of mud.

(source: Library and Archives Canada)
A wounded Canadian soldier is carried on a stretcher through the mud and water to a regimental aid post, during the Battle of Passchendaele.

(source: Library and Archives Canada)
Canadian and German wounded help one another through a quagmire of mud during the Canadian Corps attack on Passchendaele.

Chapter Twenty-Nine
BATTLE OF PASSCHENDAELE

"To those who fall I say — You will not die but step into immortality. Your mothers will not lament your fate but will be proud to have borne such sons. Your names will be revered forever and ever by your grateful country, and God will take you unto Himself."

General Sir Arthur William Currie, Canadian Corps Commander

The Second Battle of Passchendaele; also referred to as the 8th Battle of the Third Battle of Ypres, was written in the annals of the Great War as both a significant victory and a monumental waste of Canadian soldiers' lives. During sixteen days of bloody combat, field artillery batteries supported Canadian troops with 1,453,056 medium and heavy-artillery shells — each bomb carried an average of fifty-six pounds of high explosive. This massive shelling, in liaison with the fighting prowess of skilled and dedicated Canadian soldiers, ultimately forced the German defenders to relinquish their hold on the crests and ridges of Passchendaele. After the final shot had been fired and the smoke had lifted from the battlefields of Bellevue Spur and Passchendaele Ridge, Canadian Corps casualties numbered 15,654.

General Currie's reluctance to commit Canadian troops to the Passchendaele operation, in order to advance the front-line beyond the 5.4 miles established by the British Expeditionary Force, was met with General Douglas Haig's unrelenting determination to have the Canadians assume the lead role. As a result, four Canadian Infantry

Divisions found themselves cast into a hell-hole. Those who were the first to arrive on October 18 witnessed a frightening scene of death and destruction. All had been forewarned about the desolation, but what they saw was far worse than what had been described.

(source: Library and Archives Canada)
Two Canadian infantrymen survey the damage done to a German pillbox during the Battle of Passchendaele.

(source: Library and Archives Canada)
A total of 15,654 Canadian casualties was the price paid for victory at Passchendaele.

The first order of business for the 43rd Battalion, was to look for and note the number and exact location of every enemy pillbox and blockhouse. Camouflaged and painstakingly protected by barbed wire entanglements, these defensive installations had been strategically placed over the length and breadth of German-held Bellevue Spur. After a careful analysis of these enemy defence installations utilizing boots on the ground and eyes in the sky, all part of reconnoitring Bellevue Spur and Passchendaele Ridge, Canadian Field Artillery officers expressed a number of concerns.

First and foremost was the perceived effectiveness of the heavy guns to actually destroy the majority of reinforced concrete pillboxes situated between the Canadian front-line and Passchendaele. It was the opinion of both commanding officers and artillery gunners that any artillery shell measuring smaller than six inches in diameter would have negligible effect on a German blockhouse or pillbox, and likewise the defenders within. Therefore, these particular fortifications, some eight feet wide and ten feet long, required larger, more powerful shells with significantly higher amounts of explosives, to completely destroy, or at least impair, the effectiveness of enemy blockhouses and pillboxes. This was to be an enormous challenge. The Imperial German Army considered its occupied territory impenetrable, thanks to the sturdiness of those concrete, steel-reinforced structures placed along Bellevue Spur and the slopes of Passchendaele Ridge.

Persistent rain in October had transformed West-Flanders into a hideous landscape of mud, swamps, and lakes. The first Canadian soldiers who arrived in the salient, plodded through a liquefied mixture of sand, loam, and clay, ankle to knee-deep. Sometimes, they found themselves mired up to their waists in the putrid gunk. The destruction of the terrain during the early days of the war, caused by millions of artillery shells, was now made worse by the persistent rain. Imagine if you can, one million water-filled shell craters squeezed into each square mile. Troops, horses, and pack mules were overwhelmed by the condition of the salient. This was especially true for the animals, which were employed to transport ammunition, weapons, and supplies to the 3rd Canadian Infantry Division front-line positions.

To achieve the efficient movement of men and supplies, General Currie ordered the Canadian engineers to rebuild road and rail systems as well as crucial supply depots. Major-General David Watson, commander of the 4th Canadian Infantry Division, was given that assignment:

Our engineers at once started to lay our French Railways, guns were brought well forward, dumps of ammunition and supplies established, dressing stations located, and proper jumping off positions for the infantry were dug and prepared. Night and day the work progressed under most trying and difficult situations.

The transporting of medium and heavy weapons through the salient mud also played on the mind of Major Robert Massie, of the Canadian Field Artillery:

The infantry also had to go forward, and their advance was assisted by constructing duck-walks, that is, the short duck boards that are put in the trenches to form a footing for the infantry; they put them two boards wide for several miles out to form paths for the infantry; but the artillery was obliged to stick to the roads.

Major Massie's trepidation concerning weapon transportation was also shared by other members of the field artillery. They knew it was extremely important to have their field guns in position, well in advance of the pending battle. Although facilitating the movement of these weapons fell to the Canadian Corps Engineers, most of the heavy lifting was carried out by infantrymen. Working around the clock, under extremely dangerous and often difficult conditions, Canadian soldiers constructed transportation systems to handle the movement of weapons and ammunition, including narrow gauge rail lines to carry troops. Countless times, the big guns, howitzers, and mortars failed to reach their assigned location due to the mud and water. Men and horses were forced to push and drag these monstrous weapons, many weighing in excess of 2,000 pounds, to their firing sites and position them on elevated platforms. These platforms were supposed to prevent the big guns from gradually sliding into the mud, sinking and plugging the seven-foot-long cannons with sludge.

(source: Library and Archives Canada)
A six-foot Howitzer being moved by Canadian light railway at Passchendaele.

A list of priorities drafted the day before the assault, highlighted additional training, building new transportation systems, maintenance to existing roads and rail, and excavation of communication trenches. Reliable communication between front-line combat units and their headquarters during battle was germane to conducting a successful combat operation. Therefore, the Canadian Corps commander felt it was important to keep communication lines open at all cost. One of the ways to accomplish this was to excavate communication trenches to a depth of six feet, in order to protect precious wire and cable from bomb explosions. Previously, trenches had been dug to a depth of only three feet.

Another integral component of the Passchendaele plan had originally been introduced at Vimy Ridge, seven months earlier, by General Sir Julian Byng. It was General Byng who directed his officers to disseminate battle plans and operational field maps to sergeants, corporals and other NCOs attached to platoon and rifle sections. The distribution of operational material prior to going into battle, meant more men were aware of battalion objectives and critical time- frames.

This information would be important should an officer be killed, wounded, or taken prisoner. It was General Arthur Currie's intention to have his Canadian Corps prepared to the maximum level in order to meet any unforeseen challenges, while focused on achieving their objectives. Currie's plan for Passchendaele was simply to attack in a series of coordinated assaults, each with a limited objective, until such time as the primary objective and a defensible position had been secured. It was hoped that the result would be a sharp wedge, driven deep into the German positions.

As Arthur Currie said:

The greatest lesson to be learned from these operations is this: if the lessons of war have been thoroughly mastered; if the artillery preparation and support is good; if our intelligence is properly appreciated; there is no position that cannot be wrestled from the enemy by well-disciplined, well-trained and well-led troops attacking on a sound plan.

On October 21, the Canadian Corps Field Artillery commenced a four-day bombardment of the German positions. A total of 587 field guns were synchronized in stop-and-start rolling barrages, sweeping across No-Man's Land and into enemy occupied territory. The purpose of this massive shelling program was two-fold. First, it was intended to create irreparable damage to German weaponry and installations, and secondly, to produce exceedingly large numbers of casualties. In addition to the physical damage, fear, uncertainty, and low morale were expected to evolve from these massive, sustained bombardments.

The primary objective, called The Red Line, was one of a number of colour-coded objectives laid out on operational field maps. Each objective was to be captured within an allotted time frame. There were three planned stages to the Battle of Passchendaele. These stages were to commence with Phase I on October 26, Phase II on October 30, and Phase III on November 6, 1917. Chosen to spearhead Phase I were two divisions from the Canadian Expeditionary Force, under the command of Major-General Louis Lipsett (3rd Canadian Infantry Division) and Major-General David Watson (4th Canadian Infantry Division). The 3rd Division, which included the 43rd Canadian Infantry Battalion (Cameron Highlanders of Canada), launched their assault in two columns north of Ravebeek, a stream now transformed into a large pond, and containing the bloated corpses of hundreds of Australian soldiers killed earlier in the month. It was from these lowlands of water-saturated fields, abutting Ravebeek to the north of 's Graventafel Road, that the 3rd Canadian Infantry Division left their jumping-off positions and began the tortuous climb through mud and clay along a narrow strip of Bellevue Spur, in an attempt to reach their objective 1,200 yards away and 147 feet above sea level. In order to reach their objective, the 3rd Division had to overcome a number of hurtles. The majority of these challenges were in the form of heavily defended pillboxes, manned by machine-gun crews of two to four elite German marksmen. The other Canadian division, the 4th, was ordered to capture Decline Wood before advancing 656 yards to take the Ypres-Roulers Railway line.

With the passing of each day leading up to the Passchendaele battle, the field artillery batteries continued their incessant pounding of German positions, firing in excess of 3,000 rounds each night. This shelling was intended to exert pressure on the defense-minded Germans, in advance of the 8th and 9th Canadian Infantry Brigades launching their assault on Bellevue. On the first day of the Passchendaele offensive, two-thirds of the field-artillery guns directed their attention at defined enemy lines, while the remaining one-third extended their bombing range an additional 100 yards beyond those positions. Howitzer artillery teams skillfully neutralized German targets 700 yards beyond the jumping-off lines of the 3rd Canadian Infantry Division.

The minutes ticked off on Lance Corporal S.E. Shortliffe's pocket watch. Zero Hour was rapidly approaching. The Cameron Highlanders of Canada were ordered to move out under the cover of darkness, rain, and a gale force wind. Troops trudged over the swollen Ravebeek using recently assembled wooden bridges, then veered northward to where the front-line positions awaited them. Arriving at the designated jumping-off areas, each coy platoon, of between thirty and forty men, hunkered down, unsheltered from the wet and cold and waited to hear the order to attack.

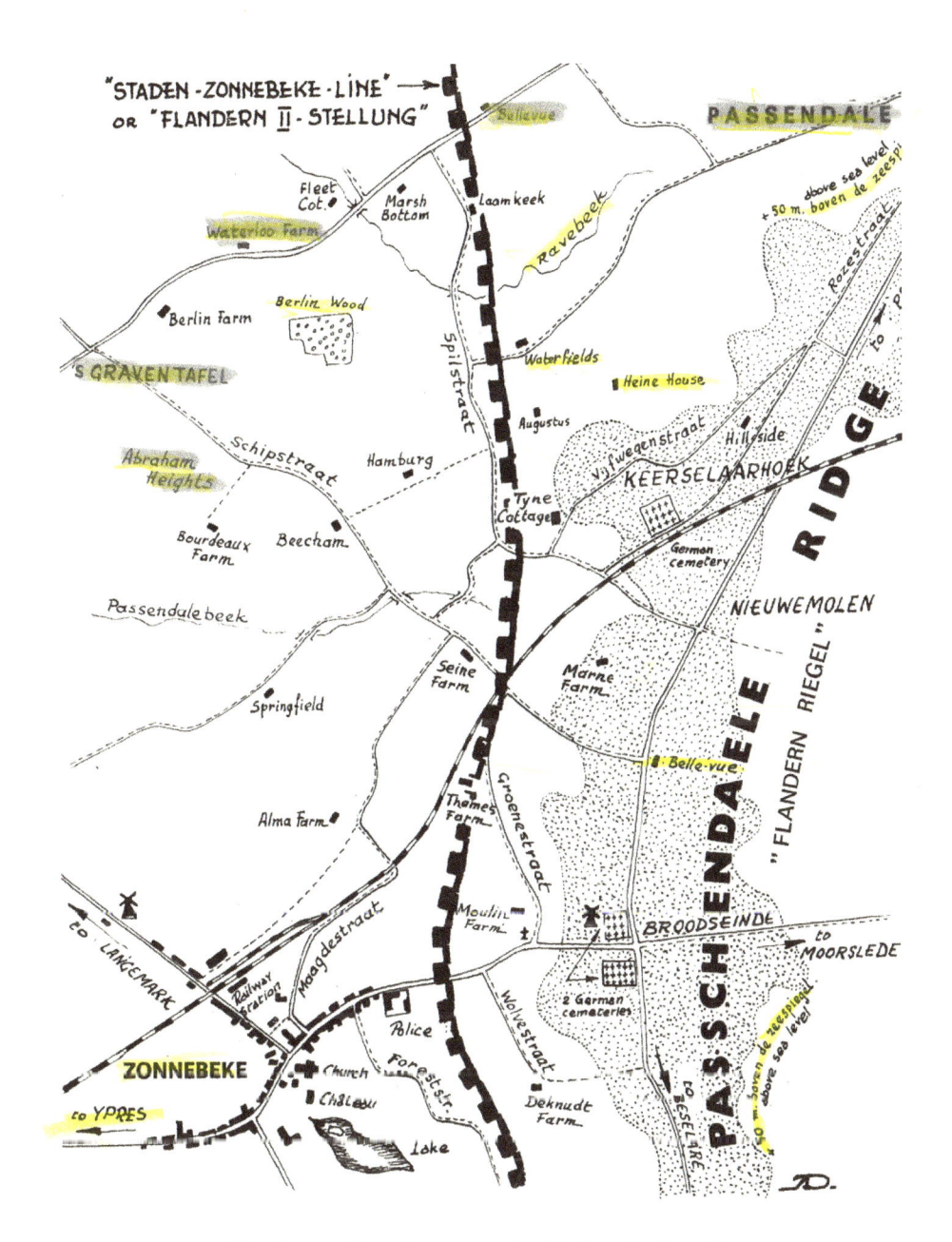

The German front line as it existed before the Canadian Corps assault, on October 26, 1917.

Private Alex Strachan, 43rd Battalion wrote in his diary:

It was a really miserable day, quite miserable. We were lying practically on the bed of the river, which had been shelled all to pieces and was just a marshy bog...our company headquarters got blown to pieces...before we started off...and the battle hadn't even begun. The first day of the Battle of Passchendaele, the Canadian infantry paid a horrific price in combat losses. Casualties quickly mounted. A total of 598 officers and ordinary regulars from the 3rd and 4th Canadian Infantry Divisions were counted as killed or missing, while an additional 2,273 soldiers were listed as wounded. Since July 31, 1917, British and Commonwealth Forces had been continually thwarted in their attempt to dislodge the kaiser's army from Passchendaele, now, after eighty days of relatively small gains made at the expense of thousands of lives, the Canadian Corps was called upon to capture Bellevue Spur, Crest Farm, and Passchendaele Ridge. It was to be a formidable undertaking, one which would take sixteen days to complete.

General Erich Friedrich Wilhelm Ludendorff, a senior Imperial German Army commander, described Friday, October 26, 1917:

The horror of the shell-hole area of Verdun was surpassed. It was no longer life at all. It was mere unspeakable suffering. And through this world of mud the attackers dragged themselves slowly, but steadily and in dense masses. Caught in the advanced zone by our hail of fire they often collapsed, and the lonely man in the shell-hole breathed again. Then the mass came on again. Rifle and machine gun jammed with mud. Man fought against man; only too often the mass was successful.

Ludendorff's observation of what German and Canadian infantrymen encountered on that cold, wet, and miserable morning of October 26 was confirmation of the terrifying hell experienced by every soldier.

Prior to the Canadians relieving II ANZAC Corps on October 18, British, Australian, and New Zealand armies had, for twelve days, been engaged in three smaller, but very deadly battles. The first was Menin Ridge (September 20 – 25), next was the Battle of Broodseinde Ridge (October 3 -4), and lastly the First Battle of Passchendaele (October 9 -12). The Broodseinde Ridge operation resulted in 6,432 Australian casualties, New Zealand 892 and the British 300. German dead were said to number an estimated 10,000, with an additional 5,000 German soldiers taken prisoner.

The Battle of Broodseinde began at dawn, on October 3, near the east end of the Gheluvelt plateau, a short distance from Ypres. Ironically, as the British and II ANZAC Corps assault was getting underway, the Imperial German Army was advancing at the same time towards the UK forces. Fierce fighting ensued between the 3rd Australian Division and the German Fourth Army. The Aussies charged the enemy with fixed bayonets and sent the Germans into a hasty retreat, until overwhelmed by heavy enemy machine gun fire, which massacred a large number of ANZAC soldiers. British artillery dispatched a wave of bombs at German Fourth Army positions, resulting in a large number of casualties. These bombardments concentrated deep within the German lines, before reverting to creeping barrages.

The British Field Artillery helped the 1st, 2nd, and 3rd Australian Divisions to finally move forward and eventually capture Broodseinde Ridge, on October 4. After reaching the top of the ridge, the Australians looked beyond the German lines to their primary objective — the occupied village of Passchendaele to the north. General Herbert Plumer, commander of the British Second Army, called the capture of Broodseinde Ridge, "The greatest victory since the Marne." The Germans referred to it as "The black day of October 4."

The First Battle of Passchendaele got under way on October 12, in a rain storm, fifty-five degrees Fahrenheit and within full view of Passchendaele village to the north. In the early stages of the assault, a section of ground was captured near Passchendaele, but was soon lost during German counter-attacks. Battlefield conditions had greatly deteriorated since October 4. The incessant rain turned the Ypres Salient into a mud bog, making movement of men and weapons extremely difficult. The heavy deluge ultimately forced General Douglas Haig to abort an afternoon attack, proposed for October 7, to the north of Passchendaele village and Goudberg Spur. Two days following the cancellation of the October 7 assault, a decision was made for October 12 to be the new date for the offensive against Passchendaele. As the decision was being communicated, the II

ANZAC Corps and the British Second Army simultaneously received misinformation concerning the extent of the troop advance made on October 9. Consequently, because of the incorrect information, the objectives for October 12 required combat units to advance an additional 1,000 yards to reach their final objectives, rather than the 1,000 to 1,500 yards originally proposed. British and ANZAC officers were surprised to discover that the German defences, on October 12, were much more effective than had been assumed.

That assumption was based on the fact that the 195th Infantry Division had suffered 3,325 casualties at Passchendaele, resulting in that particular Imperial German Army Division being relieved by the 238th Infantry Division. The 195th Division were veterans of the Flandern Schlacht (Battle of Flanders) between October 4 and October 20, while the 238th Infantry Division participated in combat operations from October 7 to October 31.

The British attack on Passchendaele was extremely disheartening and very costly in terms of dead and wounded. Artillery support was inadequate; a significant number of field guns had been taken out of action by enemy shelling, as well as many British and ANZAC bombs failing to explode in the mud.

In the meantime, the Australians were attacking an area near Tyne Cot, where they raided a number of bunkers, capturing thirty-five soldiers and four machine guns. Despite the ferocity of the battle, a small party of twenty Aussie troops did manage to reach the ruins of the historic church in Passchendaele village, however, British support situated on the right failed to be effective. The outcome saw the Australians forced to withdraw to their original front line. By this time, their field-artillery batteries were almost out of ammunition, and what shells remained fell fruitlessly in the mud. Despite the setbacks, British General Douglas Haig continued to insist on driving the assault forward in the rain and cold, even though the assault was doomed to fail. Soldiers struggled through the mud, some up to their hips in watery quicksand, unable to fire their Enfield rifles because the gun barrels were jammed with mud. This combat calamity took the lives of 3,199 troops of the 3rd Australian Division.

On October 18, the Canadian Corps relieved an exhausted II ANZAC Corps in the lowlands of Flanders, in an area between 's Graventafel Ridge and Passchendaele Ridge. The ground captured and held by the ANZAC troops became the starting point for the 3rd Canadian Infantry Division, on October 26.

Chapter Thirty
OCTOBER 26, 1917

"I died in Hell — (they called it Passchendaele).

From a poem by: Lieutenant Siegfried Sassoon

43rd Canadian Infantry Battalion War Diary —
A/Adjutant, Lieutenant A.E. Grimes
  Location: FRONT LINE D10 & 4
  Weather: Raining
  Day: Friday 26, October 1917
  Time: 01:00 hours
  Report received that Major Charlton, O.C.B. Coy had been hit just as he was preparing to go to assembly. He was brought to R.A.P. (Regimental Aid Post) at Hdqrs wounded in the legs and hand. He reported that his Company Sergeant Major and a platoon Sergeant had been wounded by a shell on his Hdqrs; that he had sent forward orders to Lieut. Scholey to take command and that the Corporal in charge of his support platoon was quite able to move the support platoon to assembly. He handed over his papers and maps. Just prior to this all B.A.B. Codes had been recalled from Coy Commanders.

While waiting for all hell to break loose, members of the 43rd Battalion used the time to write letters to loved ones, or add an entry into a small, pocket diary by the light of a trench lantern. Nearby, men were quietly asking for divine intervention from enemy bombs and bullets. Others nervously chain-smoked in silence. High above the battlefield, an umbrella of light from flares lit up the late-night sky, casting an eerie glow across No-Man's Land, Ravebeek, and Marsh Bottom. Once the flares had ended, the sky returned to its usual, sombre blackness. The cessation of flares brought a small party of Highlanders with welcomed crocks of rum to warm the stomachs and sedate the anxiety being felt by their comrades. Each rum ration was passed out with the familiar mantra, — "Never go into battle dry when you're about to die."

43rd Canadian Infantry Battalion War Diary — A/Adjutant, Lieutenant A.E. Grimes
   Day: Friday 26, October 1917
   Time: 04:30 hours
   Weather: Raining Hard
   No report having been received from Coys that they were assembled; Scouts were dispatched to locate Coy Commanders. Scouts reported in at 04:50 am that all were in position.
   It was raining hard now and had been during the assembly. The going was very hard.
   The supporting Coy of 52nd Bn, now had been reported forward in position vacated by D Coy close to Bn. Hdqrs.

On the morning of October 26, the first boots to hit the muddy ground of Bellevue Spur were worn by soldiers of the 3rd Canadian Infantry Division. Their hearts were filled with apprehension. Every soldier vividly pictured the frightening nightmare that awaited them, only yards beyond No-Man's Land. Moving in a northerly direction, troops from the 43rd, 52nd, and 58th Canadian Infantry Battalions waded through knee-deep, black muck — straight into the gun-sights of the 11.Bavarian Division (Groupe Ypern).

The 43rd Canadian Infantry Battalion (Cameron Highlanders of Canada) had been handed the task of being the first troops to breach the German lines. Their attack upon enemy-occupied territory came under intense artillery firepower, especially from the snipers and machine-gunners entrenched along Bellevue Spur and protected by coils of barbed wire. In addition to exploding bombs and body-piercing bullets, the Cameron Highlanders also prepared for the deployment of chemical gasses, such as Yellow Cross (mustard gas) and the newest chemical agent, Blue Cross (diphenylchorarsine). This particular toxic gas had been used extensively since mid-July 1917, when it was first introduced during counterattacks at Nieuwpoort, on the Belgian coast. The agent, resembling cayenne pepper, was an extremely debilitating irritant, capable of penetrating a gas mask and producing uncontrollable sneezing and vomiting. By reason of the fact the Germans had been using Blue Cross for the last three months, Canadian commanders envisioned it would also be used in the Battle of Passchendaele.

Ten minutes before the battle begins. Time to recheck my Enfield. Bullets in the clip and bayonet securely fixed. No mud plugging the barrel. Last thing before going over the top will be to remove my heavy greatcoat and leave it behind. No need to carry any unnecessary extra weight. The rain has already made the coat heavier. We are all sopping wet and covered in mud. Moments ago the Hun began shelling the 8th, 9th, and 10th Brigade lines. A few casualties have been evacuated to the regimental first aid station at Waterloo Farm. Flares are being shot above the Flandern II –Stellung Line. You can almost cut the tension with a knife. Everyone is showing a brave face, including our sergeant who says he's not afraid of dying...just afraid of how he is going to die. I think that is how we all feel right about now!

Prior to Zero Hour, Brigadier-General Frederick W. Hill, commander of the 9th Canadian Infantry Brigade, 3rd Canadian Infantry Division wrote:

In the rain and semi darkness, thousands of Canadian soldiers crouch in waterlogged shell holes or muddy ditches awaiting the signal to begin a major offensive — a battle that is destined to become one of the most famous of the First World War.

The 43rd Canadian Infantry Battalion War Diary — A/Adjutant, Lieutenant A.E. Grimes
  Day: Friday 26 October 1917
  Time: 05:40 hours

At Zero Hour 05:40 am the battle front dispositions were as follows: B Coy on Right, C Coy on Left, D Coy in Support as second wave to go through to final objective. A Coy in rear to follow to Crest of Bellevue Ridge and consolidate a support line. All Coys were assembled forward of the Ravebeek stream.

The 58th Battalion was on the right in touch with B Coy and 8th Bde. (4th C.M.Rs) were on left in touch with C Coy. Four guns of 9th M.G. Coy were attached to D Coy for consolidation and holding the final Red objective.

One Coy of 52nd Bn was in support of the battalion, and at the call of Officer Commanding.

Our barrage opened on time and the leading Coys got away. Lieut. Scholey of B Coy was hit early and Lieut. Banks as well, and very soon the command of this Coy devolved upon Cpl. Hainstock.

Lieut. Fowler, O.C.C. Coy reported in at the Aid Post wounded in the leg and reported that two of his Officers were hit, that the barrage was very ragged but that his men were going well up the slope under the charge of Lieut. Borthwick.

When dawn broke sufficiently our men could be clearly seen moving slowly over the skyline and around two formable looking pillboxes on the crest of the ridge overlooking Bn. H.Q.

Zero Hour – 5:40 a.m., October 26, 1917. The Battle of Passchendaele had begun.

One hundred and twenty seconds after the opening salvo of machine-gun fire, the roar of eighteen-pounders, 9.2 inch and 4.5 inch howitzers filled the morning air. Shells screamed across the battlefield, exploded and spewed forth plumes of mud, water, debris, and body parts. The noise was excruciatingly loud. By some accounts, individuals reportedly heard the sound of exploding bombs as far away as London. There is a question of exaggeration in such a statement. Perhaps those who said they could distinctly hear the sound of bomb explosions may have possessed vivid imaginations. It is difficult to conceive that someone actually heard bombs exploding from a distance of 130 miles away. For one thing, on October 26, it was raining and blowing hard in the salient, a climatic condition that would normally suppress much of the sound, especially over long distances. Another factor was the saturated ground of the salient. The voluminous amount of mud and water would have, in all probability, absorbed a great number of seismic waves emanating from the exploding shells. Lastly, the prevailing winds in Belgium usually blow in a west to east direction. Considering how turbulent the weather was inland, then it goes without saying the North Sea weather would have been the same or even worse. This fact alone would have reduced the chances of hearing the roar of the big guns in far-off England.

As many as seven synchronized lines of rolling/creeping barrages eased over the terrain, starting in No-Man's Land, then moviing slowly and deliberately towards the German trenches. As artillery shells pounded the enemy defensive positions, they totally destroyed trenches that buried scores of German defenders. Shrapnel from bursting shells exacted a hefty toll physically on the enemy, but it did not always entirely destroy the thousands of belts of barbed wire. In the majority of cases when the tangled wire fell back upon the ground, it lay scattered about, continuing to remain a dangerous and effective impediment to the Canadian troops in their attack against the enemy infantry.

The 43rd Battalion, with its 532 officers and other ranks, had been chosen to spearhead the 3rd Division attack against Bellevue Spur on Friday, October 26. After pushing forward and creating the first crack in the enemy defense line, the Cameron Highlanders of Canada continued their tortuous and deadly trek in the direction of the battalion's primary objective. This objective had been scheduled to be reached by nightfall. The first objective of the morning, however, was for Coy C and Coy B to capture three, heavily defended, concrete pillboxes situated directly in the path of the 43rd Battalion. The tactical plan was to have the troops follow closely behind rolling barrages. The distance between soldiers and shells was built on ground conditions at the time. Rifle sections were sent forward firing No. 23 Hales rifle grenades at the three pillboxes. Meanwhile, machine-gunners were directed to provide bombing teams, consisting of between three and four men, with light-artillery support so they could reach the pillbox blind sides without being spotted. Once in position, the soldiers hand-bombed the enemy defenders, using

Mills bombs lobbed through small openings in the concrete fortifications, called "loop holes." This was followed by muffled blasts...and then silence, the signal for the rest of the men to rush forward.

Once the first pillbox had been put out of commission, C Coy continued to race up Bellevue towards the Red Objective. Following a short distance behind was B Coy. This combat unit came under intense fire from two other machine-gun posts. The result was that B Coy temporarily called a halt to their attack until they could regroup, move on, and capture the other two machine-gun nests assigned to their company.

Northeast of the 43rd Battalion's position, on Bellevue, German snipers were entrenched along a section of wooded area called "Wolfe Copse." From there, German marksmen achieved great success. They picked off lead soldiers and officers of the 4th Canadian Mounted Rifles (C.M.R.) as they traversed their way up Bellevue. Orders to relentlessly and aggressively pursue the enemy were given to all battalions of the 3rd and 4th Canadian Infantry Divisions. It was clearly understood that such a directive, in all probability, meant the Canadian Corps would attack substantially fortified German lines, thereby causing the assault to be slowed, or even worse — halted. The 3rd Division became the pacesetter. They persistently moved forward, engaged the Germans on all fronts, successfully created large gaps in enemy positions and allowed the Canadians to surround, overwhelm, and neutralize German pillboxes and blockhouses.

As fighting raged to the north of the Ravebeek stream, the 43rd Battalion made excellent progress capturing and clearing pillboxes. It was a completely opposite situation for one particular battalion, the 58th, which was positioned on the right of the 43rd Battalion. The 58th Infantry Battalion (Central Ontario) had run into stiff resistance from German troops defending Laamkeek. Fighting roared on until mid-afternoon, when the battalion finally received much welcomed relief and support from another combat unit, the 52nd Canadian Infantry Battalion (New Ontario). The 52nd assisted in capturing Laamkeek, the 9th Brigade's intermediate objective.

Wolfe Copse, on the northern slope of Bellevue, was heavily defended by numerous snipers and machine-gunners, in fourteen pillboxes. These fourteen installations were strategically placed along the slope, together with an additional four pillboxes situated at the rear, whose job it was to protect gunners and riflemen from Canadian assault troops. Some of the fiercest fighting, on October 26, involved troops from the 4th Canadian Mounted Rifles (4th C.M.R.) at Wolfe Copse — their unit suffered 321 casualties. Despite incurring heavy losses, the 4th C.M.R prevailed and captured the Red Line on behalf of the 8th Canadian Infantry Brigade. They now controlled a major section of Wolfe Copse. Once they had captured the primary objective, the 4th Canadian Mounted Rifles dropped back 300 yards, and immediately turned toward the north flank where they linked up with the 63rd Royal Naval, a division of General Plumer's British Fifth Army.

43rd Canadian Infantry Battalion War Diary — A/Adjutant, Lieutenant A.E. Grimes
   Day: Friday 26 October 1917
   Time: 07:00 hours
   Weather: Raining
   It became evident here that something was wrong on the right side of brigade front as 58th appeared to be held up by strong fire from a strong point on right of the two pillboxes and this was confirmed by wounded coming in and subsequently by reports to 58th Headquarters that their men were all back at their Jumping Off Line (J.O.L) in consequence of sniping and machine gun fire.

The Cameron Highlanders of Canada were unwavering in their struggle to capture the battalion objective, no matter what stood between them and the knoll on Bellevue. As the 3rd Canadian Infantry Division struggled to extricate itself from the omnipresent mud, exploding bombs continued to hurl men through the air like rag dolls, depositing them in several feet of water in many of the millions of shell craters that scarred the Flanders "lunarscape." Pandemonium was happening everywhere on Bellevue Spur. It was a place of absolute desolation; a wasteland of craters and limbless trees, swamps, and untold numbers of lifeless bodies, either partially or fully submerged in the Flanders mud.

(source: Library and Archives Canada)
An armoured tank makes its way through the mud over a badly shelled area during the Battle of Passchendaele.

(source: Library and Archives Canada)
Canadian Corps stretcher-bearers with their wounded take cover behind a pillbox — Battle of Passchendaele.

This was ground zero in the war to win Bellevue Spur. As morning darkness gradually gave way to light, those watching from Waterloo Farm began to make out the body-forms of fellow Cameron Highlanders advancing up Bellevue. They were seen gallantly engaging the enemy, while facing increased and coordinated resistance. Several soldiers lurched violently backwards, their bodies striking the ground. Some remained motionless, while others twisted in pain from the impact of bullets. Other Canadian troops were ripped apart, shredded by shrapnel. Tattered pieces of blood-stained uniforms scattered about the battlefield, or on a blackened limb of a tree, were the only signs a soldier had once existed.

As we worked to secure our positions the Hun began to shell our position with "whizz-bangs," and some of the men grew panicky. Captain Arthur climbed through the mud

from group to group speaking to the fellows reassuringly. Tommy and I were digging together and watched him come near us. Dykes was working just a few feet from us. He straightened to say something to us, and the next instant a shell cut the top of his head away, leaving but the jaw and neck. The body rocked a moment and then toppled backward. Arthur saluted as he passed.[5]

Enemy machine-gunners and trigger-happy snipers made for a desperate situation for A Coy Commander Lieutenant Smart from the 43rd Battalion. The commander ordered his troops to seek cover from rifle fire emanating from a trench 250 yards beyond a group of pillboxes that had earlier in the morning been captured by the 43rd Battalion. While the lieutenant and his men came under heavy gunfire and faced the frightening prospect of being slaughtered, another group of Canadians were also being confronted by a desperate situation. The 58th Canadian Infantry Battalion reported that every officer had been either killed or wounded within the first one hour and twenty minutes of the Battle of Passchendaele.

The intensity of the fighting, on the morning of October 26, was described by Private John Pritchard, of Sudbury, Ontario:

---

5   Passage from an unnamed soldier's war diary

At last we were under enemy gunfire and I knew now that we had not much further to carry all this weight. We were soaked through with rain and perspiration from the efforts we had been making to get through the clinging mud, so that when we stopped we huddled down in the nearest shell hole and covered ourselves with our ground sheet, hoping for some sort of comfort from the rain, and also thinking that the ground sheet would protect us from the rain of shells. As the shelling grew worse it was decided we had better move on, so reloading ourselves we pushed through the mud again and amid the din of bursting shells. I called to Stephens, but got no response and I just assumed he didn't hear me. He was never seen or heard from again. He had not deserted. He had not been captured. One of those shells that fell behind me had burst and Stephens was no more.

In addition to the action at Wolfe Copse, another scene of fierce fighting happened near the centre of the main attack, on the slope of Bellevue just below Goudberg and west of Passchendaele. It was there the German divisions occupied a long line of solid, well constructed fortifications, manned by companies of elite machine-gunners. These enemy gun crews engaged the 43rd Battalion from two sides; Wolfe Copse on the left side and Laamkeek on the right. This particular area was where the Canadians successfully secured an important toehold on Bellevue Spur, while faced with suicidal attacks and stubborn resistance from dedicated Germans, willing to fight to the death. The 3rd Infantry Division generated a reasonable amount of progress along Bellevue Spur. Most of the twelve infantry battalions staked out precious ground in "bite and hold" attacks, much of it conducted in close combat. During the early going, there were the usual setbacks that commanders expected, especially considering the magnitude of the operation, however, it was a particularly surprising, strong German counter-attack from the northern section of the spur, which posed the major threat to Canadian troops. The counter-attack forced a hasty retreat of the 3rd Infantry Division to a lower and safer ground, where they consolidated and re-launched a stronger and more effective, attack against the German positions.

43rd Canadian Infantry Battalion War Diary — A/Adjutant, Lieutenant A.E. Grimes

Day: Friday 26 October 1917

Time: 08:00 hours

Our men on top of the ridge appeared to be holding on at this time although wounded coming through reported that the leading companies had been very heavily hit.

In view of the situation on both battalion fronts it was decided to send forward the supporting Coy of the 52nd Battalion. The 58th Battalion also having decided to use their Coy of the 52nd Battalion.

At this time all officers of "C" and "B" were out of action and no news could be got of Capt. Galt or his officers of D Coy.

Two scouts were dispatched to locate Capt. Galt of "D" Coy or Lieut. Smart of "A" Coy with the following message: "58th are back in their Jumping Off Lines — both Coys of 52nd are going forward to Crest of Pillboxes ridge —one right, one left; hold touch with your left if you have it now. Lieut. Fowler, MacKenzie and Verner are out at 08:00 am.

Canadian Corps battalions from the 3rd Infantry Division were the first to swarm onto Bellevue, forcing the enemy to retreat up the slope to higher ground. There, they quickly regrouped and launched a counter-attack. While Major-General Louis Lipsett's 3rd Division took the fight to the Germans on Bellevue Spur, the British 5th and 7th Divisions floundered in the flooded areas now protecting Gheluvelt. Much of the fighting centred in an area containing several pillboxes situated near Heine House and Vienna Cottages, where Canadian troops seized a large number of German soldiers.

General Currie's Passchendaele plan was carried out reasonably well, considering the horrific conditions under which the battle was fought, plus the strength of the defenders. That being said, there were specific problems in a few sectors as Canadian troops encountered the challenges of deep marshlands and miscalculations on the part of some fighting units.

One particular predicament arose during a steady, drenching rain, when the 46th Canadian Infantry Battalion (Saskatchewan), 4th Infantry Division, came under intense enfilade fire from a significant number of stubborn German troops who were defiantly resisting surrender, at Heine House-Decline Copse. That sector had been designated an objective of the 4th Canadian Infantry Division, but a breakdown in communication led to advanced posts and company positions being pulled back in order to form a defensive flank. That move precipitated an almost immediate response from the enemy, who quickly returned to re-occupy their recently vacated positions. The current situation remained at a standstill, until the night of October 27-28, when the Canadian Corps launched a counter-attack and reclaimed the positions.

43rd Canadian Infantry Battalion War Diary — A/Adjutant, Lieutenant A.E. Grimes

Day: Friday 26 October 1917

Time: 09:00 hours

Scouts reported back with message from Lieut. Smart, "Am holding ridge in touch with C.M.Rs. on left. Held up by trench approx 250 yards beyond pillboxes on ridge. 52nd Coy reported and are held back of ridge." 08:35 am

At this point things appeared satisfactory as the 52nd Coys had both gone forward and the one on the right – 58th Battalion frontage — was reported to have pushed forward ahead of the old line, but just then a report from observers came in that our men were coming down the ridge to the old line forward of the stream, and this proved to be true when it was seen that some men had actually come back as far as Battalion Headquarters while others could be seen in the old Jumping Off Line. The Coy of the 52nd Bn which had gone forward was also by this time back across the stream and in the locality of their old support line at Bn Hdqrs.

Three of the four battalions from the 9th Canadian Infantry Brigade, 3rd Canadian Division enjoyed greater luck advancing over a part of Bellevue Spur than the 4th Canadian Mounted Rifles of the 8th Infantry Brigade. The primary reason for success achieved by the 43rd, 58th, and 52nd Battalions was the fact Canadian field-artillery batteries had eliminated or at least greatly reduced the majority of barbed wire lying in the assault path of the 9th Brigade. Although Lance Corporal

S.E. Shortliffe and his fellow Highlanders had found the going slightly easier, they still had to cope with the on-going problem of friendly fire. Several shells inadvertently fell within a few yards of Canadian troops, a folly that too often resulted in scores of casualties.

43rd Canadian Infantry Battalion War Diary — A/Adjutant, Lieutenant A.E. Grimes

Day: Friday 26 October 1917

Time: 09:30 hours

Some of the men reported that they had got an order to fall back on the old line.

Here things looked very bad and the Officer Commanding — Major Chandler, ordered Major Ferguson to rally the men who had come back and take them forward to the J.O.L. and hold there.

At this point Lieut. Smart reported in to Hdqrs. that he had seen the 58th Battalion held up and fallback and likewise that the C.M.Rs appeared to have fallen back on the left and that he had a number of men in the Jumping Off Line.

Transmitted messages from battlefield operations to battalion headquarters specifically mentioned that several 43rd Battalion soldiers were observed pushing forward up Bellevue Spur, within sight of the German lines. Those reports triggered restored hope that the Cameron Highlanders would reach their 1,200-yard objective by nightfall. While battalion headquarters was abuzz with the news, a platoon of Cameron Highlanders of Canada suddenly found themselves targets in an enemy ambush. The soldiers had climbed a small knoll on their way to enemy lines, when they happened upon a section of the spur littered with decaying remains of ANZAC soldiers slain two weeks earlier. It was obvious to everyone that they had stumbled upon a killing field where snipers and machine-gunners waited to pounce on fatigued soldiers. As enemy guns opened fire, ripping apart bodies, cutting down troops where they stood, officers screamed an order to hit the ground. Each soldier looked for anything that would provide even the smallest degree of protection from the fury of the bullets. Some of that cover was found lying face down in the mud, behind the crumpled bodies of dead and wounded comrades. After what must have seemed like an eternity to those under siege, help finally arrived. Soldiers of the 52nd Infantry Battalion came to their rescue, giving firepower support and evacuating wounded men out of the line of fire. The dead remained where they had fallen. 43rd Battalion survivors retreated to safer ground to the rear, well below the hill.

43rd Canadian Infantry War Diary — A/Adjutant, Lieutenant A.E. Grimes

Day: Friday 26 October 1917
Time: 10:00 hours
Lieut. Shankland reported into Hdqrs with a full report of the position stating that he was holding the ridge about 40 yards forward of the two pillboxes with about 40 men including men of the 9th Machine Gun Coy with two of their guns which were in action.

He stated that provided his ammunition held out he could hold his position against any attack as he had already dispersed one counter attack which was forming up in the low ground 500 yards forward on his front.

He did not know where Captain Galt his Coy Commander was as he had last seen him during an attack attempting with 5 O.Rs. (Other Ranks) to capture a strong point on the right of the position he now held and suffering considerable annoyance from snipers left on his frontage and also from the direction of the strong point Capt. Galt had tried to capture. His men were however using their rifles with great effect upon isolated Germans who were seen going back and also along with the Brigade guns against the enemy assembling as before stated.

In order to report he left the position in command of Lieut. Ellis of the 9th Machine Gun Coy who though wounded refused to go out while his guns remained in action. Lieut. Shankland made his report just as a message was received from Brigade that observers of the 8th Brigade on our left had reported that some of our men were still holding the Crest and further that the contact aeroplane report was positive that a body of men were in possession of the ridge in front of the pillboxes. The map provided by the contact plane gave exactly the position held by Lieut. Shankland and also indicated that flares had been shown by some of our men forward of the intermediate objective. It appeared from this as if some men had got forward a long way before being killed by enemy snipers.

By late morning on the 26th, soldiers of the 43rd Infantry Battalion continued to persevere, keeping a steadfast hold on the precious section of ground captured during the early hours of the Battle of Passchendaele. Troops were resolute and unwavering in the determination not to surrender an inch of the sacred, blood-soaked, salient soil, which they had fought so hard and suffered so much to win. As the 43rd strengthened its hold on the newly acquired territory, the 58th Battalion was forced to declare a halt to its attack. They had been confronted with a strong, sustained resistance from a number of German infantry divisions, including 11. Bayerische Infanterie Division and 238. Infanterie Division. As a result, the 58th Infantry Battalion was pushed back a significant distance and, regretfully, were forced to leave a number of dead comrades-in-arms behind on the battlefield.

With the turbulent events transpiring on Bellevue Spur, no soldier was impervious to being killed by an enemy bullet or bomb. This was especially true when one considered high- explosive shells such as the German-made, 77mm Fuze Kanonen Zunder 11. The KZ11 was a time and percussion shell (fuze), which attained a velocity faster than the speed of sound. This low-trajectory shell was commonly referred to by the British as a "whiz-bang," named for the whizzing sound it made while speeding toward its target. German artillery guns fired thousands of these, and other deadly pellet-loaded shells, at Canadian Corps soldiers as they attacked Bellevue Spur.

As previously mentioned, friendly fire became an all-too-frequent hazard for Canadian soldiers advancing across battlefields on the Western Front. This was true as well at Passchendaele. Many infantrymen were killed or wounded, falling victim to shells fired by Canadian artillery gunners, as their comrades strained to maintain their advance in the mud, behind rolling barrages. For the most part, it was impossible for troops to sustain a proper momentum and distance between the assault force and the wall of exploding bombs. The gravity of the situation was addressed by infantry officers and artillery commanders, who immediately amended the bombing format. The artillery gunners incorporated an eight-minute continuous barrage, then every four minutes lifted and advanced the shelling fifty yards, rather than the specified 100 yards. This modification to the creeping barrage improved the situation to a degree, however, many soldiers still continued to struggle and became extremely exhausted as they wallowed in the horrifying salient mud.

The viscosity of the salient mud was an extreme impediment to all who fought on Bellevue Spur, whether Canadian or Brit, Australian or New Zealander. Troops of the Imperial German Army had to endure the mud as well. Mud and clay were the bane of the foot soldier, causing misery and hardship, although on occasion it did provide soldiers with quasi-protection from artillery shells. While exploding shrapnel bombs commonly tore apart soldiers, others were unceremoniously subjected to a bath of dark, latrine-smelling guck. On many occasions, shells landed in the deep sludge and were made instantly inert. These disabled, unexploded ordinances remained hidden and lost forever until unearthed by farm ploughs every year since the war, including present time.

The Canadian Field-Artillery commanders were prompted to try and correct the situation of the vast number of medium and heavy-artillery shells being fired at enemy lines, which were failing to explode because of the mud. The answer was found in the shell's fuse timer. Rather than rely on impact to detonate the bombs, artillery gunners set the fuse timers on approximately seventy-five percent of the Mark 1, high velocity (1,615 feet per second) shrapnel shells. Setting the fuses to explode at a predetermined second ensured that the bombs would "air burst" rather than get absorbed in the mud and clay. The solution was not perfect; air-burst shells did not generate a significant number of casualties. On the other hand, it did result in fewer wasted shells from non-detonation.

43rd Canadian Infantry Battalion War Diary — A/Adjutant, Lieutenant A.E. Grimes
    Day: Friday 26 October 1917
    Time: 10:30 hours

From this time the whole situation was clear, and Lieut. Smart taking with him the men rallied at Battalion Headquarters proceeded to the Jumping Off Line with orders to push his way forward towards the right of the slope joining up on his left with Lieut. Shankland at the pillboxes, and get in touch with the 58th Battalion throwing back his line as a flank to Lieut. Shankland's position. He was to endeavour to push in on the strong point on right of pillboxes.

The first Coy of the 52nd Bn from Brigade support had now gone forward on the low left slope of the ridge to connect up on Lieut. Shankland's left and fill in the gap between the part held on the Crest and the C.M.Rs.

During the mid-morning, thirty-five-year-old Sergeant-Major Donald Mowat of D Coy, led twenty members of the 43rd Battalion up Bellevue Spur, behind B Coy, to the location where B Coy and C Coy had earlier captured three pillboxes. As B Coy engaged German machine-gunners in their attempt to establish a Canadian position on Bellevue, Mowat and his men dug in and held their ground with rifles, grenades, and a single Lewis Machine Gun. While Mowat's party repeatedly fended off the enemy, D Coy Commander, Captain Galt selected five infantrymen and set out to attack and capture Bellevue Farm. This particular objective was an extremely important strong point, situated on the right side of the spur. Despite a determined and heroic effort, Galt's mission failed. Contributing factors in the unsuccessful mission were the extensive amount of barbed wire and the number of enemy rifles that awaited them. The small group of six were greatly outnumbered, thus their mission was doomed from the outset.

In the absence of Captain Galt, Lieutenant Robert Shankland, assumed temporary leadership of D Coy. The lieutenant's first order of business was to make a heroic and dangerous run through heavy mud and enemy gunfire, to return to the Canadian front-lines. Upon reaching the line, he commandeered a platoon of forty reinforcements and led them across No-Man's Land to a main trench line north of Mosselmarkt Road. There, Sergeant Mowat, his men, and a machine-gun crew, from the 9th Machine Gun Coy, were vigorously defending one of a number of approaches to Passchendaele. The successful defense of that particular field position held a decisive relevance if Canadian troops hoped to achieve victory at Passchendaele by the third stage of the battle.

(source: Library and Archives Canada PA-002165)
A lone soldier cautiously treks through the mud on Bellevue Spur where the 3rd Canadian Infantry Division had earlier advanced against the Germans on October 26, 1917.

After enduring hours of vicious fighting, much of it hand-to-hand combat, it was evident the Cameron Highlanders of Canada would complete the first day of battle approximately 500 yards short of their 1,200 yard primary objective. The first day of battle saw the 43rd Battalion capture several strategic positions along Bellevue. Unfortunately, during some of the heaviest fighting, they were sud denly cut off from the 8th Brigade situated on their left side. Adding to an already dire situation, the 43rd Battalion's right flank had become vulnerable. The 58th Battalion failed to reach its objective and was forced to retreat due to heavy gunfire from Snipe Hill. Miraculously, the 43rd Battalion held its position on Bellevue Spur, thanks to the courage and unselfish dedication of its troops. Lieutenant Robert

Shankland, although slightly wounded in the fighting, continued to lead the Cameron Highlanders in repelling several fierce, German counter-attacks.

43rd Canadian Infantry Battalion War Diary — A/Adjutant, Lieutenant A.E. Grimes
    Day: Friday 26 October 1917
    Time: 12:00 Noon
    Once Lieut. Shankland had filled the gap on the Crest the 2nd Brigade Support Coy of the 52nd Bn went forward through this Coy and thereafter pushed across in front of the line already established clearing out pillboxes on the left front and afterwards Bellevue and strong points on the right front. By this time Lieut. Smart had pushed forward on the right of the ridge line and established his connections having 1 Officer and 40 O.R.s with him. He succeeded in rounding up one strong point and sending back 90 prisoners, including 3 Officers.

    Lieut. Shankland although slightly wounded had by this time rejoined his command and two Battalion Scouts who had accompanied him reported back with one Officer and two O.R.s taken prisoner. The German Officer stated in English that he expected to find his Coy on the ridge as they had been ordered to counterattack.

43rd Canadian Infantry Battalion War Diary — A/Adjutant, Lieutenant A.E. Grimes
    Day: Friday 26 October 1917
    Time: 13:25 hours
    The battalion scouts also reported the position of Lieut. Smart's command on the right. Lieut. Shankland reported to the Regimental Aid Post (R.A.P.) for medical attention to his wound, stating that he had handed command over to Capt. Galt. It appears that when Capt. Galt tried to take the Strong Point in course of the attack he succeeded in penetrating the Strong Point on its left side but was unable to proceed through to a tangle of wire and iron rods on the right side of Strong Point from which the enemy were sniping down the slope on the right of the battalion. On coming out he was forced to take cover in a shell hole from machine gun fire after losing two men and the Lewis gun becoming jammed. He

was able to re-join the remnant of his command after the 52nd Battalion had come across his front and relieved Lieut. Shankland. During all this period the enemy was shelling heavily in the low ground between the point held and Bn Hdqrs.

The 52nd Battalion having pushed their line forward establishing a strong post on their left used both coys in their forward line. Brigade arranged to send one coy of 116th Battalion to support the 52nd Battalion on left of the short line held by Capt. Galt's party.

Without having experienced the Battle of Passchendaele, no one can truly imagine how frightfully terrifying it must have been on October 26 for Lance Corporal S.E. Shortliffe and the men of the 43rd Infantry Battalion. Explosions erupted everywhere. Rifle and machine gun bullets rained down upon the thousands of vulnerable, moving targets. Chlorine gas, acrid smoke, and cordite fumes filled the air. Soldiers gagged, coughed, wheezed, and struggled under the excessive weight of their combat kit, urging one foot ahead of the other through the deep salient mud. Scores of men stumbled, collapsing to their knees, coming to rest face-down in the swale-like Flanders terrain. Unable to rise up from the ground, many drew their last breath before slowly descending beneath the Ypres Salient forever. The wounded cried out for help. The dead lay silent. Bellevue Spur was, once again, a killing field.

As participants in this brutal and cataclysmic event, soldiers of the 43rd Battalion witnessed up close the tragic demise of fellow comrades and personal friends. There was no escaping death with little shelter from the bullets and bombs and especially from air-burst shrapnel and straight-line trajectory shells. It may have been either of these two artillery bombs that ultimately took the life of Lance Corporal Stephen Ernest Shortliffe, on October 26, 1917. Whichever, air burst or trajectory, it does not matter. Death would have been instantaneous, occurring within a nano-second of hearing the familiar sound of the whiz-bang. What followed was disintegration. If any human remains of S.E. Shortliffe survived the impact and explosion, they would have been lost forever in the mud of Bellevue Spur.

43rd Canadian Infantry Battalion War Diary — A/Adjutant, Lieutenant A.E. Grimes

Day: Friday 26 October 1917

Time: 19:25 hours

Capt. Galt reported as follows: "The situation looks OK as far as I can judge. The 52nd are 100 yards in front of us and in fair strength. It is to be regretted we did not get further but it was not possible. S.O.S. is in working order and conditions considered, we are OK."

The position settled down and the disposition of the 116th Battalion Coy in support was easily completed. Casualties could not be ascertained but they were roughly estimated at 13 Officers and 300 O.R.s.

Lieuts. Severn and Borthwick were known to be killed and Lieut. Banks was also presumed to be. Lieuts. Fowler, MacKenzie, N.A. Verner, Hancock, Scholey, McNally and Shankland had gone out wounded. Early in the fight a large number of men had gone slightly wounded and walking.

43rd Canadian Infantry Battalion War Diary — A/Adjutant, Lieutenant A.E. Grimes

Day: Saturday 27 October 1917

Time: 07:12 hours

Capt. Galt reported at 07:12 am as follows: "Situation quiet and unchanged. The line is well held both front and rear. Men are in a pitiable condition and while they can scarcely move will surely fight if necessary. If possible please send me up six stretchers as they will no doubt be used. Please give my runners the location of A, B and C Coys as I have some men to report."

The day was comparatively quiet and there was very little shelling by the enemy.

43rd Canadian Infantry Battalion War Diary — A/Adjutant, Lieutenant A.E. Grimes

Day: Saturday 27 October 1917

Time: 12 Noon

Battalion Scouts ordered out to scour the face of the hill over which our Coys had advanced in search of the wounded. They reported no wounded *and very few dead on the ground. The body of Lieut. Severn was found and buried by the Chaplain.*

Thirty-one hours after the first shell was fired, on the morning of October 26, a momentary lull in the fighting fell over Bellevue Ridge, allowing a number of 3rd Division battalions to search for and retrieve their wounded. Scouts from the 43rd Battalion scoured Bellevue. Amongst the smoldering rubble, craters, and damaged pillboxes they found a small number of wounded, along with the bodies of twenty Cameron Highlanders. As many as eighty-two soldiers from the 43rd Canadian Infantry Battalion had disappeared, obliterated from the face of the earth by the savage impact of shrapnel. Lance Corporal S.E. Shortliffe was such a victim. Numerous other soldiers, both dead and wounded, were sucked deep into the black salient sludge, where they were lost forever.

(Ross photo)
The author places a small flag, poppy, and photo of L/Cpl S.E. Shortliffe on Bellevue where he died on October 26, 1917.

(Ross photo)
The Passchendaele Canadian Memorial, which faces the rebuilt village of Passendale is situated on a height of land known as Crest Farm. This site marks the Canadian capture of the high ground on Passchendaele Ridge.

Between 6:00 p.m. and midnight, October 26, survivors of the 43rd, the 52nd, and 58th Battalions were relieved by three Companies of the 116th Infantry Battalion (Ontario County) and moved to the rear, in support positions on Abraham Heights. The relief was completed at midnight on the 27th with the 43rd Battalion Headquarters subsequently relocated to Otto Farm. The 43rd Battalion Adjutant, Lieutenant A.E. Grimes reported that unofficially, the 43rd Battalion's casualty count for October 26 showed two officers had been killed-in-action and one officer was missing and believed dead. A total of ten wounded officers were transported to either a regimental dressing station or a casualty clearing station, depending on the severity of their wounds. Infantry casualties were brutally heartbreaking. A total of thirty-six Cameron Highlanders were confirmed dead, sixty-six missing and 234 wounded. Those listed as "missing-in-action" were later declared in casualty reports as "killed-in-action." Lance Corporal S.E. Shortliffe was originally listed as missing on October 26, and officially declared dead on November 20, 1917.

The total of 336 dead and wounded on the first day of combat represented a battalion casualty rate of sixty-three percent.

On the evening of October 26, Brigadier-General Frederick W. Hill, commander of the 9th Infantry Brigade, 3rd Canadian Infantry Division, wrote in his diary, "It was a fine performance. We had a nut to crack and we did it."

In addition to the Cameron Highlanders of Canada who were killed on October 26, an additional fifty-nine men from the 43rd Battalion would perish between October 27 and November 15. Several succumbed to injuries while being treated at casualty clearing stations and advanced dressing stations in Vlamertinghe, Poperinghe, and Lijssenthoek. Total Canadian Corps battlefield casualties recorded during the first three days of Phase I numbered 2,481. Of these, 585 were killed in action. The combined number of casualties for both the 3rd Canadian Infantry Division and 4th Canadian Infantry Division, on October 26 numbered approximately 1,600. Included in that total were non-combat personnel, such as medical teams (stretcher bearers etc.); men transporting supplies to the troops in the field; and soldiers assigned to maintain mule tracks, roads, and light railways.

In the days immediately following October 26, an exhausted, weakened, and demoralized 43rd Battalion, together with the 58th Battalion, prepared to move to "D" Camp, in St. Jean. Due to physical and mental exhaustion, troops were permitted to take leave of the battlefield before soldiers arrived to relieve them. After settling into "D" Camp, both the 43rd and 58th Battalions organized muster parades, in which they reviewed their respective nominal rolls, in order to ascertain casualty totals. They also deployed parties of stretcher-bearers to seek out the wounded and evacuate them from the battlefield.

The Cameron Highlanders of Canada left "D" Camp in St Jean at 9:30 a.m. on October 31, and marched to the Ypres railway station where an awaiting troop transport train would take them to Clyde Camp, near Poperinghe. On the first two days at "D" Camp, the troops rested, relaxed, took a hot bath, shaved, and had a haircut. Some had duties to perform, such as kit inspections and taking inventories of stores. After the 43rd Battalion's recent tour at the front, supplies had diminished considerably and required replenishing before heading back into the line. Later in the day on November 1, Lieutenants Palmer and Ward arrived with a draft of seventy ordinary regulars to augment the combat strength of the 43rd Canadian Infantry Battalion. One of the officers, thirty-year-old, Lieutenant William Arnold Palmer, would be killed two weeks later, on November 14, during intense enemy shelling between Bellevue and 's Graventafel Road.

The Battle of Passchendaele, Phase II, got underway at 5:30 on the morning of October 30. The 3rd Canadian Infantry Division made a gallant attempt to seize the remaining stretch of Bellevue Spur from the Germans. There was a fresh chill in the air, along with a light drizzle, as troops commenced a frontal attack against the German positions. The 49th Canadian Infantry Battalion, from Alberta, began slowly snaking their way up Bellevue, heading in a north-easterly direction, along what was once, 's Graventafel-Passchendaele road, leading to Passchendaele village.

At the same time, the 5th Canadian Mounted Rifles of Quebec were in the process of securing a northern flank. In the south, near Ravebeek, the Princess Patricia's Canadian Light Infantry was aggressively engaged with the Germans near the swamps. A number of battalions with the 4th Canadian Infantry Division came under intense machine-gun fire as they attacked northward towards Crest Farm, an important German defense line located southwest of Passchendaele village. As dusk settled upon the battlefield, it was obvious to Canadian Corps commanders that, no matter how determined the troops were, the 3rd Canadian Infantry Division would not achieve its goal of reaching their objective before nightfall. Despite the failure to secure their objective, the 3rd Infantry Division did manage to advance the front-line a considerable distance up Bellevue Spur, where ground conditions were much drier.

While General Louis Lipsett's 3rd Canadian Infantry Division was engaged in close combat with the enemy on Bellevue Spur, soldiers from the 85th Infantry Battalion (Nova Scotia Highlanders), and 4th Canadian Infantry Division were being decimated. Scores of troops were killed trying to capture several strategically important enemy fortifications built along the higher elevated sections of the Passchendaele-Broodseinde Road. While the Nova Scotians were pounded mercilessly by German bombs and slaughtered in a hail of machine gun bullets, the opposite was happening with the 78th Infantry Battalion (Winnipeg Grenadiers) and the 72nd Infantry Battalion (Seaforth Highlanders of Vancouver). These two battalions out-manoeuvred and overwhelmed their adversaries — they hammered the enemy into submission. The two battalions continued their success defending Passchendaele on October 30, by flushing out German gun crews from their impenetrable fortresses atop a small height of land called "Crest Farm." This brought the Canadians to within 100 yards of what was once a village landmark, an impressive, large church, now for the most part reduced to a pile of rubble. Victory was near, but hard work and personal sacrifice would still be required to complete the job.

(source: Library and Archives Canada)
German prisoners, presumably taken during the Battle of Passchendaele, are shown receiving hot tea and biscuits.

On November 2, each Coy went about the task of filling Lewis Gun and stretcher-bearer positions, as both sections had suffered serious losses of manpower during the first two days of the Passchendaele battle. On that same day, Brigadier-General Frederick W. Hill, commander of the 9th Infantry Brigade, paid a short visit to the Cameron Highlanders and addressed the men. In his talk, he congratulated them on their fine work during the recent tour of duty in the frontline. Captain Walcot of the Transport Section was singled out by the brigadier-general for special mention, as well as Captain G.C.F. Pringle, the battalion chaplain. Captain Pringle was lauded in particular for his tireless work in attending to the wounded and encouraging the men, before and during the battle. Brigadier-General Hill's visit, of November 2, was followed five days later by Lieutenant-General Arthur Currie's. On November 7, Canadian Corps Commander Currie reiterated what Frederick Hill had said in his speech, adding his personal appreciation as well for the excellent work and professionalism of the 43rd Infantry Battalion. General Currie also used the visit to interview Lieutenant Robert Shankland for commendation of a Victoria Cross. Another VIP visitation happened on November 8, with the arrival of the 3rd Canadian Infantry Division Commander, Major-General Louis J. Lipsett. General Lipsett also bestowed his gratitude to the fighting men of the 43rd.

After nine relaxing days in Clyde Camp, the 43rd Battalion moved back to St. Jean and "B" Camp on November 10. This was the same day their compatriots from the 1st and 2nd Canadian Infantry Divisions were successfully capturing Passchendaele. The Cameron Highlanders took the short trip by train from Poperinghe to Ypres, then on foot in a cold, pouring rainstorm to St. Jean, via Kruisstraat Road. Prior to departing Clyde Camp, the battalion cheered the arrival of Lieutenant R. Henderson with another contingent of 20 troops.

The 43rd Battalion was only in St. Jean for a few short hours before being ordered to return, once again, to Bellevue Spur — this time in support lines where they were to relieve two Canadian battalions. On November 11, the 43rd Canadian Infantry Battalion replaced two companies of men from the 7th Canadian Infantry Battalion (1st British Columbia) CEF and two Companies from the 8th Canadian Infantry Battalion (90th Rifles of Winnipeg) CEF. The relief operation was completed by 9:30 p.m., except for the very last runners, who did not arrive until four hours later. Battalion headquarters was established, in an eighty square-foot, former German concrete bunker, on Bellevue Spur, while each of the coy headquarters were located in four large shell holes. During the multiple battalion relief operation, three members of the 43rd Battalion were wounded, Lieutenant Robert Shankland being among those injured.

The final drive to take Passchendaele came on the morning of November 6. It took place without the participation of the 3rd and 4th Canadian Infantry Divisions. Twelve days of difficult and deadly combat had resulted in a tremendous number of casualties. Manpower strength of both infantry divisions had been reduced considerably. It was therefore decided to withdraw General Lipsett's and General Watson's men from the battlefield. The two infantry divisions were replaced with fresh troops representing the 1st Canadian Infantry Division and the 2nd Canadian Infantry Division, under the command of General Archibald Cameron Macdonnell and Major-General Henry Edward Burstall respectively. The two divisions moved into their positions; Phase III was about to commence.

Company commanders of the 2nd Infantry Division were given orders to fight up the side of Passchendaele Ridge, in the direction of the village, and to reach the high ground before the end of day. In the meantime, the 1st Infantry Division resumed the assault on Bellevue Spur from the exact location where their comrades from the 3rd Infantry Division and 43rd Battalion had been forced to halt their advance a few days earlier. The 1st Infantry Division, under the command of General A. C. Macdonnell, launched a well-organized, strong assault on the ridge north of the village, at 6:00 a.m. This attack propelled them to the higher and dryer ground from where the Canadian Corps stormed German defence installations and effectively closed down the majority of enemy resistance using "Bullets, Bombs and Bayonets."

The onslaught of those Canadian Shock Troops storming Passchendaele quickly persuaded large numbers of Germans to signal their surrender by holding aloft and waving white flags while shouting "kamerad." In most cases, undying loyalty to the Kaiser had been replaced by a soldier's stronger desire to live. Although the Canadians appeared to have taken control of Passchendaele, pockets of fierce resistance still continued to persist in certain strategic areas of the ridge. Some of those fanatical loyalists, committed to fighting to the end, attempted to turn the tide of battle. The futility of their effort was soon apparent.

(source: Library and Archives Canada)
This is a view of a Bellevue Spur pillbox sometime in April or May 1919. Note the wooden crosses marking the location of fallen soldiers. The remains of these soldiers were later exhumed and reburied in a CWGC military cemetery near where they perished.

November 10, 1917: Four days after the commencement of Phase III, Passchendaele was liberated by the 27th Canadian Infantry Battalion (City of Winnipeg).

In addition to the 27th Battalion, the 31st Battalion (Alberta), and the 28th Battalion (Saskatchewan) captured a strategic section of Passchendaele Ridge, south of the village. Although the Battle of Passchendaele was considered to be over, it was not officially declared ended until November 15, five days later. After 103 long, agonizing, and deadly days, the guns fell silent. From many perspectives, the Third Battle of Ypres was a lengthy and costly operation, however, in comparison to the Battle of the Somme, it was actually thirty-eight days shorter. The Somme fight raged for 141 days. During the Third Battle of Ypres, July 31 to November 10, 1917, Great Britain, Australia, New Zealand, and Canada incurred a total of 244,897 casualties. It is estimated the Imperial German Army suffered approximately the same number. Canadian dead and wounded numbered 15,654. All together, Passchendaele was responsible for almost 500,000 casualties.

Despite the capitulation of Passchendaele by the Imperial German Army to the Canadian Expeditionary Force, German infantry divisions continued their aggressive pursuit and harassment of the Canadian Corps within the salient. This was especially evident in the sectors of Bellevue and Passchendaele. It was there that the enemy dispatched hour-long bombardments along 's Graventafel Road, from Bellevue to Waterloo Farm. Throughout the entire day on November 12, German howitzers shelled Flanders from Meetcheele Ridge to Bellevue and beyond; the heaviest bombing period from 6:00 p.m. and lasting until 8:00 p.m., with 's Graventafel Road again being the primary target of enemy artillery fire. Canadian batteries retaliated with a somewhat muted response of only twenty minutes. By the closing of the day, five Cameron Highlanders had been killed and four wounded. The fatalities were: Private Victor Beaver, Private John Winfield Downey, Private Angus John Gardiner, Private Charles Little, and Private William Henderson (body not recovered).

Tuesday, November 13: The sporadic chatter of machine-gun fire could be heard and felt by Canadian troops moving along the road from Waterloo Farm, to Mosselmarkt. At the same time, German heavy-artillery guns were pointed at Bellevue Spur, striking support and forward lines at the very moment the 43rd Battalion was preparing to defend the line against an anticipated ground attack. On this day, the enemy snuffed out the lives of four soldiers from the 43rd Infantry Battalion. Their names were: Private George Cleaver, Private Eric Russell, Private Sydney Percival Wright (body not recovered), and Private Murdo McAuley (body not recovered). In addition, ten Cameron Highlanders were wounded.

Under the clear, bright skies of November 14, German artillery-gunners continued shelling 's Graventafel Road and Bellevue. The intensity of the German bombing increased substantially by mid-afternoon, with enemy shells destroying a number of Canadian eighteen-pounders, in the vicinity of the Wimbledon sector. A massive number of shrapnel shells continued to create mayhem, causing large numbers of casualties throughout the day, including ten Highlanders killed and twenty-four wounded. On November 14, the 43rd Canadian Infantry Battalion lost Corporal Reginald L. C. Hawley, Corporal John McWhirter, Lance Corporal Wilfred Kendall Turner, Private Lancelot Edward Carter, Private William Edward Fowle, Private James Henry Klyne, Private William John Smallwood, Private Benjamin Smith, Private Edward Williams, and Private Ernest Edgar Wood. Except for Corporal Hawley, their bodies were never recovered.

During the height of the German artillery shelling, at 4:00 p.m., Brigadier-General Hill, 9th Canadian Infantry Brigade, ordered the Acting Commander of the 43rd Battalion, Major William Kendall Chandler, to move the Cameron Highlanders of Canada, to "B" Camp in Brandhoek. By 9:15 p.m., the 43rd Battalion had been relieved in the forward lines by the Princess Patricia's Canadian Light Infantry and were on their way to Wieltje, where they camped until morning.

November 15, 1917 was the last day the 43rd Canadian Infantry Battalion (Cameron Highlanders of Canada) CEF spent in the Ypres Salient. The battalion departed Wieltje at 8:15 a.m.; marched by company to the Ypres train station via St. Jean and Ypres. Twenty-four days earlier, S.E. Shortliffe, along with 531 of his comrades, had marched through what was once Menin Gate on their way to fight the Germans at Passchendaele. Now, only 392 Cameron Highlanders retraced their steps into the city. By 10:50 a.m., the 43rd Battalion had boarded the train at the Ypres station and forty minutes later they arrived in Brandhoek and "B" Camp. Shortly before midnight, the 43rd received orders that they would be leaving in the morning for the dreaded Somme. It was in the Somme during the fall of 1916 that the

43rd Infantry Battalion suffered tremendous loss of life, most notably on October 8, against the enemy-held Regina Trench.

Shortly before noon, on November 16, the battle-hardened veterans of Vimy Ridge and Passchendaele boarded a fleet of buses for St. Venant, France. It would be there in the Somme that, once again, the 43rd Battalion would join the British First Army on the front-lines, in what would be the start of another long and deadly tour of duty. Major combat missions in Vis-en-Artois, Arras, and in particular the battle for Cambrai, in October 1918, ravaged the ranks of the 43rd Canadian Infantry Battalion. The battalion ended the war far weaker than when the Cameron Highlanders first landed in France on February 22, 1916.

The victorious Canadian Expeditionary Force occupied Passchendaele until November 15, at which time all Canadian troops were withdrawn from the Ypres Salient and moved to the Vimy-Lens sector. The relocation from Passchendaele to a quieter battleground was part of the agreement between Generals Currie and Haig, prior to Arthur Currie leading the Passchendaele offensive. The removal of Canadian soldiers from West-Flanders brought to a close Canada's military contribution during the war, in the Ypres Salient. The country's presence initially began with the Princess Patricia's Canadian Light Infantry when they fought alongside the British during the months of October and November, 1914 in the Ypres-Zonnebeke area. Canadian troops later fought with the British Expeditionary Force in 1915 during the Second Battle of Ypres, then again at Mount Sorrel in 1916, before Passchendaele in 1917. Thousands of Canadians shed their blood to liberate Belgium from the grip of Kaiser Wilhelm's Imperial German Army. Those who laid down their lives on the battlefields of West-Flanders are forever commemorated in military cemeteries and on memorials, as well as remembered by Belgian citizens, and organizations such as the Last Post Association in Ieper (Ypres), and the Western Front Association of Belgium.

The Union Jack of the United Kingdom flew triumphantly over Passchendaele Ridge for only a few months. In April 1918, Passchendaele once again fell to the Imperial German Army, the same month that Kemmelberg, south-west of Ypres was captured by the enemy. The British, who were on the eastern front-line of the Ypres Salient (Passchendaele) were forced to withdraw towards the former front-line near Ypres. The reason for the withdrawal: the salient was too sharp, too dangerous, and easily attacked from three sides. This turn of events brought disbelief, anguish, and anger from soldiers and the families of those who had perished just six months earlier on the fields of Flanders and Passchendaele Ridge. Nonetheless, Passchendaele remained under German occupation until September 1918 when the Belgian Army, under command of King Albert, finally and decisively ended enemy control of Passchendaele.

Passchendaele, like the Great War itself, was an enigma; complex and difficult to understand. Over the years, Passchendaele provoked its share of praise as well as criticism by both historians and politicians.

Theodor Joachim wrote: "Germany had been brought near sicheren Untergang (certain destruction) by the Flanders battle of 1917."

Former British Prime Minister Lloyd George, in 1938, included these words in his memoirs: "Passchendaele was indeed one of the greatest disasters of the war…no soldier of any intelligence now defends this senseless campaign."

Conversely, the fighting prowess of the Canadians at Passchendaele and on the Western Front were praised by scholars from the Royal Military College of Canada who stated in *The Oxford Companion to Canadian History*: "Nevertheless, the competence and maturity begun in 1915 at Ypres a short distance away, and at Vimy Ridge earlier that spring, again confirmed the reputation of the Canadian Corps as the finest fighting formation on the Western Front."

The battle for Passchendaele will be remembered, not only for its horrific slaughter of some of Canada's finest young men, but also for the four officers, two NCOs and three ordinary regulars who received the Victoria Cross, for their courage, dedication, and leadership during those sixteen horrific days in October 1917. Three recipients received their Victoria Cross for combat action, on October 26. They included: Lieutenant Robert Shankland, 43rd Canadian Infantry Battalion; Major Christopher O'Kelly, 52nd Canadian

Infantry Battalion; and Private Tommy Holmes, 4th Canadian Mounted Rifles. All were members of the 3rd Canadian Infantry Division. Other Victoria Cross winners were: Sergeant George Harry Mullin, Princess Patricia's Canadian Light Infantry; Major George Randolph Pearkes, 5th Canadian Mounted Rifles; Private James Peter Robertson, 27th Canadian Infantry Battalion; Sergeant Colin Fraser Barron, 3rd Canadian Infantry Battalion; Private Cecil John Kinross, 49th Canadian Infantry Battalion; and Lieutenant Hugh MacDonald McKenzie, 7th Machine Gun Company.

The Battle of Cambrai was the final set-piece engagement undertaken by both the 3rd Canadian Division and the 4th Canadian Division in WWI. The 9th Canadian Infantry Brigade battalions, which included the 43rd Battalion, were involved in some of the heaviest and deadliest fighting west of Cambrai, but more especially during their advance in the north of the city. On October 1, 1918, the 43rd Battalion (Cameron Highlanders of Canada) CEF and the 52nd Battalion (New Ontario) pushed through the 7th Canadian Infantry Brigade line and attacked Cambrai at 5:10 a.m. Meanwhile, the Canadian line encircling the city came under heavy counterattacks by the Germans. During three days of fierce fighting, the 9th Infantry Brigade lost fifty-six officers and 1,467 ordinary regulars. The 43rd Battalion was almost annihilated. In the chaos of battle, they mustered their forces and readied themselves for yet another strong counterattack. That anticipated attack ultimately did not materialize. The Germans pulled out of Cambrai and the Canadians were hailed as liberators. Thankfully, the decision by the Imperial German Army to retreat came at a time that spared the Cameron Highlanders more loss of life.

The Cameron Highlanders of Canada continued to demonstrate their fighting skills, bravery, and tenacity in the Somme and Loos regions, fighting up until the Armistice Peace Agreement was signed, in Compiegne, France, at 11:00 a.m. on November 11, 1918. Two minutes before that ceasefire came into effect, twenty-five-year-old Private George Lawrence Price, of the 28th Canadian Infantry Battalion, was struck and killed by a sniper's bullet, in Mons, Belgium.

Private Price was the last Canadian and United Kingdom soldier to die in WWI. The first fatality of the Great War was Private John Parr, a British infantryman killed north east of the same Belgian City, on August 21, 1914.

During the battles of Hill 70, Lens, Avion, Vimy Ridge, and Passchendaele, the men of the 43rd Canadian Infantry Battalion (Cameron Highlanders of Canada) CEF fought under Major-General Louis James Lipsett (3rd Canadian Infantry Division), Brigadier-General Frederick William Hill (9th Infantry Brigade), Lieutenant-Colonel William Grassie (43rd Infantry Battalion), and Lieutenant-Colonel William Kellman Chandler (43rd Infantry Battalion).

Major-General Louis J. Lipsett, born in Bundoran, County Donegal, Ireland on June 15, 1874, rose through the ranks after his enlistment in January 1915. He became brigadier-general, lieutenant-colonel and finally major-general and commander of the 3rd Canadian Infantry Division. In September 1918, Lieutenant-General Arthur Currie insisted that all Canadian Corps divisions be under the direct leadership of Canadians. In an agreement between Currie and Sir Douglas Haig, General Lipsett, was transferred to the British 4th Division, an infantry division he commanded until his death in Saulzoir, France, on October 14, 1918. General Lipsett was forty-four years of age at the time of his death, the 59th and last British general to die in World War I.

Brigadier General Frederick W. Hill was the commander of the 9th Canadian Infantry Brigade, 3rd Canadian Infantry Division. The former mayor of Niagara Falls, Ontario continued to serve in the military until his retirement in 1930. Frederick Hill died on July 29, 1947, at the age of eighty-one.

Lieutenant-Colonel William Grassie was the highly decorated commander of the 43rd Canadian Infantry Battalion (Cameron Highlanders of Canada) CEF, 9th Infantry Brigade, 3rd Infantry Division. Born in Aberdeen, Scotland, Colonel Grassie, a former real estate agent, enlisted in Winnipeg on December 14, 1914, at the age of forty-two years. Prior to enlisting, Grassie served with the 79th Battalion (Cameron Highlanders of Canada) for five years. During his tour as 43rd Battalion Commander, Colonel William Grassie was mentioned in Despatches on three occasions.

Lieutenant-Colonel William Kellman Chandler often assumed the role of Acting Commanding Officer of the 43rd Canadian Infantry Battalion. Prior to the Battle of Passchendaele he was promoted from major to lieutenant-colonel, and shortly after, led the Cameron Highlanders of Canada into battle, on October 26, 1917.

The 43rd Canadian Infantry Battalion's proud and glorious history came to a sad conclusion on September 15, 1920. It was disbanded under General Order 149. The battalion, however, was perpetuated by the Queen's Own Cameron Highlanders of Canada until it too was disbanded at the conclusion of WWII, on November 30, 1945.

Seven months after the Armistice Treaty, the former adversaries met on June 28, 1919, to sign the Peace Treaty in Versailles. This treaty formally brought to a close, "The War to End All Wars." After four years of bloodshed and suffering, peace and security had finally returned to Europe — at least for the next twenty years.

Chapter Thirty-One
"THEIR NAME LIVETH FOR EVERMORE"

These are the names of the 161 soldiers from the 43rd Canadian Infantry Battalion (Cameron Highlanders of Canada) CEF who perished in the Ypres Salient, October 21 –November 15, 1917. (* Signifies the soldier's remains were never found.)

Lieutenant

BANKS, Robert James * — (28 yrs) died: October 26

BORTHWICK, Peter * — (29 yrs) died: October 26

HOLLIS, Oscar Harold — (24 yrs) died: October 23

PALMER, William Arnold* (30 yrs) died: November 14

SEVERN, Vernon Nicholl * — (27 yrs) died: October 26

Sergeant

DOWNIE, John Hardy * — (24 yrs) died: October 26

GEOFREY, Louis Felix * — (unknown) died: October 26

MACARTHUR, Dougall Sinclair — (29 yrs) died: October 26

WOOD, John Sutherland * — (28 yrs) died: October 26

Lance Sergeant

JOHNSTON, Joseph Gudmundor — (24 yrs) died: October 26

Corporal

EYKELBOSCH, Frank * — (20 yrs) died: October 26

HAWLEY, Reginald L.C. — (unknown) died: November 14

LEES, David — (39 yrs) died: October 26

MCDONALD, Frank * — (21 yrs) died: October 26

MCWHIRTER, John * — (21 yrs) died: November 14

STANDING, Clarence Thomas — (24 yrs) died: October 26

STEWART, David — (25 yrs) died: October 26 -Military Medal-

Lance Corporal

SHORTLIFFE, Stephen Ernest * — (24 yrs) died: October 26   page 306

TURNER, Wilfred Kendall * — (21 yrs) died: November 14

WILD, Thomas Edward * — (29 yrs) died: October 26

Private

ANDERSON, William * — (unknown) died: October 26

BAKER, James William * — (26 yrs) died: October 26

BARCLAY, Robert — (24) died: November 4, from wounds

BARKLEY, Walter Levitt — (20 yrs) died: October 26

BARR, Andrew — (28 yrs) died: October 27, from wounds

BATES, Herbert James — (23 yrs) died: October 26

BEAVER, Victor — (unknown) died: November 12

BLAIR, Archibald — (26 yrs) died: October 26

BLENKIN, Ernest * — (27 yrs) died: October 26

BROWN, William * — (unknown) died: October 26

BURLEY, Joe — (29 yrs) died: October 28, from wounds

CACHTLEY, John — (23 yrs) died: October 23, from wounds

CAIRNS, Garnet Chester * — (unknown) died: October 26

CARD, Reed * — (25 yrs) died: October 27

CAMPBELL, Peter Albert — (27 yrs) died: October 26

CAMPBELL, David — (25 yrs) died: October 27, from wounds

CAMPBELL, Robert John Mclean — (30 yrs) died: October 28, from wounds

CARTER, Lancelot Edward * — (32 yrs) died: November 14

CASSEL, Ernest Leroy — (19 yrs) died: October 30, from wounds

CHARLEBOIS, Denis Oliver * — (20 yrs) died: October 26

CHRISTIE, Alexander — (24 yrs) died: October 26

CLARK, Joseph — (27 yrs) died: October 28

CLEAVER, George — (19 yrs) died: November 13

CLEGHORN, George — (unknown) died: October 31, from wounds

CLEVETT, George Laban — (19 yrs) died: November 12, from wounds

DANIEL, William * — (31 yrs) died: October 26

DAY, Percival Charles * — (31 yrs) died: October 26

DOWNEY, John Winfield — (28 yrs) died: November 12

EDDIE, Charles * — (25 yrs) died: October 26

EDGE, James * — (27 yrs) died: October 26

ELLIOT, George Richard * — (21 yrs) died: October 24

EMMONS, Hugh Oswald * — (33 yrs) died: October 26

ENGLAND, Sidney Mark — (28 yrs) died: October 26

FRANCIS, Wheelock * — (31 yrs) died: October 26

FOWLE, William Edward * — (22 yrs) died: November 14

GARDNER, Angus John — (unknown) died: November 12

GILLETT, Lance * — (23 yrs) died: October 26

GRAY, William * — (35 yrs) died: October 26

GRAY, Henry * — (31 yrs) died: October 26

GREIG, John Rennie — (27 yrs) died: November 20, from wounds

GRAHAM, George Gordon — (35 yrs) died: October 27, from wounds

GROGAN, John — (32 yrs) died: November 15, from wounds

HANDFORTH, Henry * (35 yrs) died: October 26

HARTLEY, Gordon Walker — (unknown) died: October 23

HEALEY, William * — (43 yrs) died: October 26

HEATHER, Malcolm Charles — (unknown) died: October 27, from wounds

HENDERSON, William * — (27 yrs) died: November 12

HENDERSON, William Stuart * — (32 yrs) died: October 26

HILL, Charles William — (20 yrs) died: October 22, from wounds

HILL, Harry — (unknown) died: November 4, from wounds

JAMES, Frank Robertson * — (23 yrs) died: October 26
-Military Medal-

JONES, Andrew Cecil — (unknown) died: October 28, from wounds

KEENS, Joseph Henry * — (37 yrs) died: October 26

KENNEDY, James Patrick * — (25 yrs) died: October 26

KEOORKEIAN, Bob * — (unknown) died: October 26

KERR, Robert John * — (30 yrs) died: October 26

KIRKWOOD, James * — (unknown) died: October 27

KLYNE, James Henry * — (24 yrs) died: November 14

LAKE, Albert Edward * — (19 yrs) died: October 25

LITTLE, Charles — (39 yrs) died: November 12

LLEWELLYN, Edmund Henry * — (24 yrs) died: October 26

LOCKEY, Walter John * — (35 yrs) died: October 26

MCAULEY, Murdo * — (28 yrs) died: November 13

MCAFEE, Richard — (29 yrs) died: October 31, from wounds

MACDONALD, John * — (33 yrs) died: October 26

MACDONALD, Donald Maxwell * — (26 yrs) died: October 26

MCKENZIE, George * — (21 yrs) died: October 27

MACLEAN, Neil Houston * — (24 yrs) died: October 26

MACLEAN, Lauchlan * — (34 yrs) died: October 26

MACKIE, Alexander — (27 yrs) died: October 26

MAITLAND, Charles * — (27 yrs) died: October 27

MATHEWS, David James * — (28 yrs) October 26

MCCALL, Richard Malcolm * — (27 yrs) died: October 26

MCDOUGALL, Howard Milton * — (23 yrs) died: October 26

MCGRATH, David * — (26 yrs) died: October 26

MCLEOD, Norman — (38 yrs) died: October 26

MCQUARRIE, Neil * — (28 yrs) died: October 26

MELVIN, Robert * — (46 yrs) died: October 26

MITCHELL, Robert Edvin * — (19 yrs) died: October 26

MORRICE, Charles John * — (25 yrs) died: October 26

MORRISON, Ronald William * — (37 yrs) died: October 26

MURRAY, Douglas * — (27 yrs) died: October 26

MURRAY, Donald * — (30 yrs) died: October 26

MURRAY, Archibald * — (31 yrs) died: October 26

NELSON, Allan Gerald * — (20 yrs) died: October 26

NICHOLSON, Alexander * — (25 yrs) died: October 26

NOBLE, Andrew * — (21 yrs) died: October 26

NOBLE, John * — (27 yrs) died: October 26

NOTMAN, Robert * — (24 yrs) died: October 26

OLSON, Karl Adrian * — (29 yrs) died: October 26

PATTON, Samuel * — (45 yrs) died: October 26

PATTERSON, James * — (unknown) died: October 24

PAQUIN, Joseph * — (28 yrs) died: October 26

PEACOCK, John * — (31 years) died: October 29

PETERSON, Andrew Lewis * — (23 yrs) died: October 26

POINTEN, Percy — (34 yrs) died: October 26

POTTERTON, Ted — (27 yrs) died: November 7, from wounds

RAKE, Henry Stansfield * — (32 years) died: October 26

READ, Warren — (22 yrs) died: October 26

RENNIE, Alexander * — (21 yrs) died: October 26

RICHARD, James * — (22 yrs) died: October 26

RICHMOND, John Fraser * — (34 yrs) died: October 26

ROBERTS, Henry Edwin — (40 yrs) died: November 5, from wounds

ROBERTS, Thomas William — (unknown) died: October 28, from wounds

ROSS, Maurice * — (23 yrs) died: October 26

RUSSELL, Eric — (19 yrs) died: November 13

SCOTT, Charles * — (22 yrs) died: October 26

SCOTT, James Young * — (35 yrs) died: October 27

SIMS, Roy Harold * — (21 yrs) died: October 26

SINGER, Henry * — (25 yrs) died: October 26

SKINNER, Morden Earl * — (25 yrs) died: October 26

SMALLWOOD, William John * — (27 yrs) died: November 14

SMITH, Benjamin * — (33 yrs) died: November 14

SORNBERGER, Hollis Harris * — (24 yrs) died: October 26

STONE, William John * — (29 yrs) died: October 26

STORMONT, George Young * — (22 yrs) died: October 26

SUGGITT, Frances William * — (24 yrs) died: October 26

TAYLOR, Robert * — (32 yrs) died: October 26

TAYLOR, William — (30 yrs) died: October 28, from wounds

TETROE, Frank * — (25 yrs) died: October 26

THAIN, William * — (22 yrs) died: October 26

THOMAS, David * — (26 yrs) died: October 26

THOMAS, Thomas Otway * — (20 yrs) died: October 25

TINDALL, Clarence — (unknown) died: October 26

TURNER, Albert Henry — (29 yrs) died: November 3

TWERDUN, Tony * — (20 yrs) died: October 26

VIEVIER, Joseph * — (27 yrs) died: October 26

VINEY, Arthur Frederick — (24 yrs) died: November 4

WALKER, James (26 yrs) died: October 26

WALKER, Alexander — (23 yrs) died: October 26

WALLACE, James Emmett — (25 yrs) died: October 23

WARE, Frederick William * — (30 yrs) died: October 26

WATTS, Clarence Raymond * — (27 yrs) died: October 26

WHATMORE, John — (unknown) died: November 5

WILLIAMS, Edward * — (unknown) died: November 14

WILSON, Jonathan * — (37 yrs) died: October 26

WILTON, Howard Sylvester * — (26 yrs) died: October 26

WOOD, Ernest Edgar * — (26 yrs) died: November 14

WOOD, John Alexander — (28 yrs) died: October 27, from wounds

WRIGHT, Sydney Percival * — (33 yrs) died: November 13

WYATT, George Edward * — (20 yrs) died: October 26

Menin Gate Memorial to the Missing in Ieper (Ypres)

> LANCE CORPORAL
> GROAT A.
> HUNTER J. C.
> SHORTLIFFE S. E.
> TURNER W. K.
> WILD T. E.

Lance Corporal S.E. Shortliffe, one of the 107 members of the 43rd Canadian Infantry Battalion (Cameron Highlanders of Canada) who perished at Passchendaele and have no known grave. Their names are commemorated at the Menin Gate Memorial.

These are the names of 54 Cameron Highlanders of Canada soldiers who are buried in a Commonwealth War Graves Commission Cemetery in the Ypres Salient.

BARR, Pte. Andrew — died of wounds — (1) Nine Elms British Cemetery, Belgium

BARCLAY, Pte. Robert — died of wounds — Etaples Military Cemetery, France

BARKLEY, Pte. Walter Levitt — died of wounds — (2) Vlamertinghe New Military Cemetery, Belgium

BATES, Pte. Herbert James — (3) Poelcapelle British Cemetery, Belgium

BEAVER, Pte. Victor — (4) Tyne Cot Cemetery, Belgium

BLAIR, Pte. Archibald — Poelcapelle British Cemetery, Belgium

BURLEY, Pte. Joe — died of wounds — Nine Elms British Cemetery, Belgium

CACHTLEY, Pte. John –died of wounds — Nine Elms British Cemetery, Belgium

CAMPBELL, Pte. Robert John McLean — died of wounds — Nine Elms British Cemetery, Belgium

CAMPBELL, Pte. David — died of wounds — Vlamertinghe New Military Cemetery, Belgium

CAMPBELL, Pte. Peter Albert — Poelcapelle British Cemetery, Belgium

CASSEL, Pte. Ernest Leroy — died of wounds — (5) Lijssenthoek Military Cemetery, Belgium

CHRISTIE, Pte. Alexander — Tyne Cot Cemetery, Belgium

CLARK, Pte. Joseph — Boulogne Eastern Cemetery, Boulogne-sur-Mer, France

CLEAVER, Pte. George — (6) Passchendaele New British Cemetery, Belgium

CLEGHORN, Pte. George — died of wounds — Nine Elms British Cemetery, Belgium

CLEVETT, Pte. George Laban — (7) Bedford House Cemetery (Enclosure 4), Belgium

DOWNEY, Pte. John Winfield — Tyne Cot Cemetery, Belgium

ENGLAND, Pte. Sidney Mark — Passchendaele New British Cemetery, Belgium

GARDINER, Pte. Angus John — Tyne Cot Cemetery, Belgium

GRAHAM, Pte. George Gordon — died of wounds — Nine Elms British Cemetery, Belgium

GREIG, Pte. John Rennie — died of wounds — Lijssenthoek Military Cemetery, Belgium

GROGAN, Pte. John — died of wounds — Lijssenthoek Military Cemetery, Belgium

HARTLEY, Gordon Walker — (8) New Irish Farm Cemetery, Belgium

HAWLEY, Cpl. Reginald Leicester — Passchendaele New British Cemetery, Belgium

HEATHER, Pte. Malcolm Charles — died of wounds — Nine Elms British Cemetery, Belgium

HILL, Pte. Charles William — died of wounds — Nine Elms British Cemetery, Belgium

HILL, Pte. Harry — died of wounds — Nine Elms British Cemetery, Belgium

HOLLIS, Lieut. Oscar Harold — Tyne Cot Cemetery, Belgium

JOHNSTON, L/Sgt. Joseph Gudmundar — Tyne Cot Cemetery, Belgium

JONES, Pte. Andrew Cecil — died of wounds — Nine Elms British Cemetery, Belgium

LITTLE, Pte. Charles — Passchendaele New British Cemetery, Belgium

LEES, Cpl. David — Tyne Cot Cemetery, Belgium

MACARTHUR, Sgt. Dougall Sinclair — died of wounds — Nine Elms British Cemetery, Belgium

MACKIE, Pte. Alexander — Passchendaele New British Cemetery, Belgium

MCAFEE, Pte. Richard — died of wounds — Nine Elms British Cemetery, Belgium

MCLEOD, Pte. Norman — Passchendaele New British Cemetery, Belgium

POINTEN, Pte. Percy — Tyne Cot Cemetery, Belgium

POTTERTON, Pte. Ted — ** Epsom Cemetery, Surrey, United Kingdom

READ, Pte. Warren — died of wounds — Nine Elms British Cemetery, Belgium

ROBERTS, Pte. Thomas William — died of wounds — Nine Elms British Cemetery, Belgium

ROBERTS, Pte. Henry Edwin — died of wounds — Lijssenthoek Military Cemetery, Belgium

RUSSELL, Pte. Eric — Passchendaele New British Cemetery, Belgium

STANDING, Cpl. Clarence Thomas — Passchendaele New British Cemetery, Belgium

STEWART, Cpl. David — Poelcapelle British Cemetery, Belgium

TAYLOR, Pte. William — died of wounds — Nine Elms British Cemetery, Belgium

TINDALL, Pte. Clarence — (9) Ypres Reservoir Cemetery, Belgium

TURNER, Pte. Albert Henry — Etaples Military Cemetery, France

VINEY, Pte. Arthur Frederick — St. Sever Cemetery Extension (Rouen), France

WALLACE, Pte. James Emmett — Tyne Cot Cemetery, Belgium

WALKER, Pte. Alexander — died of wounds — Lijssenthoek Military Cemetery, Belgium

WALKER, Pte James — Tyne Cot Cemetery, Belgium

WHATMORE, Pte. John — Etaples Military Cemetery, France

WOOD, Pte. John Alexander — died of wounds — Nine Elms British Cemetery, Belgium

YPRES SALIENT MILITARY CEMETERIES

(Final resting place for troops of the 43rd Battalion)

1. Nine Elms British Cemetery is situated in the western section of the town of Poperinghe. This cemetery was used by casualty clearing stations from September 1917 until October 1918. Nine Elms British Cemetery contains 1,556 Commonwealth burials, 289 are Canadian and of that number, 16 are from the 43rd Canadian Infantry Battalion (Cameron Highlanders of Canada) CEF.
2. Vlamertinghe New Military Cemetery is located 3 miles west of Ypres (Ieper) and less than 2 miles south of the village of Vlamertinghe. This cemetery was also a hospital burial ground for 1,813 Commonwealth soldiers. Most died of their wounds, suffered during the Third Battle of Ypres. There are 155 Canadians buried there, 2 are from the 43rd Battalion.
3. Poelcapelle British Cemetery, 5 miles northeast of Ypres (Ieper), contains the graves of 7,469 Commonwealth soldiers. More than 400 of the 525 Canadian soldiers buried there are unidentified. The majority of Canadians, buried at Poelcapelle British Cemetery, were members of the 3rd Infantry Division, who were killed during the Battle of Passchendaele. There are 4 soldiers from the 43rd Infantry Battalion buried in Poelcapelle.

4. Tyne Cot Cemetery is located less than two miles south west of the village of Passchendaele and 5.5 miles east of Ypres (Ieper). It is the largest Commonwealth war cemetery in the world. A total of 966 Canadian soldiers are buried there. 900 of those men were killed in the Battle of Passchendaele, 554 are unidentified burials. There are 10 identified Cameron Highlanders of Canada buried in Tyne Cot Cemetery.

5. Lijssenthoek Military Cemetery is the second largest Commonwealth War Graves Commission Cemetery in Belgium. Located in the small hamlet of Lijssenthoek, 1.2 miles southwest of Poperinge and six miles west of Ypres (Ieper), this cemetery contains the bodies of 9,829 soldiers, Canadian burials accounting for 1,051 of that number. There are approximately 300 Canadians buried at Lijssenthoek, who died from wounds incurred in the Battle of Passchendaele and were brought to the cemetery from Casualty Clearing Stations. There are 5 soldiers from the 43rd Infantry Battalion buried in the Lijssenthoek Military Cemetery.

6. Passchendaele New British Cemetery is located on the road to 's Graventafel, a short distance north of the village of Passchendaele and is situated on the Bellevue Spur, at Mosselmarkt. This cemetery was established in 1920-21 and contains the remains of soldiers removed from small burial plots, unmarked graves and unidentified bodies retrieved from the battlefield. Of the more than nearly 2,100 burials, 77% are unknown. Canadians number 650 and all were casualties of Passchendaele. The number of unidentified is 452. There are 64 graves containing the remains of soldiers from the 3rd Infantry Division, 7 Cameron Highlanders of Canada.

7. Bedford House Cemetery, 1.2 miles south of Ypres (Ieper) is a huge cemetery encompassing four enclosures; the fourth and largest is located on eastern part of the cemetery and contains the graves of 3,860 Commonwealth soldiers, 17 of which are Canadian soldiers killed at Passchendaele. There is 1 soldier

from the 43rd Canadian Infantry Battalion buried in enclosure four at Bedford House.

8. New Irish Farm Cemetery is located 2.4 miles northwest of Ypres (Ieper) in an open field. Originally the cemetery contained only 73 graves, however today there are 4,678. There are 254 Canadians buried in New Irish Farm Cemetery, 89% (227) of those soldiers have never been identified. Of the 27 identified burials, 6 were killed in action at Passchendaele, one being a member of the 43rd Infantry Battalion (Cameron Highlanders of Canada) CEF.

9. Ypres Reservoir Cemetery is located almost in the heart of Ypres (Ieper), a short walk from Menin Gate Memorial. This cemetery was used throughout the war and contained 1,099 graves, however, years later, it was enlarged to accommodate battlefield clearances and soldiers' remains from smaller cemeteries, thereby increasing the number of buried soldiers to 2,611. There are 151 Canadian soldiers buried in the Ypres Reservoir Cemetery, half of the graves representing soldiers killed in the Battle of Passchendaele. One member of the 43rd Battalion is buried there.

** Epsom Cemetery is situated in Surrey County, south east England, far from the killing fields of Passchendaele. While researching each of the casualties of the 43rd Canadian Infantry Battalion, the author noted one soldier in particular who served with the 43rd Battalion was not laid to rest in a military cemetery near Passchendaele or in a casualty clearing station cemetery close to Ypres. Twenty-seven-year-old, Private Ted Potterton, husband of Emma Potterton, 76 Bracken Path, Epsom Common, died on November 7, 1917, within days of being evacuated from Belgium to a military hospital in England. The medical facility possibly may have been the Woodcote Park Military Convalescent Hospital, in Epsom. It would have been there that Private Potterton finally succumbed to wounds incurred in combat on October 26 or soon thereafter. Private Ted Potterton is buried in Epsom, approximately 16 miles from London. The Epsom Cemetery contains the graves of 189 WWI Commonwealth soldiers, 62 of which were Canadian burials. It is presumed that all officers and other ranks, buried in Epsom Cemetery died as a result of their wounds received in battle between 1914 -1918.

> "They shall not grow old,
> As we that are left grow old;
> Age shall not weary them,
> Nor the years condemn.
> At the going down of the sun
> And in the morning
> We will remember them."

Acknowledgements

I would first like to express my gratitude to Fernand Verstrate, who not only served as my battlefield guide in May 2012 in France and Belgium, but also as a sort of history professor, imparting his knowledge on the historical facts of the Great War as we retraced my great-uncle's wartime journey across Nord-pas-de-Calais, France; to West-Vlaanderen, Belgium. In addition, I will be forever grateful for Fernand's assistance in providing advice, historical material, and unrelenting support for *Bullets, Bombs, and Bayonets*. His knowledge of WWI combat operations, especially in the Ypres Salient where the 43rd Canadian Infantry Battalion (Cameron Highlanders of Canada) CEF played a major role in the Second Battle of Passchendaele, was immensely important in the writing of this book.

I would also wish to add my sincere appreciation to the following individuals who assisted me with my book project: Olivia J. Ross, Charlene Stevens, Sonia Jensen and Dorothy Outhouse. Without your help, *Bullets, Bombs, and Bayonets* may never have come to fruition.

Thank you for helping me to realize my dream.

Bibliography

Ancestry.ca

Allied Weapons of WWI — Digger History

Battles of WWI — author, Martin Marix Evans. Arcturus Publishing Limited 2008

Cameron Highlanders of Canada (43rd Canadian Infantry Battalion) War Diary

Canadian Military Heritage Project

Canadian Great War Project

Canadian Expeditionary Force Study Group

Collections Canada — War Diaries

Commonwealth War Graves Commission

Canadians at War — author, Susan Evans Shaw, Goose Lane Editions 2011

Canadian Battlefields 1915-1918 - co-authors, Terry Copp, Matt Symes, Nick Lachance, Wilfred Laurier University Press 2011

First World War.com

For King and Empire, The Canadians at Passchendaele — author, Norm Christie, CEF Books 2007

Ghosts Have Warm Hands — author, Will R. Bird, CEF Books 2002

Hell in Flanders Fields — author George H. Cassar, Dundurn Press 2010

Library and Archives Canada

Lee Enfield Rifle– History Learning Site

NZ History. net

On This Day: The Battle of Passchendaele — CBC Archives

Old Enough to Fight — co-authors, Dan Black and John Boileau, Publisher James Lorimer & Company Limited 2013

Passchendaele — The Fight for the Village — author, Nigel Cave, Publisher Pen & Sword Military 2011

Passchendaele — author, Norman S. Leach, Coteau Books 2008

Slaughter in the Mud — The Canadians at Passchendaele, 1917- author, N.M. Christie, CEF Books 1998

Sacred Places Vol I *Belgium- Canadian Cemeteries of the Great War-* author, Norm Christie, CEF Books 2010

Shock Troops — Canadians Fighting The Great War 1917-1918 - author, Tim Cook, Penguin Group 2008

The Canadian Encyclopedia.com

The Long, Long Trail — The British Army of 1914-1918. Sir Douglas Haig's Passchendaele Despatch.

The Queens Own Cameron Highlanders of Canada.net

The War Walk — author, Nigel Jones, Cassell Military Paperbacks 2004

The Great War in Ypres — Images of Flanders — author, Jacky Platteeuw, Tempus Publishing Limited 2007

The War That Ended Peace — author, Margaret MacMillan, Penguin Group 2013

The First World War-authors, Peter Simkins, Geoffrey Jukes & Michael Hickey, Osprey Publishing Limited 2013

The Great War — author, Robert Hamilton, Atlantic Publishing 2014

They Called it Passchendaele — author, Lyn MacDonald, Penguin Books 1993

Underground Warfare 1914-1918 - author, Simon Jones, Pen & Sword Books Limited 2010

Veterans Affairs Canada

Wikipedia

World War 1 – A Day in the Trenches — Hubpages.com

Winning The Ridge — The Canadians at Vimy Ridge, 1917- author, N.M. Christie, CEF Books 2004

CPSIA information can be obtained
at www.ICGtesting.com
Printed in the USA
LVHW09s0125300918
591900LV00001B/5/P